The Power to Spring UP

To Paula,
Thank you for
help! Here's to a
long & prosperous
collaboration.
Dee Katovitch
7/29/15

The Power to Spring UP

Postsecondary Education Opportunities for Students with Significant Disabilities

Diana M. Katovitch, M.S.

Woodbine House 2009

All rights reserved. Published in the United States of America by Woodbine House, Inc., 6510 Bells Mill Road, Bethesda, MD 20817. 800-843-7323. www. woodbinehouse.com

Cataloging-in-Publication Data

Katovitch, Diana M.
  The power to spring up : postsecondary education opportunities for students with significant disabilities / Diana M. Katovitch. -- 1st ed.
     p. cm.
  Includes bibliographical references and index.
  ISBN 978-1-890627-95-9
  1. People with disabilities--Education (Higher)--United States. 2. College students with disabilities--Services for--United States. I. Title.
  LC4813.K37 2009
  378.0087--dc22
                                                                2009027979

Manufactured in the United States of America

First edition

10 9 8 7 6 5 4 3 2 1

"If I have seen far, it is because I have stood
on the shoulders of giants."
—Sir Isaac Newton

In loving memory of my mother, Lee Tibbetts,
the shortest giant I ever knew,

and to my husband, Dale Katovitch,
who is my giant still.

Table of Contents

Part Two: Program Profiles

Acknowledgements

It would be almost impossible to name and individually thank everyone on the many campuses and associated with the remarkable programs I visited between January 2007 and February 2009 while writing this book. I was amazed and humbled by their willingness to share information about their programs, their successes, and their struggles. In some cases, especially with the parents and students who shared their stories via email, I cannot thank them by name, because they have asked me to preserve their privacy. For everyone who took the time to speak with me, if I named you in the book, I express my gratitude here. I sincerely thank the students and staff of the following programs:

- College Based Transition Program, Buffalo State College, Buffalo, New York
- College Experience Program, Ontario County ARC, at Fingerlakes Community College, Canandaigua, New York, and Hobart William Smith College, Geneva, New York
- Threshold Program, Lesley University, Cambridge, Massachusetts

- Transition Program, Middlesex Community College, Bedford, Massachusetts
- College Internship Program and Aspire Program, Lee, Massachusetts
- Berkshire Hills Music Academy, South Hadley, Massachusetts
- University of Rochester, Monroe Board of Cooperative Educational Services #1, Rochester, New York
- Roberts Wesleyan College, Monroe-Orleans Board of Cooperative Educational Services #2, Rochester, New York
- College Experience Program through Living Resources, Inc., College of St. Rose, Albany, New York
- Cayuga Onondaga Board of Cooperative Educational Services, Cayuga Community College, Auburn, New York
- Occupational Training Program, Eastern New Mexico University, Roswell, New Mexico
- Chapel Haven, New Haven, Connecticut
- Vista Vocational Center, Westbrook, Connecticut
- Job Corps, New Haven, Connecticut
- Venture Program, Bellevue Community College, Bellevue, Washington
- Career and Community Studies Program, The College of New Jersey, Ewing, New Jersey
- The College Program for Students with Asperger's Syndrome, Marshall University, Huntington, West Virginia
- Kelley Autism Program, Western Kentucky University, Bowling Green, Kentucky
- ABIRP (Acquired Brain Injury Resource Program), Western Kentucky University, Bowling Green, Kentucky
- Graduate Transitions Program, Montgomery Community College, Rockville, Maryland
- D.R.I.V.E. (Diversity, Responsibility, Inclusion, Vision, and Experiential Learning) Program, Keuka College, Penn Yan, New York
- The Transitions Class, Wayne Finger Lakes Board of Cooperative Educational Services, Newark, New York
- Camphill Soltane, Glenmoore, Pennsylvania

A few people, however, I can thank by name. Thank you to the women of Woodbine House Publishing, for taking a chance on me—acquisitions editor Nancy Grey Paul, publisher Fran Maranaccio, and editor

Susan Stokes. Thank you to one of my former students, Rachel O. Myers, for giving me feedback on the chapter addressed to students, for letting me give her one last homework assignment, and not complaining!

To my stepfather, Richard Tibbetts, sister, Kathy Belanger, and stepdaughter, Celie Katovitch, writers all, for understanding what is involved in writing a book and offering encouragement. To my dear friends, Bill and Nancy Grow, Laurie Finch, Patty Hurlburt, and Nick Bessette, and my sisters from Delta Kappa Gamma International who supported this project unfailingly from day one, I appreciate your kindness deeply.

Finally, to my son Sam, thank you for being proud of me—what a compliment for a mom. Sam and my husband Dale kept the home fires burning during my travels and during my long, long stretches at the computer. As for Dale, the dedication says it all—thank you and I love you.

Prologue

"I believe in human beings, but my faith is without sentimentality. I know that in environments of uncertainty, hunger, and fear a human being is dwarfed and shaped without being aware of it, just as a plant under a stone does not know its own condition. Only when the stone is removed can it spring up freely into the light. But the power to spring up is inherent and only death puts an end to it. I feel no need for any other faith other than my faith in human beings." —Pearl S. Buck, 1951

Long before I began writing this book, I read and loved this quote written by Pearl S. Buck for the Edward R. Murrow radio series *This I Believe*. I have it framed in my classroom. There is something about the metaphor of the stone that speaks to the importance of environment and expectations—good growing conditions, in other words—that appealed to me as a teacher of students with significant special needs.

As a young teacher, I believed first and foremost that environment was the key factor in creating good outcomes for students with disabilities. After more than twenty years of working in the field, I still do to a point. While the world is not without responsibility in becoming more accessible and more welcoming to individuals with significant disabilities, the solutions are more complex and the role of environment more subtle than I assumed when I opened the door to my first classroom.

Pearl S. Buck was one of the earliest and most prescient advocates for people with significant disabilities. Although Ms. Buck is best known for her Pulitzer Prize-winning novel *The Good Earth*, I first encountered her in her memoir *The Child Who Never Grew*. The title referred to her daughter and to Ms. Buck's search for a decent life for a child born when the ground was covered with metaphorical stones for those with disabilities.

Caroline Grace Buck, called Carol by her family, was the first and only biological child born to Pearl and John Lossing Buck. She was born on March 4, 1920. Her life was equal parts seminal and searing for her mother, because in the words of the book's title, Carol was "the child who never grew." Born with phenylketonuria (PKU), a metabolic disorder, in the days before neonatal testing and effective dietary treatment, Carol became significantly intellectually disabled. Ms. Buck "came out," for lack of a better expression, about Carol in 1950 in her short book. It was a daring move at the time, since intellectual disability was terribly misunderstood and regarded as shameful. Ms. Buck wrote about her quest for reasons for her daughter's delays and for a place where she might live her life safely. Ms. Buck placed Carol at the Vineland Training School in New Jersey when her daughter was nine years old. Carol lived at the Training School until her death in 1992. Ms. Buck began writing professionally in order to pay Carol's fees at Vineland, and the experience of having a child with a disability is widely believed to have been her inspiration for becoming an international advocate on behalf of children in need.

I first read *The Child Who Never Grew* as a teenager because of my interest in becoming a special education teacher. I found it appalling. Ms. Buck described her then thirty-year-old daughter as a "helpless child," incapable of learning. I had already worked with several children with significant intellectual disabilities, knew them to be capable of growth, and had seen enough of institutional conditions to condemn them. Reading the book again while preparing to write this book, I saw through the dated language and antiquated expectations for people with intellectual disabilities and recognized the pain of a dream permanently deferred for a dearly loved child. Ms. Buck realized that her daughter would never be able to live a normal life. Carol had significant disabilities, it's true, but she was further handicapped by the time in which she lived. In addition to coping with the shock of her daughter's diagnosis, Ms. Buck faced a world with virtually no options for individuals with significant disabilities.

Fearful of Carol being left bereft if something should happen to her (Carol's father had distanced himself from her care), Ms. Buck searched for a high quality caretaking institution. It was simply the best—and in many ways, the only—choice for Carol to live and to learn. The title notwithstanding, an epilogue written by Janice C. Walsh, Carol's sister and guardian after her mother's death, tells of how Carol did learn and did grow, given the support of the staff at Vineland.

• •

I like to think that Pearl S. Buck would approve of the current climate that exists for individuals with disabilities, certainly not stone-free, but far less rocky than it once was. I derived the title of this book from the quote at the beginning of the prologue. I believe, as Ms. Buck did, that individuals with significant disabilities, given opportunities and environments in which to grow, can spring up to levels previously thought impossible. One of those previously unheard-of levels is higher education. Young adults with significant disabilities, such as intellectual disabilities, autism spectrum disorders, and a variety of learning disabilities, are seeking to further their education and increase their prospects for independent and productive lives.

Pearl S. Buck was almost prophetic in her belief that people born with these disabilities have something to contribute to the world. She believed in their right to learn, in spite of the efforts that might be needed on both sides for the learning to happen.

Normal impatience burst forth time and again, to my shame, and it seemed useless to try to teach. But justice reasoned with me thus: "This mind has the right to its fullest development, too. It may be very little, but the right is the same as yours, or any other's. If you refuse it the right to know, in so far as it can know, you do a wrong." (The Child Who Never Grew, pp. 77-78)

I think Ms. Buck would have supported the drive of students with significant disabilities to develop their minds to the fullest extent possible. I think she would have believed that even if a student could not meet all of the requirements of a degree program, the student should not be denied the chance to know what he or she can know.

She also recognized that a life is more than just intellectual development.

> *My child taught me to know, too, that mind is not all of the human creature.…What I am trying to say is that there is a whole personality not concerned with the mind.…While IQ may be very low indeed a child actually may function a good deal higher because of his social sense, his feelings of how he ought to behave, his pride, his kindness, his wish to be liked.…A high intelligence may be a curse to society, as it has often been, useless unless it is accompanied by qualities of character which provide social maturity, and the less brilliant child who has these qualities is a better citizen and often achieves more individually than the high intelligence without them.…We have to thank the helpless children for teaching us that mere intelligence is not enough.* (The Child Who Never Grew, pp. 78-79)

This observation was extraordinary in its time. We now recognize that "soft skills," those that cannot be measured on an IQ test, are tremendously important in personal success, and spill over into the areas of learning, employment, and personal relationships. I have seen these qualities supersede academic achievement and IQ scores in the overall success or failure of my students' lives. "Social maturity," as Ms. Buck referred to it, can and must be taught and fostered in young adults with significant disabilities (SD), as much as it is taught and fostered in young adults without SD.

• •

How does any young person living in this country today become learned, socially mature, and a contributing member of society? Increasingly, by going on to postsecondary education. Eventually, 70 percent of high school graduates in this country will attend some kind of college or vocational program. Although not all will graduate, they will have the opportunity to pursue the training and education needed to reach their personal goals. In the 2005-2006 school year, 2.8 million students in the United States graduated from high school; 66,275 students exited high school with other credentials, such as a certificate of attendance or an IEP (Individualized Education Program) diploma or "aged out" of school eligibility (Planty et al., 2008 and 2009). Presumably most, if not all, of the members of this second group had some type of disability. This group of students, too, has the right to the "fullest development" of their minds and the responsibility to learn "social maturity," but they have limited opportunities to do so without the benefits of education beyond high school.

I continue to disagree with Ms. Buck about people with significant disabilities being "helpless" or "eternal" children. They are not. They have the ability to learn, and, I believe, have the same responsibility as anyone else to contribute to the world. We often speak of human rights, but I believe that human responsibilities are even more empowering in the long run. While I once put all of the responsibility for removing the stones of low expectations and limiting attitudes about individuals with significant disabilities on society, I now equally believe in raising expectations and insisting on contributions from them. But I am not so naive that I believe that these young people can meet these goals simply by raising our expectations. They need instruction, they need appropriate support, and they need the opportunity to follow the same paths as their peers who do not have disabilities.

We must, as a society and as an education system, begin to insist that these paths become more widely known and available and to insist that young adults with disabilities take their place in building their own futures and in helping to lift their share of the world's load. We must make the opportunities available and then we must expect them to take advantage of those opportunities. The denial of those opportunities and the denial of appropriate responsibility placed on young adults with significant disabilities are the final stones holding down the plant.

* *

Notes to Facilitate the Reading of this Book

To simplify reading, I have used male and female pronouns by alternating chapter.

The following abbreviations and terms are used throughout:

PSE: Postsecondary education, which refers to any education or training beyond high school, including vocational training, two- or four-year colleges, both public and private.

SD: Significant disabilities, a term which refers to conditions that significantly affect the ability of the individual to engage in life activities such as learning and carrying out activities of daily living. These disabilities include, but are not limited to, the conditions listed in Chapter One.

IDEA: Individuals with Disabilities Education Act. A federal law governing the right to education for all children with disabilities in the United States from birth through age 21 (final age may vary by state). This law is primarily concerned with education in grades kindergarten through twelfth grade, but may also cover some students with SD who are dually enrolled in high school and PSE.

ADA (Americans with Disabilities Act, 1990) and **Section 504** (Section 504 of the Rehabilitation Act): laws that concern the rights to employment, education, and access to public services given to all individuals with disabilities, both temporary and permanent, in the United States.

IEP (Individualized Education Program): a document required under IDEA to list the services that must be provided by a school to a child with a disability (transportation, special education services, speech therapy, test modifications, etc.). The IEP also outlines the child's disability and the effect of the disability on the child's functioning, and lists annual educational goals and the progress on these goals that the child has made. A transition plan is required as part of the IEP when the child turns 16 (again, this may vary by state) and must list the child's future goals and a coordinated set of activities that will help the child achieve these goals.

A further word on the organization of this book is needed. The initial chapters outline reasons to make PSE available to students with SD, and research about some of the issues involved in how to make these opportunities happen. But this book is not primarily about numbers or studies. Special education, because it concerns itself with especially unique learners, has many achievements that are difficult to quantify with ordinary statistics. It is not that evidence is not available; special educators, even more than professionals in other educational disciplines, are experts in defining goals, teaching to specific outcomes, and gathering data, but we do this on a student-to-student basis. Goals are specific to the student involved. So, with such a group of students, who are working diligently to learn things that many typical students learn instinctively or would find hopelessly mundane, numbers will only tell part of the story.

Special educators measure success with a different yardstick than general educators and administrators. I doubt this reality will come as a surprise to the teachers, families, and advocates of young adults with SD who are turning to this book for guidance. I will include such research when it is available, because evidence of the efficacy of PSE opportunities will help to bring about more opportunities. Changing policies because it is the right thing to do is noble, but changing policies because it is the right thing to do and it works is even more powerful.

However, to quote from the introduction to the second edition of *The Child Who Never Grew* written by Martha M. Jablow, "More than all the statistics, charts, and research data, personal stories that tell 'the real truth' as my six year old niece says, can move mountains and change lives." To best describe the opportunities available to these students, and their achievements within these opportunities, the second half of this book profiles programs I have had the privilege to visit and students and professionals I have met. I tell these stories intentionally, in an effort to tell "the real truth" about the challenges and triumphs involved with launching young adults with SD into the world. The stories are continuing—these programs and services are constantly being improved and expanded, in response to the needs of the students who are seeking them out. I was impressed and humbled by the willingness with which these stories were shared. These students and professionals want their stories told so as many students as possible can benefit. I regret that I was not able to gather more stories from more programs in the limited scope of this book. However, I hope that the reader finds the story, or one quite like it, that will be of greatest use to him or her in achieving a goal of PSE for a student living with SD.

The book closes with short chapters listing advice directed to students with SD, their parents, and their secondary school teachers on how to make PSE happen for this particular group of students, and an epilogue that discusses the continuing issues related to students with SD in higher education. A final caution to the reader: this field is in constant evolution. Programs, available services, admissions requirements, tuition, and options for funding are changing all the time. Please check to make sure that the information you have is up to date.

Part 1

Students with Significant Disabilities in Postsecondary Education

"A Life Worth Living"

Postsecondary Education and Students with Significant Disabilities

Of the many functions our colleges and universities serve, most need little explanation or defense. The advancement of research... vocational training, at all levels...the cultivation of the habits of respectfulness and tolerance on which responsible citizenship in a diverse democracy depends....

This is an impressive list of goods. But there is another that must be added to it. It is harder to define but just as real. It is the good of helping students come to grips with the question of what living is for—the good, as Alexander Meiklejohn, the president of Amherst College, described it a century ago, of helping young people fashion "a life worth living" from their given endowments of desire, opportunity, and talent (Kronman, 2001).

In spite of the decades-long trend in this country to view acceptance to the right college as an end in itself, acceptance to college is and has always been the beginning of a powerful period of new learning. I believe that the only appropriate motto for any college worth its endowments is "Forget everything you ever thought you knew for sure." Students with significant disabilities are beginning to take their places in colleges and universities across the country. That students with SD do not belong in college is one of those notions we always thought we knew for sure—be prepared to forget it.

This book is geared toward students with significant disabilities (SD) who want to pursue the benefits of postsecondary education (PSE), but due to a variety of circumstances, would struggle to be admitted to or to find success in college, even with accommodations allowed under the Americans with Disabilities Act (ADA) and Section 504 of the Rehabilitation Act guidelines. These students include:

- Students with intellectual disabilities (score on an IQ test of 70 or below with deficiencies in adaptive behavior). These students may be identified as having mental retardation, cognitive impairments, or developmental disabilities, or as having a genetic syndrome with intellectual disability as an associated feature.
- Students with severe or multiple learning disabilities, with or without an intellectual disability
- Students with acquired brain injuries
- Students with nonverbal learning disabilities or autism spectrum disorders
- Students who have any of the above disabilities, as well as speech/language, sensory, or physical disabilities

These students may also face the following challenges in pursuing PSE:

- They do not meet the criteria for protections under the Americans with Disabilities Act (ADA) or Section 504 of the Rehabilitation Act because they are not "otherwise qualified individuals" due to 1) a lack of a traditional high school diploma or GED (although the students may have received a certificate of attendance or IEP diploma from their high school), and/or 2) difficulty achieving a minimum score on a college entrance exam, such as an Ability to Benefit Test or reading/math placement exams, which may be prerequisites to matriculation in a PSE program.
- They may have delays or deficiencies in social skills, self-care skills, employment and employability skills, and self-awareness, especially about the nature of their disability and how it affects their daily life.

However, they also have the following:
- A desire to go to college, for the same reasons that their peers want to go to college
- Personal motivation to work hard and to learn new things
- A desire for as independent and self-determined a future as possible

My introduction to the possibility of postsecondary educational opportunities for young adults with SD came in the form of a *New York Times* article in a limited series called "A Dream Not Denied." The story was about a young woman named Katie Apostolides who was in her third year of attending Becker College in Massachusetts. The description of her morning and her classes was very typical, except that Katie, who describes herself in the article as "just a normal girl," has Down syndrome. It was my personal "forget everything you ever thought you knew for sure" moment.

As a secondary special education teacher since 1990, I thought I knew for sure that none of my students would ever attend college. The very mention of the topic made me wince. How many times had I sat across from students, asking them to tell me about their plans for the future, hoping against hope that they would not mention college? They always wanted to go. College held the same appeal for them as for any other high school student—the chance to live away from home with their peers, to take classes, to have a rich and exciting social life. However, it was a clear if seldom-spoken part of my job description to help them face reality. College just wasn't going to happen for them.

Most of the students I had worked with as a teacher for seventeen years and a job coach for five years before that could not meet the graduation requirements for a high school diploma in New York State or in any state. They had profound academic delays—sometimes barely reading or writing at the first grade level. They were socially immature. I heard their parents complain about how helpless they were at independent living skills. It was hardest of all with the students who were the most capable—the kids who had academic skills near the middle school level, but for a variety of reasons could not stay afloat in general education classes in high school. At graduation, they received an IEP (Individualized Education Program) diploma as their credential, evidence of progress for sure—often enormous progress—but not a diploma that would be recognized for admittance to college.

I knew of a few forward-thinking districts who placed their special education classes for students ages 18 to 21 on community college campuses; the district where I taught at the beginning of my career had such a program. The alternative was for students to remain in high school, on the same campus where they had spent four years already. Some students stayed in high school for seven years. Others decided to leave school with their graduating class, turning away from three more years of free public education to try to make it on their own. These were the students who were the least prepared, who still had so much to learn—but who adamantly did not want to learn it in high school.

Year after year at annual reviews, I would dutifully inform the students and their parents before graduation at the end of twelfth grade that they were entitled to return to school under IDEA regulations until they turned 21 or received a high school diploma. The students would invariably say, "Yeah, right, Mrs. K." and their parents and the members of the Committee on Special Education would laugh knowingly. I would attend graduation, watch my students cross the stage, and step off into the abyss. I was often tearful, both with pride and dismay. While many of them worked after graduation, they often struggled along in low paying, low status jobs, unable to move higher up the ladder due to limited education and skill development. Their difficulties with social and independent living skills often left them living with their families, although they desperately wanted to be on their own. A few got into trouble with the law, starting an even grimmer downward spiral.

I tried to counsel some students who really seemed determined to give college a try to pursue a GED. In seventeen years, I had one student receive a GED. I counseled others to go to our local community college to attempt an Ability to Benefit Test to see if they could bypass the diploma requirement. The teacher who had my position before me told me that she actually had a student who was able to pass the test and enroll in college.

"How is he doing?" I asked.

"He flunked out his first semester," was the answer. It seemed the only answer. Students with those kinds of disabilities just didn't go to college.

And still, here was this story about a young woman who had a significant disability actually enrolled in college, earning credits, living in a dormitory, with greater prospects for a full life due to her education.

I was puzzled and skeptical, then delighted. This story was what my students had been asking about for years. How could this be? I began my education all over again.

My education has always been book driven. The Internet is mostly a way for me to read stuff, without endangering my marriage by bringing more books into the house. Although there were excellent websites (they are listed in the resources) and people to contact by email, I kept looking for a book that pulled together what was known about college opportunities for students with SD in one place.

I couldn't find one, so I'm writing it now.

In a quiet revolution, students with significant disabilities (SD) have been realizing the goal of PSE. The reasons to make this goal a reality for more students with SD are as compelling as the stories of the students who are meeting the goal now on campuses across the country.

Improving Adult Outcomes: "It Works. It Really, Truly Works"

Even after more that thirty years of free and appropriate public education, students with SD face uncertain adult futures. The National Organization on Disability reported the following outcomes in 2004:

- 35 percent of people with disabilities are employed full or part time (78 percent of people without disabilities are employed full or part time).
- Three times the number of people with disabilities live in poverty (household income of less than $15,000 per year) than the number of people without disabilities.
- People with disabilities are less likely than people without disabilities to socialize outside the home (attend church, eat out, etc.).
- People with disabilities report lower levels of life satisfaction (34 percent are very satisfied, compared to 68 percent of people without disabilities). (Getzel and Wehman, 2005)

Three separate research studies (2004, 2001, and 2000) have been able to show that students with intellectual disabilities who participate in PSE have a greater chance of becoming competitively employed. Another study, conducted by Frances T. Yuan, addresses the other outcomes.

In 2006, Yuan surveyed graduates of the Threshold Program at Lesley University in Cambridge, Massachusetts. Threshold, founded in 1982, was one of the first comprehensive, nondegree programs for students with SD on a college campus in the United States. Yuan surveyed 125 graduates and 93 parents of graduates, representing 10 years of graduating classes (1996-2005) to determine the impact of the program on adult outcomes.

- 80 percent of the students were employed, with an average hourly wage of $9.84 per hour. This hourly rate translates into roughly $18,000 a year per individual. 55 percent of the students reported that they had not been unemployed for more than three months since graduating from the program.
- 76 percent of the respondents were living independently, although some still received financial support from their parents. 96 percent of the students and 83 percent of their parents were satisfied or extremely satisfied with their current level of independence.
- Parents reported an improvement of 55 percent or greater in their adult children's abilities to manage money, shop for and prepare food, carry out household chores, and manage their own health needs.
- 68 percent of the students were satisfied with their social life, 20 percent were married or engaged to be married, and 80 percent of their parents reported that their adult children "always or mostly" demonstrated appropriate social skills. (All data taken from *Beyond Threshold* survey compiled by Frances T. Yuan.)

For a researcher to ask the question, "Why do you believe in a program like this?" is to risk crossing the line from professional to warm and fuzzy. I asked it anyway when visiting programs, since creating, refining, and maintaining comprehensive programs and working to create such positive outcomes for students with SD is extraordinarily challenging. Helen McDonald, Director of Admissions at Threshold, summed it up after sharing the above results with me: "Because it works. It really, truly works."

The Next Logical Step

"You know, none of them are really mentally retarded anymore."

The Director of Special Education in my school system made this remark rather casually one day, watching my class work. The definition of mental retardation (increasingly called intellectual disability) has always had three parts: an IQ of 70 or below and deficits in adaptive behavior (generally, the ability to manage the details of daily life), both occurring before the age of 18. She knew the birth dates and test scores of the students in the room as well as I did. But, watching the kids socialize, surf the Internet, and make their way through the day, the adaptive behavior deficits were not evident. They looked and acted just like their typical peers. By attending their neighborhood school, and living and learning side by side with nondisabled siblings and peers, the adaptive skills deficit had been minimized to the point that, for the most part, they functioned just like their peers.

Often, my colleagues would not know that a student was one of "my" students until the student was faced with an academic task or they received an IEP (Individualized Education Program) in their email. By the same token, every student in the school who had what might be tactfully called "social skills challenges" was assumed to be mine.

"Dee, I have one of your kids in my class, and I'm afraid the kids will eat him alive by the end of the week," a teacher would tell me on the first day of school.

I would ask the student's name. Then, I would say, "Sorry, he's not one of 'mine' —he's all yours."

The movement to include students with SD in neighborhood schools and general education classrooms has contributed to rising expectations for typical futures for individuals with SD. Increasingly, teenagers with SD expect to do what their peers are doing, when their peers are doing it, whether it is drive a car, date, work part time, or move out on their own. At age 18 or 19, after the excitement of senior events such as picnics, proms, and trips, students with SD expect to graduate and go into the world. Seventy percent of high school graduates in the United States go on for PSE at two- or four-year schools or technical programs, and many students with SD expect to do the same. However, only about 8 percent of students with intellectual disabilities currently go on to any kind of PSE (Getzel and Wehman, 2006).

It's not that students with SD must leave school at 18 with their graduating class, since IDEA grants them the right to stay longer. But, if we as teachers, parents, and advocates have done our job right, students with SD don't want to remain in high school until their early 20s, any more than any other student would.

A young woman in a college-based transition program in Rochester, New York, said it bluntly: "We're not babies. Don't treat us like babies." She and her classmates were adamant that programs like theirs had no place on a high school campus. No matter how good the program was, four years of high school was enough. Even if it means graduating with a certificate of attendance instead of a diploma, many students will take that option rather than stay in high school.

Opportunities for Self-determination, Responsibility, and Failure

In early June of my senior year, my high school sponsored a Senior Week to keep us out of trouble in that heady week before graduation.

In addition to the senior prom and dinner dance, we had the Senior Boys' and Senior Girls' Luncheons.

It was the last time anyone called me a girl.

Two short months later, when I arrived at Syracuse University, I was called a woman. Ready or not, acting like it or not, we were men and women. It was symbolic of the sudden increase in freedom and responsibility we were facing.

It was risky, but it was controlled risk. After all, we had a paid room to return to at night, food on the table through a meal plan, a limited number of bills to keep straight, and mentors around if we ran into trouble. But we had to control our worlds, even those limited to a dorm room. We had certain classes and certain credit requirements for graduation, and we needed to make sure we met them. We could screw up, even screw up royally, but there were some safety nets in place that helped avert complete disaster.

Postsecondary education for students with SD provides the same opportunity for freedom and responsibility in a way that the best high school program cannot. Colleges are not 9-3 operations and bells do not ring to remind students when to go to class or lunch. There are no administrators around to check passes or prevent fights in the cafeteria. Professors are there to teach, not to remind students of deadlines or to badger them to do their homework.

A certain standard of behavior is expected among college students, since people had to apply and are paying to attend. But many students find that the rigid social order of high school does not exist in college, and a wider variety of clothing, interests, and beliefs are tolerated. As long as one student's purple hair, musical taste, odd clothes, or fervent political beliefs don't interfere with other students earning their credits on time, most of these differences will be regarded benignly or at least maturely.

The freedom to make decisions, to take risks, and to move through the day independently is essential if students with SD are going to learn self-determination. After reading many definitions, I would define someone who is self-determined as the leading actor and director of his own life. A good actor and director knows what he can do for himself and when he needs to seek the help of the experts around him. He knows how to make choices and decisions, and is able to set and to achieve personal goals. He can watch himself and decide if everything is going well or poorly, and act accordingly to fix it. He can problem solve. He stands up for himself appropriately when needed. He has an internal locus of control—he feels that his effort makes things happen, not fate or bad luck (Getzel and Wehman, 2005). All successful adults, with and without SD, have self-determination skills.

Some PSE programs for students with SD provide direct instruction or support groups to practice self-determination skills, especially self-advocacy. Perhaps for the first time, students will need to self-identify as a person with a disability. They need to be able to tell the Disability Support Services staff, professors, and employers the name and nature of their disability if they are going to request their accommodations. This information can be extremely hard for students to accept themselves, and quite intimidating to explain to a relative stranger. Many students benefit from instruction in understanding and articulating their disability.

Many other self-determination skills can be practiced in natural environments during a typical semester. Students make choices and decisions on a regular basis, from what program of study to engage in to what flavor of latte to buy. They have to continually evaluate whether the choices are working or not, and cope with decisions that did not work out as well as hoped.

Risk is controlled, but not eliminated in PSE opportunities for students with SD. It often begins with the application process. The very requirement of an application means that not everyone who applies will be granted entrance. Although admissions requirements have blocked the door to college for many individuals with SD, admissions requirements are still integral to programs and services. One director referred to this reality as "the movement from entitlement to eligibility." IDEA services are "no cut"; postsecondary programs, often even those funded by school district funds, can and do cut students. Due to limited slots available for programs and the level of independence and behavioral self-control expected, not every student who applies to a PSE program will be accepted. This reality reflects the real world focus of PSE—after all, not every student without SD is admitted to a first choice college, either. In the real world, not everyone will get the job they want or be able to buy their dream house. Adults need to realize that they will not always get a trophy just for showing up.

Once a student is admitted, colleges and PSE programs retain the right to set the course of study and prerequisites for desired courses. While these requirements may be waived on an individual basis or as an accommodation under ADA or Section 504, colleges and PSE programs maintain a fair amount of discretion in these matters. Particularly for certain degree or certificate programs, waiving an academic requirement, such as foreign language for a degree in international relations, may undermine the academic integrity of the program. Institutions cannot be compelled to make such modifications.

Colleges and PSE programs also have the right to set and enforce a code of conduct. The programs I visited told stories of students who had been "asked not to return" for a variety of reasons. Internships on and off campus had additional rules, such as dress codes and employee procedures to be followed. Students who failed to comply were fired. In other words, the students with SD could fail, in some cases for the first time, just like everyone else. And, hopefully, they would learn from the experience just like everyone else.

What You Can't Learn in High School: Expanded Opportunities for Classroom Study and Natural Learning

Colleges offer a wider variety of courses than high schools. Even within the required core curriculum, there are many courses to choose from to meet the requirements. Within this variety of courses, there are options for students of different ability levels to learn about subjects they have never had the chance to study before.

The common academic wisdom is that for every hour in class, a student should spend two to three hours outside of class studying and preparing. That translates into an additional nine hours of preparation for a typical course, almost 45 hours per week for a full-time course load. The onus is on the student to work independently or with a study group to complete readings, review information, and prepare assignments. Most learning, then, takes place outside the classroom.

I call this phenomenon the 90% -10% principle. Not to diminish the role of inspiring and knowledgeable professors, but most learning in college does not happen on their watch. It happens in the library, the student union, and in the dormitory. While I don't deny the importance of a low student-teacher ratio in learning, it is far more important at the K-12 level, where much of the work and learning happens in the classroom. In college, most professors are fairly amenable to adding students to classes if space and equipment permit. After all, the students will be doing the majority of the work outside the room.

The 90 percent principle is also at work during the 108 hours a week that students are not studying or in class. Learning is happening naturally all over campus. Even when a student is living in a dorm room with a meal plan, he needs to juggle many activities of daily life. He must plan time for meals, laundry, showers, cleaning, rest, and exercise. Add a job and a few organized social activities and the balancing act becomes even more challenging. The student may be living with a roommate for the first time and will need to negotiate differences in needs and preferences. It may be the first time he has encountered people from other countries or cultures, or who have very different outlooks on life than he does, and he will need to find ways to positively interact with them.

Students living in their own apartments have to add the skills of cooking, shopping, and traveling to and from campus. All of the skills are practical preparation for independent adulthood. Many of these skills appear on transition plans in IEPs for students with SD. What better way to learn them than in the natural laboratory of a college experience?

The 90 percent of time spent outside the classroom holds even more potential for real-life learning for students with SD than the 10 percent of the time spent inside it.

Increasing Competence Fosters Lifelong Inclusion

Individuals with SD want to have the same lives and choices as anyone else. Overwhelmingly, they want to live, learn, play, and earn in their communities as full members. People with SD are more visible and involved in all roles in the community than ever before, but full and comfortable inclusion, especially at work, remains elusive. What are the critical elements, then, that make inclusion really happen for individuals with SD?

A study in *Exceptional Children* (summer 2007) surveyed 5,837 middle school students about their attitudes toward the inclusion of peers with intellectual disabilities in their schools. Unfortunately, the findings were that, although the students realized that they needed to be "nice" to students with intellectual disabilities and that they behaved for the most part in a nice and accepting way, they did not perceive the students with ID as being truly capable of carrying out complex tasks (including academics) or as being socially desirable companions.

However, the authors also found:

*The most important finding of the present study is that youths' perception of a person with ID is the pivotal factor (in middle school students wanting to include peers with ID in classes or social experiences). More specifically, the results strongly show that neither contact nor exposure per se leads to more positive attitudes, **but rather contact and exposure that provide youth with the opportunity to witness the competence of individu-***

als with ID. Youth who perceive students with ID as being more competent are also more positive about the inclusion of those students in academic classrooms. This finding suggests that youth primarily base their judgments on whether students with ID should be included in academic classes on their percep- tions of competence (Siperstein, Parker, Bardon, and Widaman, 2007—emphasis mine).

Note the two-part conclusion: simply having students with intellec- tual disabilities in classrooms was not enough to change the attitudes of their peers. The middle school students had to be able to see the students with SD behaving in a competent way, whether socially, behaviorally, or academically. Competence, then, is critical for forming positive attitudes of middle school students toward peers with SD. Positive at- titudes based on the competence of individuals with SD will follow the middle school students throughout life and influence their acceptance of people with SD as coworkers, neighbors, and friends. Fortunately, competence, in all of its forms, can be taught. The types of competence needed by young adults with SD and ways those competencies can be taught in PSE are subjects for later chapters.

Benefits to Higher Education

Including individuals with SD in opportunities clearly benefits those individuals. But colleges and universities are in the business of education and research, not charity. However, students with SD can be far more than just passive recipients of a college's good graces. They have much to offer receiving institutions.

Institutions of higher learning are concerned about diversity on campus. Their students are going to be functioning in an increasingly global world, among people of different backgrounds. As it stands now, colleges and universities have professors and students from all over the world, of different races, ethnic identities, religious traditions, and increasingly, socioeconomic backgrounds. As people with SD become more integrated into the world, they also become a group with a history and background to be understood. Graduating students will find that people with SD become their coworkers, neighbors, customers, congregants, employees, or employers. Diverse societies have room for people of differing abilities as well.

Students with SD on campus can contribute to the education of those professionals who will eventually serve them in the community in the fields of education, psychology, medicine, human services, and hospitality. My degrees in special education, elementary education, and reading required that I actually work with students who needed those services. I spent time in local schools and working with local agencies—all off-campus. These requirements were quite a challenge, since I did not have a car until I started student teaching in my senior year. I would have jumped at the chance to do my practicums and observations on campus.

Many PSE programs on campus for students with SD actively recruit and depend upon regularly enrolled students majoring in many disciplines to work with their students as study partners, coaches, or mentors. Often, when the regularly enrolled students finish their required course hours, they continue to volunteer to work with students with SD in the programs simply because they enjoy it. They have become friends.

As I discovered while researching this book, students with SD are eager and quite capable of giving feedback on ideas and participating in research. Those participating in programs on typical college campuses might consent to be part of a graduate student's research into a disability-related topic or they might provide feedback that would be useful in expanding the concept of Universal Design (see below).

Universal Design

Universal Design (UD) is a concept developed by Ronald Mace in the early 1970s to make buildings and products user-friendly for all users, regardless of ability or disability. The principles of Universal Design are:

1. Equitable use
2. Flexibility in use
3. Simple, intuitive use
4. Perceptible information
5. Tolerance for error
6. Low physical effort
7. Size and space for approach and use

Universal Design as a philosophy maintains that ease of use and accessibility for all can be included into the design of a building without creating special accessible spaces specifically for people with disabilities. All parts of the building are designed to be used easily by everyone, regardless of need. A building conceived using UD, for example, would be designed to have entrances used easily by people who have age-related mobility problems, or who are pushing a baby stroller, carrying too many packages, or using a wheelchair. A building or computer program designed to be easily usable by all can be tested by a student with SD who may have specific access needs. Prototypes or models can receive real-time feedback from students with SD.

Although the principles of Universal Design were originally meant to improve physical access, they are now being expanded to improve access to college-level instruction. Universal Design for Instruction (UDI) uses the seven principles above and adds two additional principles specific to the classroom—a community of learners (principle 8) and instructional climate (principle 9) (Getzel and Wehman, 2005). For example, a professor might seek to enhance the classroom community and climate by encouraging communication among students and modeling respect for diversity.

Using these nine principles, college-level course work can also become more accessible for students with a variety of needs. With the explosion of online resources available to students and professors, information that used to be disseminated in a paper syllabus on the first day of class and work that involved paper textbooks and course readings in a physical library can now be made available wherever a student can log onto a computer. Professors can now make large amounts of information available to students, including course notes (principle 1: equitable use). A student with SD who must use software that reads information aloud, a student with a learning disability in spelling who struggles to take notes, a student without a car who cannot easily get to the library to get course readings, and a student who missed the day's lecture due to illness can have equal access to the information in the class notes. The additional principles concerning classroom climate can make a college classroom a more welcoming environment for students with SD and other nontraditional students by actively recognizing that diversity exists.

While applying UD in creating new buildings on campus and UDI in the classroom has great benefits for students with disabilities, every person on campus can benefit from the principles. The presence of students with SD can put positive pressure on the college environment to make maximum use of the principles.

"Eruditio Gratis Eruditio": Learning for Learning's Sake

Colleges are more than just degree factories and education is more than just a ticket to a well-paying job. While a good job is a worthy goal, education has historically been about more noble aims than just some day earning a good paycheck. Young adults with SD seem to understand this fact instinctively. I did an informal poll of my students in the spring of 2007, asking them for reasons to attend college other than the standard "to get a good job some day." Their answer stunned me in its simplicity—"I want to go to college to get smarter." They perceived that college was where you learned more than just how to be employable, but also how to be educated.

The liberal arts, originally called artes liberales, were the skills learned by freemen in the Roman empire. Slaves learned to build walls and dig ditches—they needed to have skills. If a man was free—a citizen of Rome—he had the liberty to develop his mind, as well as his body.

Christina Mailhot, a graduate of STRIVE U, a program for adults with intellectual disabilities, audited a German class through the University of Southern Maine, with a goal of understanding her family heritage. No vocational goal in international relations for her, just an interest in where she came from. Many students with SD have the same desire as their peers to learn simply for the sheer joy of learning. With apologies to the MGM studios for the use of their quote, these students believe in eruditio gratis eruditio—learning for learning's sake. This idea is learning in the truest sense of the word.

Can students with SD learn abstract concepts and participate in higher level thinking? At one time, I had my doubts. For years, I kept my classroom instruction very concrete and focused on life skills. High school students in New York State are required to study global history. My students were still struggling to remember what county and state they lived in—how could I ask them to learn about countries they would never see?

The rise of the Internet, the events of 9/11, the war in Iraq, and a realigning of learning standards for students with special needs in New York combined to change my mind. How could my students, fast approaching the age of majority, make good decisions as citizens if they did not know more about the wider world? I set out to try to find a way to teach them.

I bought a handbook on international etiquette and brought it in to class.

"Did you know that it is illegal to chew gum in Singapore?" I asked.

That's all it took. Students who fought against much-needed reading practice in the classroom were now fighting over a book. They were fascinated by the fact that other places in the world were not like their hometown. Now they know that information and much more. And, yes, they still struggle to remember their county and state. We're working on it. Now, though, I balance my instruction to address both what they need to survive in the world and what they need to thrive as people in a free society.

Components of Postsecondary Education for Students with SD

Try to picture a student with significant disabilities on a college campus. What would their day look like? What does the day of any college student look like?

Academics

An academic component is critical. College students are on campus to take classes. The type of academics offered depends upon program goals.

- Programs connected to a technical school or emphasizing majors in business or human services will offer courses related to these professions, teaching specific skills in the career field.
- Programs that emphasize transition will offer courses addressing skills needed to address the ten components of transition (see Chapter 2).
- Programs that focus on college preparation may offer specific courses in study skills and time management while students are concurrently enrolled in college-level foundation courses.
- In individually supported inclusive programs or when a student with SD is attending college without the support of a program, student interests and goals drive course selection from the standard college offerings.
- If the student is pursuing a specific degree or certificate from the college, credit requirements for the degree will determine course selection.

Program founders and directors have reported with regret that some students with SD are no more willing to accept the reality of academic demands than are some regularly enrolled students. "Some students just wanted to come to campus to 'hang out,'" said Lynne Sommerstein of the College Based Transition Program at Buffalo State College in New York. But college students take classes, and the program requires that students audit at least one class a semester. Students who balked at the requirement were asked to leave the program.

It seems obvious to say so, but college level work is hard, much harder than many students with SD have had to do before. However, continued instruction in academics is important for students with SD at the postsecondary level. Unlike some other skills, reading and writing can continue to improve throughout life, given instruction and, especially, practice. Difficulty should not be a deterrent, even if students have historically struggled to master academics. Dr. Edward Taub's research on improving motor function in stroke patients by strapping down a functional arm so that the patient was compelled to use the paralyzed arm demonstrated that consistent and intensive use of a disabled body part could restore function, even if only partially. It stands to reason, then, that students with SD could also gain skills when intensively challenged.

Work Experiences

Organized PSE programs for students with SD have an employment component.

This reality may rankle advocates who have fought for academic opportunities and have battled the "vocational track" so often used to educate students with SD. But most college students work. They work to pay expenses or work at internships related to their field of study to fulfill course requirements. Colleges have also embraced the values of volunteerism and community service and urge students to participate in these projects.

Postsecondary education programs for students with SD use a combination of these experiences to address the vocational goals and needs of their students. The number of hours spent on work experience each week depends on the program goals. Some students will work as many as twenty-five hours per week.

Social and Recreational

PSE programs encourage students to participate in campus activities, both formal and informal. Students often receive a campus ID, so that they can access fitness centers, the library, and other student centers. Many programs for students with SD have an affiliation with Best Buddies, an organization that pairs college students with young adults with intellectual disabilities, whether or not those young adults are enrolled in PSE programs.

Programs often use regularly enrolled students as peer mentors or assistants in program activities, based on the idea that structured, scheduled interactions will lead to increased comfort and respect between students with and without significant disabilities, and that natural friendships will form. This philosophy follows the Circles of Support or Circles of Friends models of social support.

Other programs hold a completely opposite philosophy. The Threshold program at Lesley University, for example, does not use regularly enrolled students as program assistants, feeling that helping relationships will hamper rather than help the formation of friendships between students with and without SD. Lesley has a liberal policy on campus clubs—as few as two students with an esoteric interest can set up a club. Threshold students can and do join these clubs, just like any other Lesley student.

Residential/Independent Living

The component of a PSE experience that is the most challenging to access, to set up, and to support for students with SD is also the component most deeply desired by the students. This component is residential life. Even many community colleges— traditionally commuter schools—are seeing regularly enrolled students who want to live on campus, and the community colleges are responding by building campus dorms and apartments. Demand for on-campus housing almost always exceeds supply. Students must meet certain enrollment criteria (admitted to a program, usually carrying a minimum number of credit hours) in order to apply for housing. Unfortunately, these criteria almost always exclude students with SD.

However, there are a number of programs in the U.S. that have a residential component that is either program specific or by special arrangement with the hosting college. The options include either traditional dormitory arrangements or small group apartments.

Students with SD want a college-living experience as much as their regularly enrolled peers do. They need it as much, or more than, the regularly enrolled peers. As programs and services for students with SD increase on college campuses, hopefully this option will become more readily available.

What's Transition Got to Do with Postsecondary Education?

Every year, millions of people around the world finish their second-ary or high school studies and go on to something else. But, if you have Down syndrome or a related disability, we have named it. We have named it transition. Otherwise, it is just "What are you doing next year?" (Simons, 2004).

Transition planning is mandated for all students with disabilities in the United States as they enter the last few years of free and appropriate public education (FAPE) under the Individuals with Disabilities Education Act (IDEA). Transition sounds formal and intimidating, but, as Jo Ann Simons wrote in the quote above, transition is really just the answer to the age-old question, "What do you want to do when you grow up?" Often, the answer includes college.

Ask a student with significant disabilities that question in child-hood, and you will hear a familiar litany of dreams. Like their peers without SD, they want to be famous actors, professional athletes, astro-nauts, doctors, and lawyers, all earning great salaries. They want to be rich, live in beautiful homes in exotic places with adoring spouses and children, and go to Disney World every year. Don't we all?

The reality of adulthood, of course, is quite different for most of us. But, as we moved from childhood to adulthood, we learned how to control and manage our lives and make what dreams we did have become reality. Although we did not know it at the time, we participated in ten different components of transition (in parentheses following each example). In the course of our independent adulthood, most of us have done the following:

1. Many of us attended college or trade schools to earn degrees or certificates in subjects that interested us. Many of us continue to take adult education classes on topics of interest or when we need to update our skills. (Postsecondary education/continuing education)
2. We work or have worked in jobs that we applied for because we liked them or liked the benefits such as the salary or the schedule that came with them. Many of us volunteer in our communities. (Employment)
3. We have some experience with the legal system. We have wills, we sign contracts, we serve on juries, and we appear in court when summoned. We know our rights and responsibilities. We have lawyers or legal advisors to help us stand up for our legal rights. (Legal/advocacy)
4. We live in our own homes. We handle the day-to-day tasks of cooking, cleaning, laundry, and paying bills. (Personal independence/residential)
5. We join clubs, go to sporting events, shop, go out to dinner or the movies by ourselves or with others (Recreation and leisure)
6. We have doctors, dentists, and medical specialists. We make and keep appointments and pick up and take prescription medications. We know about the importance of exercise and healthy diet, although we may not always follow through! (Medical/health)
7. We may have sought counseling for personal problems or mental health issues. (Counseling)
8. We have a regular source of income. We have checking accounts, savings accounts, and credit cards, and we know how they work. (Financial/income)

9. We know how to drive and/or use public transportation to get where we want and need to go. (Transportation/independent travel skills)
10. We do many other things, especially responding to unexpected good or bad fortune. (Other)

Don't Leave It to the Last Minute—Transition Planning in High School

Under IDEA, many of these transition components are addressed for children and young adults with SD at school. For ten or even twelve months of the year, the school bus arrives to take the child to school, where she receives needed instruction, therapies, and nursing services. Counseling may be available if she needs it to learn effectively and to control her behavior. In addition to academics, the child can socialize with friends, join clubs, participate in sports, attend dances, and go to concerts and plays. As the child becomes a teenager, she may be able to go on "job shadowing" visits or have a work study job; through some state programs, she may be able to get a summer job. She may even be taught independent living skills, such as cooking, cleaning, or caring for clothes in a special class setting or an inclusive home and careers class. In addition, the school district is legally obligated to identify all children who need these services and to provide the services free of charge.

The end of Free and Appropriate Education (FAPE) (see glossary) will leave a huge gap in the life of a student with SD, unless she, her family, and teachers have made a comprehensive plan for life after high school. Under IDEA, the planning process is known as transition services.

Transition services are preparation for the hand off that occurs when the student is no longer eligible for services under IDEA. Once the entitlement to FAPE comes to an end, usually in a student's early twenties or upon receiving a diploma, the student and her support system must manage all of the details of adult life. Beginning at age 16 (earlier if needed or if dictated by state law), school district personnel must begin the conversation about, what we called in the early days of the regulation, "what happens when the school bus doesn't come anymore."

Waiting until school ends to plan for adulthood is foolhardy. In the late 1980s, before the reauthorization of IDEA reminded school districts and parents to plan for transition, I worked in a vocational training program in Massachusetts. I watched the effects of a failure to plan for adult life on a student I will call Trisha. Trisha was tiny, thin, and cheerful and she looked and acted more like a child of 7 than a young woman of 21. Her family apparently thought of her that way, too, judging from how often her job coach needed to remind her that bringing toys to work was not appropriate. According to her teacher, the family was very reluctant to discuss the next step for Trisha. After all, the school bus kept coming—why worry?

In June before her exit date, Trisha participated in the program's graduation ceremony. She continued to attend the program—as she was entitled to under Massachusetts state law—until her twenty-second birthday. As the months passed, the staff reported with increasing alarm and frustration that there was still no plan for Trisha. She continued playing happily with her toys, at home and at work. She was delighted on the day of her birthday, anticipating a party at home that night. The staff was grim, knowing what would happen next.

Trisha did not come to school the next day, because she was twenty-two years old. I can only imagine the panic in her house that morning, because Trisha was not capable of being left at home alone and her parents needed to go to work. I remember her father was extremely angry with the program staff—all because the school bus stopped coming.

Later, no doubt after much scrambling, hurried meetings, and frantic phone calls, Trisha's family was able to enroll her in an adult program that allowed her to return to our program for additional vocational training. I doubt that her family even then was making plans for the next step for Trisha. The best they could do was return her to a program for teenagers that she had attended for several years already. I don't know what happened to Trisha after that temporary fix expired.

Even in the early 1990s when I was teaching in New York, parents were allowed an "out" in transition planning. In many meetings, when future plans for employment, education, and independent living were discussed, parents were allowed to say that some plans were "too far off to discuss at this time." Many did, even parents of students who were between the ages of 18 and 21. The students themselves had not gotten much beyond their dreams of "being rich and living in a beautiful house."

Times have changed. I seriously doubt that my current students would allow their parents to say that their transition to adult life was "too far off to discuss at this time." Most of them have been plotting to move out and run their own lives since middle school and they realize that they will need training and a job that pays a living wage to meet that goal. Wanting to reach the goals of independence and self-determination and actually doing what it takes to reach them is the substance of transition planning.

Postsecondary education is considered a single component of transition. However, as we are discussing in this book, PSE is not just an end in itself, but is a powerful tool for learning and practicing all of the components of transition. Secondary transition planning services can lay the groundwork for PSE and the other transition components by preparing students with SD and their families for the legal differences between services guaranteed under IDEA and those guaranteed under the Americans with Disabilities Act and Section 504.

· ·

Changes in Legal Protection after High School

The reason for the change from comprehensive services provided by schools to often patched-together services for adults is that different laws apply to different age groups. IDEA—the law that applies to students aged 3 to 21—is about entitlement. A little entitlement can be a dangerous thing; total entitlement can be even worse.

Imagine a nineteen-year-old high school senior with significant disabilities. Consider the entitlements and protections that this student has under IDEA:

1. The school district must provide free and appropriate educational services, in the least restrictive environment possible. Often, services are provided in the student's home district, in the

neighborhood school. If appropriate services can't be provided there, the district will pay tuition for an appropriate program.

2. The district is responsible for ongoing assessment by psychologists, certified teachers, and therapists, to make sure the right services are being provided.

3. Teachers are responsible for modifying instruction, modifying content, and modifying assessment conditions, as needed to maximize student success. If appropriate, districts may waive certain graduation requirements, such as a foreign language or mathematics course.

4. The district pays for transportation.

5. The district is held accountable for identifying students who have disabilities and making sure the students receive their services, modifications, and accommodations. In my district, if a student waives a service (such as test accommodations) teachers must document that the accommodations were offered and the student declined them.

6. The district is required to hold an annual meeting with all stakeholders (the student, her family, school staff) to update plans, to review progress, and to address questions and concerns. Parents must be notified of the meeting in a timely fashion, interpreters must be provided as needed, and parents may bring any experts or advocates that they wish to the meetings.

Note the responsible party for students who are still in high school—the school district. Now, consider the rights of the same student one year later, after receiving her diploma and considering college, when her rights as a person with SD are protected by the ADA and Section 504. To use a colloquial expression, suddenly the student is not in Kansas anymore!

The Americans with Disabilities Act and Section 504 of the Vocational Act are antidiscrimination laws. They provide legal protection if someone is discriminated against at work or at school on the basis of their disability and require that public services and buildings be accessible as well (i.e., have ramps or elevators, use of Braille labels, or flashing fire alarms). The key ideas here are preventing discrimination and providing for accessibility; nowhere in either law does it say that people with disabilities are entitled to anything other than the same treatment under the law as people without disabilities.

Look at the changes in rights and entitlements before and after graduation for the student mentioned above.

1. Educational services are no longer free or guaranteed. The student must apply for admission to college and find a way to pay for it. The college retains the right to accept or reject applicants based on their eligibility or number of spaces available in the program.

2. If the student needs an educational assessment, she must arrange for it and may need to pay for it.

3. Colleges retain the right to refuse to modify course content or to waive program requirements.

4. Transportation is the responsibility of the student, although campus transportation must be accessible to people with physical disabilities.

5. The student must self-disclose her disability in order to receive academic accommodations. The student is responsible for following up to make sure the accommodations are being provided and are effective for her needs. This follow-up can include meeting with disability support staff, speaking to professors about the need for accommodations, advertising for a paid note taker or tutor, scheduling a time in advance at a testing center, etc. Personal care attendants must be hired and funded privately—the college is only required to provide academic accommodations. Academic support services such as tutoring or organizational coaching may or may not be available on campus through the college, and if they are privately available, the services may require an additional fee.

6. The student must advocate for any meetings necessary. Parents are no longer considered part of the decision making team. All privacy laws about grades, performance evaluations, and health status apply, unless the student has a court-appointed guardian or has signed permission to share the information with her parents. Unless a parent has been granted guardianship by a court, a young adult with SD is her own guardian at age 18. (Note to parents: your young adult will love this fact as much as you will hate it. See more on the complexities of guardianship in Chapter 17.)

7. There are no allowances in the ADA for behavior that is a manifestation of the disability.

Throughout this book, pay close attention to the discussions of changes in legal protection. These changes are among the hardest that families of young people with SD will face as adulthood begins. This transfer of responsibility will happen as the calendar turns the page to the day the student exits from IDEA eligibility.

The transition from childhood to young adulthood is overwhelming for every family, not just families of individuals with SD. Enrolling in a postsecondary program with other young adults going through the same process, whether they have SD or not, is a tremendous opportunity to master transition components in a natural environment.

In addition to attending academic classes, students with SD may have the opportunity to work in work study jobs (which can help with funding PSE), internships, practicums, and service learning/volunteer opportunities. These experiences can be noted on a resume. They can offer the chance to try out different career paths, including those not typically open to individuals with SD.

Many students live in dormitories or campus apartments during college. Living away from home provides tremendous opportunities for practicing independent living skills in a supervised setting. Students can also practice traveling to, from, and around campus safely and independently.

College campuses have numerous age-appropriate social events. Media depictions of wild partying and drinking notwithstanding, campuses have a lot invested in providing many options to help students avoid the dangers of overindulging in alcohol or drugs. Campuses host movies, dances, clubs, shows, and athletic events on a regular basis.

Programs for students with SD are keenly aware of their role in transition to adult life and offer a variety of supports so that students can gain experience in transition components. Every program I visited planned transition practice or instruction into its offerings, but they delivered the services in a variety of ways.

For students who need direct instruction in transition components, some programs offer specific classes. These classes may make up part of or the majority of the postsecondary program. Classes in human sexuality and health are popular offerings, as are classes in employment seeking, social skills, financial management, self-advocacy, and mental health issues. Some students need this level of support, while others will benefit from targeted coaching as issues arise (e.g., managing a checkbook, planning what to say to a professor). However, I cannot stress enough the importance of teaching these skills (see Chapters 15, 16, and 17 for a more complete discussion of how to begin). Young people, with or without SD, can quickly stumble into financial, social, professional, or academic difficulty without the guidance of their mentors.

College is an interlude before the rigors of adult life. Including training and practice in skills that will be needed throughout life—whether it's called "transition" or "what are you doing next"—is a critical aspect of making a college education count.

Addressing the Elephant
in the Lecture Hall:
Inclusion and Postsecondary Program Options

This chapter is one I wanted to avoid, but the topic sat there like the proverbial elephant in the lecture hall, and no matter how studiously I ignored it, the topic came up in every interview and in every article I read on the subject of postsecondary options for students with significant special needs. To fully include or not to fully include—that was the question.

The Think College website (www.thinkcollege.net), which has the most comprehensive listing on the World Wide Web of available programs for students with intellectual disabilities, has classified the programs into three model types: inclusive individual support model, mixed model, and substantially separate model.

- **Inclusive individualized support model:** students participate in classes with students without disabilities and are provided with supports and services to maximize participation and learning opportunities.
- **Mixed model:** students participate in social activities and/or academic classes with students without disabili-

ties and also participate in classes with other students with disabilities (sometimes referred to as "life skills" or "transition" program).

- **Substantially separate model:** students only participate in classes with other students with disabilities (sometimes referred to as "life skills" or "transition" program) (From www.ThinkCollege.net)

I have had experience working in all three models. I began my work with individuals with SD in substantially separate programs, ranging from a summer camp to a job training program for young adults. While I was working on my bachelor's degree at Syracuse University, I had the opportunity to observe and to work in a fully inclusive second grade classroom. Since then, my teaching experience has been in mixed programs, where my students were included in a variety of classes and social situations, but received daily instruction in life skills and modified academics in a special class setting.

My training at Syracuse University advocated full inclusion. Full inclusion is where students with disabilities learn side by side with typical students in classrooms and participate in age appropriate clubs and activities at school. Any needed special education services or modifications to curriculum are provided in the general education setting. After being fully included in classrooms from preschool through high school, some students and parents want full inclusion to continue at the college level. They want to take the same classes, join the same clubs, and live in the same residence halls and apartments as regularly enrolled undergraduates.

Differences in Philosophy

As I researched this book, I found that interviews with program coordinators and articles about postsecondary education always returned to the full inclusion/not full inclusion debate. To me, the arguments on both sides were compelling. Some of the reasons for differences in philosophy follow. I began to realize that the debate was just that—one of philosophy. I learned in graduate school to be suspicious of single philosophies of education. While studying reading education in the early 1990s, I watched caring, committed educators nearly come to blows in the "decoding" versus "whole language" debate. At the time, it struck me as a pointless argument. Obviously, both methods had their merit—many students learned to read using decoding methods and many learned to read by immersion in whole language experiences. Many students learned using a combination of both. Wasn't there room in classrooms for a combination of effective methods?

In the course of my research for this book, I met intelligent, informed, and experienced people who feel extremely strongly that either full inclusion or substantially separate models are the only right way to educate students with significant special needs. I heard full inclusion advocates denounce separate programs and describe the amazing growth of students immersed in general education with natural supports. I heard advocates of significantly separate programs bemoan full inclusion and speak of the amazing growth of *their* students who were taking specialized classes. I listened attentively to compelling arguments on both sides, and came to the only conclusion that I could—both sides were right.

However passionate the arguments for one type of program being "right" for all students, I have decided after long consideration that I will not prescribe a specific program type. The decision on program type must be made on the individual level, made by students and their families and based on the student's goals, preferences, needs, and desires. I do not expect this decision to be popular with either camp, but my reasons follow.

To prescribe a single type of program to a young adult with SD is paternalistic. I would not say to a typical college applicant, "Because you are a woman you should/should not attend an all women's college"; or, "Because you are a student of color, you should/should not attend a historically black college." The choice to attend a college program where you will or will not be in the minority is up to the individual student. It should be the same for students with SD. I'm certain that we as a society would never say to a non-intellectually disabled adult that he did not have the fundamental right to choose how and where to pursue higher education, even if that choice will separate that student from the full range of student diversity. In fact, if a student is exceptionally able or is pursuing a specialized course of study, college advisors may urge the student to enter honors programs or specialized colleges that will almost guarantee that the student will be in a homogeneous group.

People with disabilities have chosen, at times, to separate themselves from the mainstream. The Deaf (meaning culturally Deaf) community has chosen to engage in significantly separate education for many years to teach and to preserve a rich legacy of language, history, and the arts to Deaf children and founded Gallaudet University and the National Technical Institute for the Deaf as largely separate institutions. Deaf students who meet the "otherwise qualified" designation under ADA can apply for and attend colleges and universities with hearing students and receive interpreter services, or may choose to attend college where Deaf people will be in the majority. There are solid reasons for people with disabilities to choose to be educated or to socialize together. Support groups all share the cardinal principle that, sometimes, no one understands what it is like to be deeply challenged than someone else who is facing the same challenge.

But, by the same reasoning, I don't think society would ever say that people without disabilities must be completely separate in all areas of their life, only interacting with others who are like themselves. We are different from one another but must share the same world. Sooner or later, we must all develop the coping skills that are necessary to deal with these differences, and college is a good time to do that. We may choose to be with people like ourselves for some parts of the day and to immerse ourselves in the wider society for other parts of the day. As adults, we claim the right to choose how and when to join in and to pull away. That choice should be available to people with SD as well, and no one else's philosophy should interfere with it.

I have had students make choices that I disagree with strongly—to drop out of school, to become teen parents, to break the law, to move out of their parents' home. At times like these, I find myself frustrated and angry, but remind myself that young adults must make their choices and learn from them. This truth, after all, is at the heart of self-determination philosophy. The only rule I insist upon for my students is that although they can make poor choices for themselves, their behavior should not negatively affect other people. You want to waste time in class and fail the year? Fine, but don't spend your time disrupting other people who want to pass and can't focus because you are acting up. You can choose for yourself, but you have no right to choose for anyone else. Perhaps that needs to be the philosophy we embrace when talking about PSE for young adults with disabilities.

Lynne Sommerstein, lecturer in Exceptional Education at Buffalo State College, made this observation about the students in the inclusive individually supported model at Buffalo State, when people observed that the program students tended to spend their free time together: "If they choose to be together, that's fine. But it is about choice." Marc Ellison, the director of the College Program for Students with Asperger Syndrome at Marshall University, expanded on this idea to say, "Students with disabilities should have a menu of options to choose from, and it should be a rich menu." Here, then, are the postsecondary options that are currently available to students with SD in U.S. colleges and universities.

Inclusive Individual Support Model

In a fully inclusive individual support college experience, students with significant special needs attend classes, side by side, with typically enrolled peers. The courses are chosen by the student and his advisors, based on interests, abilities, and future employment goals, often arrived at through person-centered planning (see glossary). Students often participate in the course activities, but not for credit (often called "auditing" or "sitting in" on the course); the option for credit is available if the student completes the same course work required of other students. When a student audits a class, assignments and readings may be adapted to meet the student's individual abilities.

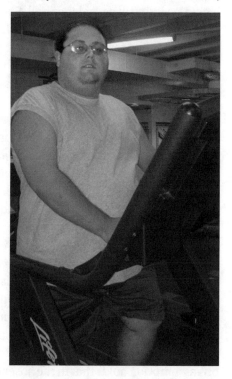

Students receive academic and personal supports through a variety of methods. An on-campus facilitator and support staff may have primary responsibility for adapting curriculum, providing tutoring, guiding self-advocacy, and approaching professors about student inclusion. Some programs work with a team of volunteers, who are regularly enrolled students. These regularly enrolled students often begin their work as part of a field study for a course in education or psychology, and are seeking experience working with people with disabilities. The College Program for Students with Asperger Syndrome at Marshall University and the College Based Transition Program at Buffalo State College are two examples of fully inclusive experiences with an organized support system on campus.

Other students with special needs choose to create an educational program of their own, at colleges and universities that have no set "program" to help them do so. Given support from parents, peers, supportive college professors, and college administrators, these students create an individualized experience, taking classes toward a certificate or degree or for their own personal enrichment. Katie Apostolides, the student with Down Syndrome mentioned in Chapter One, applied to and was accepted as a general admission student at Becker College in Massachusetts and was able to take part in all of the usual college programs and services, including living in a residence hall. She arranged tutoring and other academic accommodations through the Disability Support Services office.

Advocates for full inclusion, at all levels of education, view it as a human rights issue. They argue that separate programs cannot be equal and are tantamount to special education at the college level, rather than college level education. They argue the undeniable fact that the adult world is not "special," or at least, that the parts of it that are "special" (sheltered workshops, group homes) can be demeaning and undesirable. Some full inclusion advocates are people with SD who were educated in separate schools and compelled to live in separate environments in adulthood. In order to prepare for an inclusive life, advocates believe, all students should learn, live, and socialize side by side from preschool through college.

Assuming that students with intellectual disabilities have the ability to fully participate in classes and campus life follows what researcher Anne Donnellan (1984) calls "the criterion of least dangerous assumption." Donnellan wrote about individuals who had significant and multiple disabilities, including communication disabilities, whose understanding could not be measured by standard tests involving speaking, writing, or even gesturing. She wrote that "the criterion of least dangerous assumption holds that in the absence of conclusive data, educational decisions ought to be based on assumptions which, if incorrect, will have the least dangerous effect on the likelihood that students will be able to function independently as adults" (Donnellan, 1984).

INCLUSIVE POSTSECONDARY PROGRAMS IN CANADA

Full inclusion in postsecondary education has a long history in Canada. Canadian universities began fully including students with intellectual disabilities in 1987, beginning with eleven students at the University of Alberta, using a process known as IPSE (Inclusive Post-Secondary Education). Students have been included in a wide variety of courses, academic as well as nonacademic. A longitudinal study of the graduates of IPSE programs has found that 70 percent of them are competitively employed (Uditsky and Hughson).

Even if the course work did not culminate in a degree or certificate, one study found that achievement of employment and independent living goals could be attributed to the strengthening of student resumes through academic course work. Other positive employment outcomes came from networking with peers without disabilities who were able to help the IPSE students find work in their fields (Biersdorff, Bowman, and Weinkauf, 2004).

Tim Weinkauf from the University of Alberta listed the following principles of IPSE:

1. IPSE is open to any adult with an intellectual disability.
2. IPSE is totally inclusive and is coherent with what other students experience.
3. Students in IPSE programs assume Socially Valued Roles.
4. IPSE programs provide Individual Student Support(s).
5. IPSE programs provide support to others (professors, volunteers, peers) as well.
6. IPSE programs encourage self determination of students.
7. IPSE students involve families.
8. IPSE programs view students as adult learners.
9. IPSE programs see friendships as educational outcomes.
10. IPSE is a tool for community education.
11. IPSE programs believe that education extends beyond the classroom (Weinkauf, 2002).

But what about students who can gesture, speak, and even read and write to show what they know? Wouldn't IQ or achievement testing be able to determine what the student is capable of learning and preclude full inclusion in college level classes?

IQ testing is not as definitive as has been claimed, although the score on an IQ test is one of the criteria used to diagnose people with a learning or intellectual disability. The National Council on Educational Outcomes, in its 2004 study of expectations for students with cognitive disability, reports that "IQ test scores, under optimal test conditions, account for 40% to 50% of current expected achievement. Thus, 50% to 60% of student achievement is related to variables 'beyond intelligence'" (NCEO, 2004). In other words, students can achieve at levels higher than their IQ would indicate based on factors such as motivation, social skills, and learning strategies, as well as environmental factors such as the amount and quality of instruction available, family influences, and other experiences that influence learning. Given high expectations and the multiple, rich opportunities for learning for students who are immersed in a college setting, wouldn't students logically outperform their IQ score?

Advocates are extraordinarily passionate about accepting nothing less than full inclusion, for all students at the postsecondary level. Candee Basford stated at a Postsecondary Education Conference sponsored by the Ohio Down Syndrome Advocacy Network (ODAN) in May 2007 that:

> "Unfortunately . . . in spite of warnings of the negative consequences, special programs on campus have proliferated. We believe that these special programs are akin to special education in the basement. Special programs only reinforce our culture's historic patterns of segregation and false assumptions. Special programs are the easy way out for higher education, saving them from the need to invest in any meaningful change. The special program has been harmful to the future of inclusion at college by becoming THE place to send students with significant disabilities. We do not support the development of these special programs on campus and we ask that others join us in adopting an inclusive approach."

Greg Palmer writes of his son, Ned, who has Down syndrome:
> "His own intellectual and even physical abilities rise or fall depending on the crowd around him. . . . I want the best for him, and from personal experience I truly believe that he

*is happiest and most functional when he's around people
without disabilities. . . . I don't think Ned is any better than
[other people with disabilities] but because of his abilities,
the experiences he's had, and the friends he's made outside of
the developmentally disabled community, I think he is a little
different"* (Palmer, 2005).

Parents and teachers of young adults with SD have reported this
effect many times. They have seen adolescents with special needs rise to
the occasion far better in academic and social environments when they
are completely included, and for these young people, a fully included
postsecondary experience may be indicated.

Substantially Separate Model

Postsecondary programs that use a substantially separate model
provide all instruction in small groups only to students enrolled in the
program. The course work offered depends on the program goals, as
well as the individual goals of the students.

Substantially separate programs may offer training in a particular
career field, such as business, auto mechanics, childcare, food service,
musical performance, etc. The course work specifically teaches the
skills needed in that career area, at a reduced pace, with repetition
as needed for the students to achieve mastery. In many cases, a major
program component is internships in the field of major. The programs
arrange the internships at local places of employment, and supervise
or support students in their job sites as needed. Some programs require
two to three days per week at internships.

Other programs have a more general instructional program, focusing on transition areas and skills. (See Chapter 2 for a discussion of
typical transition areas.) Continuing instruction in basic academics is
sometimes provided.

Far fewer education professionals are willing to publicly state
their stance on separate programs, for fear of seeming discriminatory.
However, advocates of substantially separate programs are just as passionate as full inclusion advocates about their specialized instruction.
One program's director even went so far as to decry what she termed
the "inclusion illusion."

"I can't see the benefit of simply allowing students to sit in a college class just to sit there, when they could really be learning skills," said one director whose program has a greater than 80 percent employment rate among its graduates.

Another director has questioned students who entered her program after attending a fully inclusive college setting about what they had learned in the classes. "They say to me, 'Oh, I don't know. I just sat in on the class.'" The director felt that the students' time had been wasted, since they were unable to explain the goals they had achieved in their inclusive college courses.

Ann Christy Dybvik, a speech-language pathologist and autism resource consultant, acknowledged the argument in favor of full inclusion over separate programs this way:

"The fiercely emotional nature of these arguments renders it difficult to criticize the practice of inclusion. Those who make the attempt often find their fundamental beliefs regarding tolerance and diversity coming under fire. But those harboring doubts about inclusion do not generally question the values behind it, only whether the practice is effective."

Diane Twachtman-Cullen from the Autism and Developmental Disabilities Consultation Center in Cromwell, Connecticut, created a list of "worst practices in inclusion," including:

1. Insisting on inclusion at all costs
2. Settling for a mere physical presence in the classroom
3. Giving priority to the inclusive education model over the individual needs of students
4. Providing little or no training to staff.

All of these poor practices could exist on a college campus that was not prepared to educate students with significant special needs.

Michael F. Gliona, Alexandra K. Gonzales, and Eric S. Jacobson in their article "Dedicated, Not Segregated" write that the concept of least restrictive environment (LRE) under IDEA has been misinterpreted. The continuum of alternative placements (CAP) has typically been presented as a top-down diagram, with the regular classroom in the most favored position at the top and a separate residential program at the bottom. Therefore, the authors argue, the range of choices has stopped being a continuum and started being seen as best to worst based on where the student is educated. Gonzales writes that, "Every option on the continuum of alternative placements is some child's least restrictive environment," based on the level of independence and involvement that the student can have in the situation:

> "If a disabled student must be personally escorted everywhere on a general education campus but can get around with relative independence on a more protective special education campus, then probably the special campus is the LRE for that student. . . . **Special schools are not segregated, and they are not needlessly restrictive for the students they serve** [authors' emphasis]. . . . On the contrary, these schools serve students of many cultures. They provide students with real opportunities to form friendships, to participate in school activities and to participate in community life. Students at special schools do not need 'Circle of Friends' committees or 'person-centered' assessment procedures to oversee their social life" (Kauffman and Hallehan, 2005).

Greg Conderman, associate professor of special education at the University of Wisconsin, has made the argument that full inclusion has focused on "equal treatment instead of equal opportunity," meaning that all students should be educated in the same way, rather than in the way that works best for the student in question. This situation is just what advocates for students with SD want to avoid.

It is worth noting that some substantially separate programs offer more contact with regularly enrolled students than others. Depending upon the program, the time spent in class may be separate, but internships and social interactions are inclusive. Parents and students will need to ask about the opportunities for inclusion if this issue is a high priority in their decision-making process. One service that is more readily available in substantially separate programs is campus living in program residences. Some programs offer a dormitory type of experience and others offer apartment-style living. These options are much more difficult (although not impossible) to come by in a fully inclusive experience, since students who are not pursuing a degree or carrying a full-time course load may not be permitted to apply for housing. Instruction in independent living skills (cooking, cleaning, paying bills, doing laundry) is intensive in separate programs and is usually not provided as part of the program in fully inclusive programs.

Substantially separate programs are working toward the same outcome as fully inclusive programs—independent and worthwhile futures for the students they serve. Their emphasis is on developing competence in a specialized situation *first* in order to maximize inclusion later on. Adult outcomes (employment, independent living, personal satisfaction) for students who graduate from substantially separate programs are equal to the outcomes for fully included programs, so the bottom-up approach has validity for some students.

Mixed Model

In a mixed model, students with disabilities participate in some classroom and social activities with students without disabilities and in some instruction and social activities with other program participants. Many programs that began as substantially separate have added these elements, and could now be classified as mixed models.

Mixed models can draw from the best practices of substantially separate models and fully inclusive models. Students can receive specialized instruction in areas of need and follow their strengths and interests in inclusive settings. In many mixed model programs, program staff teach subjects required for the special program in separate classrooms, usually on the college campus. Then, the students with SD spend part

of the day in regular college classes and inclusive internships or social settings (clubs, working out in the campus health club).

There are mixed programs with residential components, as well. In some programs, students live on college campuses in a dormitory where they are supervised and supported by residential staff. In others, they live in housing specifically for students with disabilities. The majority of the programs listed on the Think College website are mixed models, so this model is the most readily available to students with SD and their families.

I had hoped in the course of my research to find that mixed models were "the best of both worlds," and therefore, the best model to use for students with SD at the postsecondary level, but I did not find that to be the case. Once again, it is the best model for some students, but not all.

Some students may not benefit from a mixed model, because they may feel that they do not socially belong anywhere, and would prefer to either be fully included or just among other students with SD. Other students may feel over- or under-challenged by the academic and social demands. Still others may stay too much within their "comfort zone"

DUAL ENROLLMENT

· ·

In many communities, high school students without disabilities can take advantage of college level programs while still enrolled in high school. This is called "dual enrollment" and has been used for many years to allow students to take courses and earn credits that would otherwise not be available to them in high school. Students are often able to transfer these earned credits and apply them towards a degree.

Many forward-thinking school districts have begun to use the dual enrollment concept to allow their students with SD the chance to spend all or part of their school day on college campuses. These dual enrollment students can audit courses or take courses for credit or participate in a specialized program with on-campus service coordination.

The advantage of dual enrollment is that districts might be able to use IDEA funding to pay for tuition, books, and even staff members on campus (see Chapter 6). Sometimes, several school districts combine resources or work with adult service agencies such as the ARC to create a program like this for their students with SD who are between the ages of 18 and 21.

(whether that zone is substantially separate or inclusive) and refuse to address issues that they need to address to become fully independent. If a student is "hiding" his disability, for example, and is not willing to do the hard work of really understanding himself and what he needs to do to learn and function as an adult, a mixed model may not be the best choice. Better to face those realities in a fully inclusive or significantly separate program than allow the student to put off the inevitable growth in personal understanding.

For students who adapt easily and have a good understanding of their strengths and weaknesses, who are willing to stretch themselves at times but recognize when they are in need of more help, a mixed program might be the best model. Mixed programs can vary widely in the types and the amount of inclusion they provide. Some programs have a lot of social mixing, but little academic inclusion. Other programs may include students for one or more courses, but not facilitate much social inclusion. Parents and students should visit any program they are considering to see how the program handles the mixture and judge whether it fits the student's needs and goals.

* *

What Program Is Best for an Individual Student?

The most important aspect of choosing a program is what I call "buy-in." I learned long ago that we as educators could create the most supportive and welcoming inclusive experience or the highest quality, service-rich special class experience, or anything on the continuum in between, but if the parent and/or the student really did not want that type of experience, it was not going to work—period.

Over the years I have had a few students who were working toward a regular high school diploma, and their parents advocated for them to enter my special class and pursue an IEP diploma instead. One mother told me that when her daughter was in general education classes, she spent hours on homework each night, stressed out and in tears, only to fail every test and barely pass her classes. They decided to focus on her vocational training instead, much to the young lady's relief. She became a star student in her vocational program, and continued to build her academic skills in a special setting with a slower pace of instruction. In another case, I had colleagues repeatedly consult with me about a young man they were certain would never pass the state graduation tests, but he and his mother were insistent that he should attempt a regular diploma. He is now thriving in a two-year college pursuing an associate's degree. Students will work hard to make their preferred situations work, and their parents will work hard to encourage and support them, and outcomes will tend to be better in these cases.

Please note that I say that outcomes *tend* to be better. Students with SD and their families are not immune from what Anne Ford in her book *On Their Own* calls "the nay-sayer" and "deluded optimist" phenomena. To freely apply her concept in this situation, the nay-sayer parent and student underestimate the student's abilities and potential to grow in postsecondary education, and the deluded optimist parent and student may overestimate the student's abilities and potential to grow. Ford initially fell into the nay-sayer category when considering PSE for her daughter, Allegra, who has severe multiple learning disabilities:

"'She'll never be able to go to college,'" I said, and I firmly believed it, even though Allegra had not yet turned ten. Over the years I learned more about children with LD and their potential, and I saw that hopes for college did not have to be abandoned, only revised. My notions of 'college' needed revising as well" (Ford, 2007).

Parents and students in the nay-sayer category are looking for college to be an emotionally and intellectually safe situation, where the students will not be challenged or frustrated. These students and their families need to gain an understanding of the "dignity of risk" concept—that success in college, regardless of the type of program chosen, is by no means guaranteed, but there is much to be learned from challenge and failure.

Ford also writes of an extreme example of a deluded optimist, who had a son with severe learning disabilities and was pursuing a degree at a high profile college:

". . . When I wondered aloud how the young man got into such a high powered school, he [the mother's boyfriend] told me that the boy's mother wrote the essays for his college application. I then asked how the young man was doing, and he told me things were beginning to spiral out of control. He was in way over his head, but rather than allow him to transfer to a college more appropriate to his level, the mother chose instead to pack up everything and move to the college town, not only to keep an eye on her son, but to do all his homework for him!" (Ford, 2004)

This situation has happened more often with students with SD in inclusive situations than some programs would like to admit. For example, program coordinators of the On-Campus Program at Syracuse University had to face this issue. In well-meaning efforts to assure the success of the students with SD in inclusive settings, a few program staff did the homework for students and had the students copy it (Walker and Rogan, 2007). A student with SD will benefit more from taking a less challenging academic course and doing the work independently than having someone else do the work or having the course work watered down to the point that it is of no benefit to the student.

Choosing the Right Setting for Your Student

What do all of these options mean when choosing what to do about PSE for students with SD? As a first step, you may want to fill out the checklist on pages 57-61. Then, list all of the choices of PSE programs you are considering and choose the one that will best meet the student's needs and desires.

Jo Ann Simons, the President/CEO of the St. Coletta and Cardinal Cushing Schools of Massachusetts and the mother of Jon, a young adult with special needs, described an enviable list of options that Jon had to choose from at the end of his senior year of high school:

1. attend a 4-year college in Massachusetts, as a non-degree student (the first at that college),
2. attend college at a program in New York state,
3. attend a postgraduate independent living skills program at Riverview School, or
4. live in his community and get a job (Simons, 2004).

Jon decided to take the third option, while concurrently enrolling in Cape Cod Community College in a mixed program for students with special needs. He had a genuine choice, from a rich menu of choices, and as we said at the opening of this chapter, it really is about choice after all.

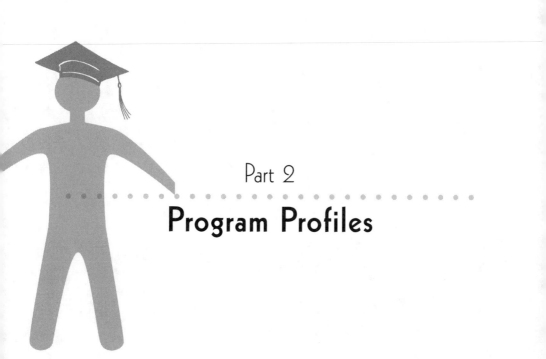

Part 2

Program Profiles

More about Options

Programs and on-campus services directed toward students with significant disabilities exist all over the United States and more become available every year. The following chapters profile a few of the programs that I have had the privilege to visit. They represent a variety of experiences that are currently available to students. For brevity's sake, I was not able to include all of the programs I visited, but a complete list is included in the Acknowledgements.

Students with significant disabilities are as different from one another as other students. I have had many transfer students enter my class over the years; the accompanying IEP, as required by law, lists their classification on the first page: "mental retardation," "learning disability in language arts/math," "autism." Most of the time, the student's shoe size would have given me more insight into who she was and what she needed. Obviously, students have some similarities in their needs, but not as much as a common classification might suggest.

The supports and options that will address the goals and needs of one student with SD will not address the goals and needs of the next student with SD, even if they share a common disability. Their level of independence, their academic skill level, the level of supervision they need for safety—all of these areas will vary from student to student.

In the interest of creating a common vocabulary, I have classified the programs discussed in the book into the following categories. Occasionally, programs will straddle categories.

Instructional Focus

Academic. Most of the classes available in a program with an academic instructional focus are those offered in a typical college program (English, sociology, art, biology, mathematics, etc.) and/or they build academic skills for the sake of academic development, rather than to teach skills needed on the job or for independent living. There may be nonacademic classes available and some emphasis on transition and independent living, but these are not the dominant focus of the program.

Vocational/Technical. The classes available in a program with a vocational/technical focus are required for students who wish to meet the training requirements for a specific career area. Other classes available may address employability skills (interviewing, resumes, social skills) and there may be some nonacademic courses available for personal enrichment. Internships are often a big component of these programs.

Transition/Independent Living. The classes and programs available in this type of program are geared toward teaching students the skills needed for future independent living and self-management (see Chapter 2). Course work may be offered in a traditional classroom setting, in the community, through internships, or in social activities offered by the program.

Living Options

Commuter Program. Commuter programs are day programs, where students must travel back and forth between campus and home daily. Students may live near campus in their own apartments or houses supported by agencies or people other than the college.

Residential Program. I use this term to apply to programs that provide living options on or off campus (dormitory, apartments, rented house). In some cases, these programs require that students enrolled in the program live on campus.

• •

Supervision and Support

Note: Many postsecondary education programs for students with SD offer more than one level of supervision and support, depending on the individual student's needs. Often, program goals will include moving students to lower levels of support as they become more independent.

High Support. Students who need this level of support are directly supervised by program staff at all times while on campus, traveling,

---

PERSONAL CARE ASSISTANTS

• •

Some college students with significant disabilities may need the help of a personal care assistant, also called a PCA (see glossary) to help them eat, bathe, dress, or use the bathroom while they are on campus. Many students with SD receive these services from teachers, teacher aides, and school nurses while they are in high school. Because these services are considered part of a free and appropriate education, high school students and families do not have to arrange or pay for this care.

Postsecondary education is a different story. Colleges and programs are not required to arrange or pay for the services of a PCA for a student, even if the student needs these services to attend classes. The student and his family must hire, manage, and find a way to pay for the services of a PCA.

Fortunately, there are public funding sources for paying for PCA care (e.g., Medicaid). PCAs may need to get permission from the Office of Disability Support Services (ODSS) to attend classes with the student with SD and to enter the dormitories and dining halls to provide care. Some colleges and programs may limit access to classes, except if the PCA is needed for the student's health and safety in class. (For example, a student who has a severe seizure condition may need the PCA to stay in class.) ODSS can also help in making arrangements for parking permits for PCAs.

or in campus residences. However, students are expected to be independent in self-care. Academic support may be directly provided in the classroom by program staff.

Moderate Support. Students are supervised for a certain number of hours per day, but are allowed and expected to move or travel independently on campus when they have demonstrated capability. Students may be taught how to travel off campus independently. Academic support may take the form of tutoring.

Low support. This level is closest to the life of a college student without SD. Students have access to program staff or resident advisors in emergencies, and staff may be available in residences overnight. A high degree of personal independence is expected for admission. Academic support may be available, but students must seek out help as needed.

Level of Inclusion

Inclusive. In an inclusive program, there are no specialized or separate classes for students with SD. Social experiences with peers without disabilities are often facilitated by staff members (through programs such as Best Buddies, peer mentoring).

Mixed. Both specialized classes and inclusive classes are provided in a mixed program. Social experiences with students who do not have disabilities may or may not be facilitated, but inclusive experiences are often available.

Specialized. In a specialized program for students with SD, classes are program specific and limited to program participants. Social experiences may be inclusive or may be specialized for program participants only.

Readers may want to know my opinion on the best program I visited, but I saw many "best programs." I can assure you that I would not have included a profile unless the program was of high caliber and providing good services for its students. I also visited excellent programs that I could not include in the profiles for the sake of brevity. But, I cannot in good conscience call any program the "best." During every tour, during every conversation with the young people enrolled in the programs, I saw places that would fit one of my students, past, present, or future. But remember, I have almost twenty years' worth of students to place and at least ten more to go. Most families will only be placing one or two children. What is important is that you and the student find the best place for her to reach her goals.

Readers should also keep in mind that the programs and options described in this book are in constant evolution. Any information on programs or laws can change without warning. Always, always check the information to ensure its accuracy.

. . . .

What's the Best Type of Program for My Student?

Answer the following guiding questions to narrow down the possibilities for postsecondary education for your student. Involve your teenaged or adult child as much as possible in answering the questions. Answer "yes" or "no" to all of the questions.

1. How much supervision does she need for her safety and health?
  - ➤ Is she able to move from place to place independently (walking or using mobility aids):
    - within a building?_____
    - Between buildings (no street crossing)? _____
    - Crossing streets? _____
    - Using public transportation (programs will usually teach students to use public transportation systems in their area) or driving ? _____
  - ➤ Is she able to eat, dress, shower/bathe, and use the restroom independently and without prompting? _____
  - ➤ Is she able to stay home alone safely:
    - for short periods of time (a few hours or less)? _____
    - overnight? _____
  - ➤ Is she able to self-medicate (take out correct dose, self-administer the dose, remember when to take the medication)? _____
  - ➤ Is she able to control her behavior without harming others, property, or herself? _____
  - ➤ Is she in good health? (free of seizures, breathing difficulties, diabetes, etc.) _____

8-10 "no's" in the list above indicate that a **high** level of support and supervision is probably needed. If this level of support is not available through the program, you may want to consider hiring a PCA to meet these needs.

If your student has most of the above skills, she will probably be able to function safely in a **moderate to low** support program. **Life skills/transition** programs are often able to teach skills in independent travel and personal health care (taking medication), and gradually allow students to have more independence on campus.

2. *What daily living skills does the student already have?*
   Circle the skills that are priorities that she needs to/wants to learn to be an independent adult.
   Can she:
   - Do cooking and meal planning? _____
   - Do laundry? _____
   - Shop for groceries or other necessities? _____
   - Perform banking tasks (make deposits, use ATM, etc.)? _____
   - Pay bills? _____
   - Clean an apartment/house? _____
   - Arrange for appointments (doctor/dentist/therapist)? _____
   - Exercise regularly? _____
   - Use free time appropriately (alone or social events with others)? _____
   - Handle minor home repairs and emergencies (changing a light bulb, shutting off water, using a fire extinguisher, etc.)? _____

Most PSE programs with a **residential option** will teach all or most of these skills in apartments or program residences. **Independent living/transition** programs will also teach many of these skills in both residential and commuter programs. **Academic and Vocational/Technical** programs may offer specialized courses in these areas, but you should ask if these courses are available. Look at the skills you circled in the list above; ask if these skills will be taught in the program.

If you and your student want to pursue a largely academic program, you will need to either teach her these skills or seek instruction elsewhere (such as through an adult agency or working with a PCA).

3. *What communication skills and social/emotional skills does the student need to learn to be an independent adult?*
   Can she:
   - Ask for help appropriately? _____

➤ Use common courtesies (please, thank you, table manners)? _____

➤ Have conversations? _____

➤ Soothe herself appropriately when she is upset? _____

➤ Identify her disability and her needs accurately? _____

➤ Self advocate for her accommodations, needs, desires? _____

➤ Follow the hidden curriculum (see glossary) in the classroom and on campus? _____

➤ Use technology for communication and information (Internet, cell phone, email, instant messaging, etc.)? _____

➤ Interact appropriately with authority figures (boss, professor)? _____

➤ Interact appropriately with possible romantic partners? _____

➤ Recognize abuse or mistreatment and know how to seek help? _____

Most organized PSE programs for students with SD realize that the students they serve will have delays in most of these areas. The above skills and more will often be taught directly during real-time interactions during the day (by instructors or peer mentors), in small discussion groups, or in formal classes (human sexuality, communications classes, etc.). If you and your child wish to pursue an individually supported, inclusive PSE program, you may want to hire a peer mentor or use the services of a speech/language therapist to target areas of need.

4. *What job skills does the student need to/want to learn?*

Does she want to/need to

➤ Earn a degree, certificate, license, or credit hours to qualify for a desired job? _____

➤ Learn specific skills related to a career of interest, such as keyboarding, making a spreadsheet on a computer, using tools, repairing engines, commercial food preparation, welding, etc.? _____

➤ Learn "soft skills" (see glossary)? _____

➤ Learn basic employability skills, such as attendance, following directions and routines, showing initiative, etc.? _____

➤ Learn how to apply for and interview for a job? _____

➤ Write a resume? _____

➤ Gain work experience in campus or community sites? _____

Obviously, **vocational/technical** programs will emphasize skills in specific vocational areas, will include internship hours, and will provide instruction in employability skills. Check program descriptions, however; internships or volunteer opportunities are part of many PSE programs, even if work preparation is not the primary focus of the program. Work experiences, even those that don't emphasize a particular career path, can be valuable to your student, by building his resume and giving her a chance to practice her "soft skills" as an employee.

5. *What are the student's current academic skills? What are his goals for PSE?*
Does she/do you:
> Know if she *wants* to continue learning academics? _____
> (A caution to parents: pay close attention to what your student wants to do. Some students have simply had enough class work and would prefer to spend the majority of their time on nonacademics. Postsecondary education does not have to be heavily academic.)
> Know her current reading, writing, and math skills and current academic accommodations (e.g., speech-to-text software, recorded books, use of a calculator)? _____
> Know her current ability to complete long-term projects, such as papers, speeches, and preparing for tests? _____
> Know how much help she needs to stay organized, to plan ahead, and to prioritize academic assignments? _____
> Know what specific academic skills and/or information she would like to learn (e.g., courses not available in high school, which academic skills to strengthen and how much)? _____
> Know how hard she wants to work (college courses, even those the student will audit, will cover a great deal of information in a short time and the classes themselves will last an hour or longer)? _____
> Know the best program for the student to learn these academic skills (specialized, mixed, inclusive)? _____

When exploring possible placements, ask specific questions about the coursework available. If you or your student wants to improve skills, look for courses or individual tutoring that will teach skills. If the goal is to explore new topics (art history, film, sciences, languages), find out what classes are available and if there are prerequisites to enrolling in the classes.

A degree- or certificate-bearing program will have certain requirements that the student must fulfill. It is a good idea to find out what the requirements are before beginning the program and also whether the student is likely to be able to meet them.

6. *Where does the student want to live during her PSE experience?*
   Answer "yes" to all acceptable options.
   ➢ At home? _____
   ➢ With family or friends near the campus? _____
   ➢ In a dormitory or group living situation? _____
   ➢ In an apartment? _____
   ➢ Is the college/program within easy reach for daily commuting? _____
   ➢ Is the student likely to want to change her living situation (e.g., from home to school) within the next year? _____

For many students, living away from home is the main reason for pursuing PSE. Every program I visited had been approached by parents and students looking for an on-campus living experience. A **residential program** will be a program with apartment or dormitory living for students enrolled in the program. **Commuter programs** may be a good choice for students who don't want to live away from home or who want to wait a few years before trying independent living. However, some students move away from home to live in their own apartments, in agency-supported residences, or with family or friends who live near the program. They spend their days studying and their evenings and weekends in their own living situations.

When you find a few programs that look like they would be a good fit for your student, it's time to take a closer look. Call the program to ask specific questions and ask for an information packet. Ask if you can have the contact information for a few parents and ask them about their student's good and bad experiences.

A campus visit is a must. Programs may require applicants to spend time visiting the program before they decide to accept them as students, since the programs, too, need to ensure that the student is a good fit. Even if a visit is not required, go anyway. Try to imagine your student on the campus—would she grow and learn there? Would you be comfortable having her there? This decision is a major investment of time, money, and emotion; don't make it without having all the information you need.

Storming the Ivory Tower
College Based Transition Program
Buffalo State College

The College Based Transition Program at Buffalo State College in Buffalo, New York, is based in a tiny office. The compact space is intentional.

"I didn't want the office to be big enough to hold a class," said lecturer Lynne Sommerstein. The CBTP was designed with inclusion in mind. A three-way partnership (Buffalo Public Schools, an adult service agency called People Incorporated, and Buffalo State College), the project began in the fall of 2001. The aforementioned tiny office is large enough for record-keeping and paperwork for the program coordinators. The transition students sign in every morning and promptly leave to follow their individually designed and fully inclusive schedules. Several of the students are dually enrolled in Buffalo Public Schools and the CBTP; others are over 21 and are clients of People Incorporated.

Mary Lou Vaughn is a teacher for Buffalo Public Schools, a dynamic woman, and the unofficial keeper of the program's stories—the poignant, the funny, the astonishing, and the hair-raising. She modifies coursework and tests for the students, trains student mentors drawn from

the ranks of Buffalo State college students, facilitates discussions between students and professors, works with parents, and keeps IEP and assessment data. (In her own words, she also does windows.)

"Our motto is: only as special as necessary," she reported. Transition students work toward earning a certificate of continuing education. They select their courses based on interests and personal areas of strength, and at times, only minimal modifications are required. Professors are approached and are given the option to allow CBTP students to sit in on their classes.

Mary Lou escorted us across campus to meet some of the students during their lunch break. The student union building was busy and somewhat confusing. Mary Lou told the story of a frantic phone call from campus officials early in the fall semester.

"One of your students is lost and upset in the student center," the official reported. The CBTP staff accounted for all of the students, and then traced their movements during the day to see who had gotten disoriented. None of the transition students had any problems that day.

"Turns out, it was just a lost freshman," said Mary Lou.

Mary Lou introduced me to Christian, who obligingly gave me an interview during his lunch break in the student union. Christian has a talent for math, and has successfully passed two 100-level math courses. In one course, he was required to participate in a four-student study group—in the role of tutor to some regularly enrolled students who were struggling with the material. While the math concepts come easily, Christian, who has autism, faces his own struggles with traveling independently, giving presentations, and getting motivated to pursue employment internships (all required elements of the program).

Presentations are a recruiting tool for the CBTP. Transition students present to classes of regularly enrolled students about the program and ask for volunteers to act as study partners for the program. The benefit is two-fold: the transition students get help for homework, assistance on campus, and opportunities for socialization, while the regularly enrolled students can earn service credits for their study partner hours. Several programs of study at the college require a certain number of service hours with a human services agency. For undergraduates without a car, a campus-based opportunity to fulfill this requirement is a great benefit. Christian summed up the role of study partners in the program succinctly, "I help them or they help me."

Some volunteers continue on after their service credit hours are met, simply because they enjoy the experience or because they believe in the program's merit. Others are, to use Mary Lou's term, "touched" or have a personal connection to a person with an intellectual disability, and perhaps are storing up information for someone's future.

Keeping track of a busy campus schedule is a challenge for all students. Apparently a stickler in this regard, Christian, knowing that I am a school teacher, asked me, "Shouldn't you be teaching a class right now?" I assured him that I was on mid-winter break. His study partner needed a reminder as well. As our conversation drew to a close, Christian contacted his study partner by cell phone, because the study partner (a regularly enrolled student) had missed their appointment. Christian left a message, and left the union for his next responsibility.

Students from CBTP have gone on from the program to make their place in the larger world. Mary Lou told me about a student who desperately wanted to be a police officer, but could not meet the academic requirements for the job. While exploring the possibilities, he learned about a training program for security officers. With the help of the CBTP staff, he enrolled in the program and passed the certification test to become a security guard. Another student named Terrence serves on two self-advocacy boards in Albany, New York, to advise the state government concerning issues for people with developmental disabilities.

Postsecondary programs for students with SD often begin with the vision of a person who has seen a void in opportunities for a loved one with a disability. The chief visionary of the CBTP at Buffalo is lecturer Lynne Sommerstein. Her area of expertise is exceptional education, and her vision for postsecondary education for students with significant disabilities comes from the early 1990s, when Lynne

was seeking a PSE program for her daughter Michelle, who has developmental disabilities.

Lynne and Michelle's story is very much the story of the CBTP and postsecondary education for students with SD.

Michelle began participating in fully inclusive classes in high school, after many years in a substantially separate setting. Lynne noticed that when Michelle was included in academic classes, her overall abilities began to improve. When Michelle approached the end of high school, her family searched for a way for her to continue her education in college.

"I spent a year on the phone. Literally," said Lynne. She contacted colleges in New York State and in New England, explaining her vision for her daughter's future education and meeting dead end after dead end. The colleges had never fielded such a request before, and the few substantially separate programs that did exist were lacking some critical features that Michelle and her family were seeking—the chance to audit college-level classes and the chance to live in a residence hall.

Finally, Lynne located a program called ENHANCE, which operated through the now defunct Trinity College in Vermont. (Referring to the college's closure, Lynne joked, "The special program was not the reason the college closed—it wasn't our fault.") The program was not as inclusive as the Sommersteins would have liked, but there were opportunities for program participants to audit academic classes, as well as participate in separate classes. Although most participants in the program were day students, the college did allow Michelle to live in the dormitories. With the help of Trinity College President, Sister Janice Ryan, the family was able to arrange a room in a residence hall for Michelle and to hire a roommate to help her learn how to live on her own. Michelle learned to fly from Vermont back to New York for school breaks by herself, as well.

In 1995, after two years of study, Michelle completed her experience at Trinity College with a Certificate of Continuing Education. She returned to live in Buffalo, lives independently with her husband, and works in the Commissioner of Jurors and Clerk's Office of the Buffalo courthouse. Lynne proudly reports that, although her daughter has faced some challenges living independently, Michelle now handles life on her own, and is making too much money to qualify for SSI. "People have gotten used to thinking that it's a bad thing (to earn too much for government assistance)," said Lynne. "It's not. It's a good thing."

Lynne is very familiar with the challenges, both of logistics and attitudes, in creating opportunities for students with SD in college. Funding is a big hurdle, and Lynne feels that local school districts should be held accountable for PSE expenses for students between the ages of 18 and 21, even those students who have already earned an IEP diploma. (This is currently not the case in most of the country.) Families have a significant role as well. "Parents have to be educated consumers (of special education services)." When we discussed the tendency for schools and parents to help students with SD too much, she stressed the need for high expectations. Giving students a one-to-one aide is "like putting up a force field around them," she said.

For Lynne, this expectation that her daughter would learn from experience extended to discipline issues, as well. She told a story of Michelle being suspended in high school for smoking on campus. When the principal called Lynne to report the incident, she insisted that Michelle be disciplined as any other student. When the principal protested that Michelle had been influenced to break the rules by other students, Lynne assured him that the other students knew enough to hide in the bushes to avoid being caught; Michelle hadn't learned that part of misbehavior yet.

Attitudes on the Buffalo campus present challenges as well. Although many professors have been welcoming and encouraging, Lynne hears some colleagues' quiet comments that the CBTP students are "just playing college." They do not realize that the students must earn 72 continuing education units (CEUs) by participating in internships, making class presentations, auditing classes, and meeting other program requirements. While the ivory tower is beginning to crumble, it has not fallen yet.

FACTS & STATS

Name of program: College Based Transition Program (coordinated cooperatively with Buffalo City Public Schools, People Incorporated, and Buffalo State College) at Buffalo State College, Buffalo, New York

Instructional focus: Academic; vocational internships are arranged by program staff according to student interests on and off campus

Living options: Commuter program

Level of support: Moderate to low support (in-class support provided by program staff acting as classroom aides; tutoring is provided by study partners)

Level of inclusion: Inclusive. Social interactions are supported by study partners, field placement volunteers, and a chapter of Best Buddies

Number of students enrolled: 12

Admissions requirements: Admissions decisions are individually considered by a committee, although students must be residents of Buffalo City School District or clients of People, Incorporated, which serves people with developmental disabilities in the Greater Buffalo area

Program staff and credentials: Coordinated by a certified special education teacher from Buffalo Public Schools and staff from People, Inc. Inclusive classes are taught by professors of Buffalo State College

Tuition or fees at the time of press: Buffalo students ages 18-21 are funded by the district; tuition for People Incorporated consumers is covered by that organization; private pay is $114 dollars per day

Day in the life: Most students travel to campus by city bus and sign in at the CBTP office. Students audit at least one course a semester, eat lunch on campus, attend internships, plan and give presentations to classes, and meet with study partners. Students keep a daily journal of their activities.

A Matter of Degree
The Venture Program at Bellevue College
and ReThink Higher Education's Passport Program

Pick up the classified ads section of any newspaper and find the columns labeled "Employment: Professional." Jobs that qualify as professional, with all of the connotations of that term, usually require an applicant to have a degree from an accredited institution of higher education. Although specialized training at a technical school or on the job can gain an employee access to a good paying job with desirable benefits, there is still something in our culture that confers great status to a degree.

For students with significant disabilities, a degree is proof that they have achieved something real and tangible they can hang on a wall, write on a resume, or present at an interview. Without a degree, even college attendance pales. If a person attends college but does not graduate, the common belief is that he or she has been playing around, wasting time and money taking classes that will not amount to anything, whether or not that is true. For many careers, a degree is the ticket to entry. No degree, no consideration for the job.

Advocates for students with special needs often have a greater focus on the process of learning and growing than on the final credential, but a degree is common ground—we all know what it represents. It represents a skill set, the meeting of certain criteria at a certain level. For better or for worse, a degree confers gravitas a certificate does not. The two programs described in this chapter offer two different approaches to help students with SD earn a bona fide college degree.

The Venture Program, Bellevue College

The Venture Program in Bellevue, Washington, is the first degree-granting college program for students with significant disabilities in the U.S. The program had an enrollment of 55 full- and part-time students in the 2008-2009 school year. The North Campus building is a former Microsoft building, and is modern and airy. Venture graduated its first

degree recipients in the spring of 2008. However, the program is experiencing what director Marci McGinnis calls "growing pains." There has been a massive turnover in staff (Marci herself had only been the program director for three weeks at the time of my visit) and the pressures of accreditation of the program and maintaining the standards of the associate's degree (Associate in Occupational and Life Skills or AOLS) were starting to be felt.

One of the challenges of offering a degree to students with SD is the reality of failure. In spite of tremendous efforts on the part of students, parents, and faculty, some of the enrolled students will not be able to meet the requirements for the degree. Some of these students were among the first class admitted to the Venture Program. This reality is sobering, especially when students whose parents advocated for a PSE program in the first place are among those who fail. In an effort

to recognize the achievements of these students, BCC and Venture are working to create a certificate option for students who can meet some but not all of the degree requirements.

The benefits to students, degree seeking or not, are still substantial. Marci told me, "The students learn how to push themselves, self-advocate, and function a lot better in society. Previously, the world was completely adapted to them. Pushing beyond that, they grow ten-fold." Students can study subjects they were never able to study before: film interpretation, disability issues, workplace controversies, and communication and relationship skills.

Critical thinking is emphasized throughout the curriculum. I was able to observe several classes where students were urged over and over again to articulate not just correct answers but the reasons why their answers were correct. Multiple answers and interpretations were encouraged. The classes emphasized engagement; students completed individual assignments and then discussed the work in round table discussions. Faculty members provided clarification, but pushed students to seek their own answers and back up their opinions.

For example, in a career exploration class, the students had completed individual interest inventories in which they listed ten areas of activity in which they were most interested (art, building things, animals, problem solving, designing) and the challenge to the class was to generate possible careers that would incorporate the interests. Students had to explain the career and how the career used their classmate's areas of interest.

Christina, who describes herself as a Venture "old timer," told me about how this type of inquiry learning had helped her develop. "I've learned a lot about myself, about my weaknesses, but also about my strengths."

This structure was repeated in other classes I observed. In News and the Citizen, students read a newspaper article of their choosing and reported the information and why it might be important to the class. A media class watched an online video about advertising techniques and students then answered written questions to explore how the techniques affected their purchasing decisions.

The students in the Venture program gather with the other continuing education students at Bellevue College in the Café at lunchtime. Like the classes, the discussions I witnessed were lively and open. The students gave me permission to take candid photographs and expressed sincere interest in my coming book.

In the afternoon, I sat in on a group discussion on Problem Solving in the Workplace. The instructor, Nathan, separated the group into men and women. The women represented management and the men represented the employee in a sensitive workplace issue—how to handle an employee with serious hygiene problems. The management group had to brainstorm how to address the issue with an employee, and the employee group had to brainstorm reasons why an employee's poor hygiene might be justified.

The small group discussions were animated. Nathan commented at one point, "I think the women in management group getting sinister," which sparked knowing laughter from the group. I mentioned that maybe it was time to take cover behind my briefcase.

"If it gets ugly, there are two exit doors in the front of the room," Nathan offered helpfully.

One of the students, Will, added, apropos of a flight safety presentation, "And remember, the closest exit may be behind you!"

FACTS & STATS

Name of program: The Venture Program at Bellevue College, Bellevue, Washington

Instructional focus: Academic (several classes have a focus on workplace preparation); vocational internship required in fourth year of program

Living Options: Commuter program

Level of support: Low

Level of inclusion: Specialized, culminating in an Associate in Occupational and Life Skills (AOLS) degree. The college has given preliminary approval for a certificate option for students who complete the first two years of requirements.

Number of students: 55 full- and part-time students

Admissions requirements: Students must be at least 18 years old, complete an application (with $50.00 fee), submit two letters of recommendation, a completed parent questionnaire, and the results of the following tests performed in the last three years: Peabody Individual Achievement Test (PIAT) or Kaufman Test of Educational Achievement (KTEA); or Woodcock Johnson A or 3, achievement section; or other approved tests (see website for list).

Program staff and credentials: 3 special education teachers; other staff are specialists in their field of study (science, literacy, and employment preparation); internship coordinator.

Tuition and fees at the time of press: $350 per credit hour (typically, students take between 6 and 9 credits per quarter)

Day in the life: Most students travel by public transportation to the college. Classes are held in classrooms throughout the building on a rotating schedule (Monday, Wednesday, Friday and Tuesday, Thursday) Students often eat lunch on campus. Fourth-year students will have internship hours.

Website: http://bellevuecollege.edu/venture

Although this was a fun activity, the groups had to engage in higher level thinking to generate perspectives. The men's group understood that poor hygiene in the workplace was not acceptable, but the group had to try to take the perspective that it was. The women's group had to consider the employee's need for privacy and respect concerning the sensitive personal issue.

In their fourth year, Venture students are placed in a field placement in their area of vocational interest. A great deal of classroom-based time is spent on determining student interests and strengths so that the field placement will be as successful as possible.

I also spent time in a physical education class. At the beginning of the Quigong class, I watched students approach the instructor, Ken, to advocate for their needs. One student shared that he had a visual impairment and would need help to understand the poses and stretches. Another student explained that he would have to leave early to catch a 4:00 ferry. Ken discussed the issues with each student and together they agreed on how to best accommodate the needs.

Jody had been a Venture student for one week at the time of my visit. He was a nontraditional student, even in this nontraditional program, since he was 30 years old and had moved across the country in order to have this opportunity for continuing education. "I have a quote for you," he said. "It's sensational."

The Passport Program

"Attitudinal issues remain the largest barrier to postsecondary students with intellectual and learning disabilities. I have heard more times than I can count that *college is for smart people*," Cynthia Johnson told me over coffee in downtown Seattle.

Cynthia was the founding director of the Venture Program at Bellevue Community College in Bellevue, Washington. A group of six parents had approached BCC with a desire for a postsecondary program for their students with SD.

"I have always felt that this was a civil rights issue," she said. "It is about access to an underrepresented population. I believe access to students with intellectual and learning disabilities is the last bastion of prejudice in higher education," Cynthia said. She had the opportunity to testify before the U.S. Department of Education Commission on the

Future of Higher Education and to ask for funds in the form of demonstration grants for postsecondary students with intellectual disabilities. In the summer of 2008, the Reauthorization of Higher Education Act was signed and indeed included these grants. She believes this population is underprepared for postsecondary work, and that specialized postsecondary programs provide the avenue for the students to be successful in developing their skills. For Cynthia, the students are redoing a cultural paradigm.

"The students [attending the Venture Program] came in with learned helplessness," she said. "They had been told that they were wonderful and perfect and they were given perfect scores on every assignment. I believe that true learning takes place between challenge and frustration." They had not learned how to struggle to understand and how to put forth the effort needed for higher level thinking.

Even though Cynthia is a supporter of the Venture Program, she sees a need to create a new type of postsecondary program that will help students with SD learn skills they are typically not taught in high school. She sought to create the competency the students with SD were lacking by creating a new program that would include a rigorous curriculum of academic skills (reading, learning strategies for independent study); workforce preparation skills (how to have conversations, computer applications); and social/life skills (exercise and wellness).

Because Cynthia feels so strongly that postsecondary education for students with SD needs to be rethought, she founded an organization called ReThink Higher Education and developed a degree program called Passport—a Degree Program for Unique Learners (the degree is an Associate's in Essential Life Skills). Passport is designed to be implemented at colleges and universities across the country or used by transition programs or organizations. Cynthia has done the painstaking work to ensure that a degree program for students with SD can be replicated in colleges across the country and to plan how this may best be done.

She has also created a consistent alternative assessment system where the students' progress is monitored in each class, and their competence proved by demonstrating specific skills in the classroom that will also be helpful in the workplace. Colleges that follow the Passport model would offer specialized classes taught in such a way that the students get the needed repetition of information and skills to gain mastery. Students can repeat courses when they do not meet certain

FACTS & STATS

Name of program: Passport: A Degree for Unique Learners culminating in an Associate's Degree in Essential Studies. Intended to be replicated at interested institutions of higher education throughout the country.

Instructional focus: Academic

Living options: Will vary based on cooperating college or organization—can be either commuter or residential.

Level of inclusion: Specialized

Number of students: Will vary based on cooperating college or organization

Admissions requirements: "Passport was created for individuals who have received extensive special education services in K-12, and are considered higher functioning special education students with diagnoses involving intellectual and learning challenges. The program focuses on students who would have difficulty navigating in a traditional college classroom because most participants in this selective program generally attain scores below the typical range on specific standardized tests of intellectual ability and academic

criteria. This is in keeping with Cynthia's belief that, for students with SD, "your best teacher is your last mistake."

While creating this curriculum, Cynthia thought, well, why not make it a degree program? In addition to all of the benefits of degrees discussed above, degree programs allow students to apply for and receive federal financial aid. Allowing students of modest financial means the chance to receive federal funding of their education was another of Cynthia's goals.

She feels strongly that the decision to offer the degree must come from the administration of a college or university so that it will be accepted by the faculty and staff. ReThink Higher Education has a readiness assessment for colleges to determine whether the Passport Program would be a good fit for them. The Passport degree may be offered on college campuses as early as 2010.

performance. Functionally, the ideal candidate for the Passport Program will have an ability in the low-average to borderline range of intelligence as measured by standardized I.Q. tests (70-90), reading in the fifth to eighth grade level with math typically lower. Most students are 18-25 and have had some work experience, either volunteer or paid. Students have a variety of diagnoses including those within the autism spectrum, high functioning multiple learning disorders involving reading, mathematics, and expressive writing, and developmental or cognitive disabilities. Passport is not a match for all students and is not appropriate for individuals diagnosed with severe mood disorders, conduct disorders, or personality disorders (from www.rethinkhighered.com)

Staff and credentials: Instructors will be experienced in working with students with special learning needs

Tuition and fees: Will be established by individual sites, but is intended to be self-supporting with student tuition (i.e., not funded by the college or adult agency) and affordable with federal financial aid

Day in the life: Will vary based on cooperating college or organization, but Passport is meant to be a largely classroom based program

Website: http://rethinkhighered.com

Taking Care of Business
The Occupational Training Program
Eastern New Mexico University

...If the goal is an economically and personally rewarding career, the goal should not be education per se but rather gaining the requisite skills necessary to compete for high skill/high wage work.... Just as high skill/high wage professional work requires prerequisite skills, so too do these occupations require specific occupational skills. Unlike professional work, however, for which requisite skills are certified by baccalaureate or graduate school degrees, the skills required to obtain technician level employment can be learned either in 1- and 2-year postsecondary technical programs or in school to career programs that include formal work based preparation (Gray and Herr, 2006).

A majority of jobs paying a living wage will not require an advanced college degree but rather will be accessible through short term training programs. By the year 2010:

    1. The greatest number of job openings will fall into two categories: a) lower skill jobs that offer low wages and (b) higher skill jobs that offer living wages

2. Short term training and bachelor's degrees will be the types of training and education needed to obtain jobs that offer living wages

3. Almost 60% of living wage jobs will be obtainable through short term training that includes some combination of basic literacy and computer skill instruction, occupationally specific classroom and on the job training and related work experience (Flannery, Yovanoff, Benz, and Kato, 2008)

Vocational education and special education have long been uncomfortable bedfellows. Vocational education (currently called career and technical education or CTE) was considered the court of last resort, a place to send students who weren't going to make it in college preparatory programs or gain admittance to a four-year college. The often-

told story of an insensitive guidance counselor telling a student with significant disabilities that he was a "J.I.T."—a Janitor In Training—does have an element of truth. CTE students were frequently given the impression that they were studying a trade because they could not achieve academically. Fortunately, many had the strength of mind to continue their studies in a specific trade, regardless of the opinion of unenlightened professionals, and had the last laugh when they gained good-paying employment directly out of high school.

Families of students with special needs also bear some responsibility for the negative reputation of CTE options. Many have a knee-jerk reaction to their children receiving training in jobs involving "food, flowers, filth, and folding" (people with developmental disabilities have often been relegated to entry level jobs in food service, plant and building maintenance, and industrial laundries). While the chance to explore jobs beyond these narrow options should be provided, advocates should not forget that a number of young adults with SD will want to be cooks, florists, and custodians and their desires need to be respected.

Over the years, many of my students with SD have wanted to pursue training in the trades rather than continue along an academic track. Several have made the decision about a career path as early as middle school. There are a variety of post-secondary options that allow students to pursue specialized training in the trades or service industries, some of which also incorporate the opportunities of a two- or four-year college.

Since 1986, students with SD have been gaining technical skills that have opened doors to economically and personally rewarding careers through the Special Services Occupational Training Program (OTP) at Eastern New Mexico University in Roswell. The campus, in typical southwestern style, is made up of low, modern buildings. The program office is in the Arts and Sciences Building, but classes are held in buildings around campus.

Although I usually meet with program or admissions directors, I met in the program offices with Stephanie Mainello-DeLara, a sign language interpreter for the program. I could have met with any staff member or student—the ownership of the program by the staff and students was evident throughout my visit, described by a student named Tim as a "big, huge college family." The OTP is a large program in terms of enrollment with more than seventy students who have a wide range of needs and abilities, so all staff and students need to work together to meet the program's high standards.

Stephanie outlined the scope of these standards. Students can meet the requirements to earn a Certificate of Occupational Training in as few as three semesters (fall, spring, and summer session, with graduation held at the end of the summer session) through a combination of classroom study and work in the community called practicums. OTP offers training in eleven vocational areas (see list at the end of the chapter), with two additional special topic areas that are still under development. The students must complete 45 credit hours in their area of study, general job skills, and independent living skills. After a week-long orientation that includes travel training to take the city buses to their practicum job sites, the students plunge right into their programs of study.

"We have supports, but they are weaned away," Stephanie reported. It can be overwhelming for the students, some fresh out of high school, to suddenly take on all of these adult responsibilities.

Lauren, a student in the child care program, commented on her adjustment while showing me around the campus. Since arriving at Roswell, she has learned to ride the city bus to a local child care center, to fly home to visit her family in Texas over breaks, and has also learned how to manage her on-campus schedule. "But pretty soon, you're just boom, boom, boom," she said, snapping her fingers to illustrate her ability to follow her daily routine.

The majority of the OTP students live on campus in suite or apartment-style arrangements, where they must manage their own laundry, personal hygiene, and eating arrangements. (Apartments have a full kitchen, whereas students living in the suites must sign up for a meal plan through the university's cafeteria.) All of the students I interviewed found homesickness a challenge in their early days on campus. "My biggest change was being away from home," Cheyenne told me in our conversation. Cheyenne is due to earn her certificate in veterinary assistance, and has already been offered a full-time position by her practicum employer, so next fall, she will move to her own place near Roswell.

Class attendance and punctuality are high priorities, and extra tutoring is required if students' grades begin to fall. Chris and Brooke, both students in the Office Skills program, emphasized the need for students to have personal responsibility in order to be successful in their employment training.

"My advice to high school students is learn to study," Brooke said during our conversation.

"Students should do the same thing as other high school students do when they plan to come to college: get up early, go to classes on time, and go to practicum," Chris added.

Brooke plans to seek work as a legal secretary and Chris wants to apply his business skills as a film director of historical dramas.

Although students can earn their certificates after completing 45 credits, a few choose to stay an additional year or two to complete training in other occupational strands. Once they have successfully completed the common program requirements (Job Skills, CPR, adaptive physical education, and independent living skills), students can take courses from the Eastern New Mexico University catalog for credit or audit. For example, Tim, who plans to own a Mexican restaurant, has received a certificate in food service and is completing the requirements for an office skills certificate. R.L. has earned a certificate in food service and is working toward a certificate in child care. (Tellingly, he told me he plans to work in food service because the pay is better than in child care!) Both young men spoke of the need to balance their work loads and social life. "I've been going to parties," Tim enthusiastically reported, with R.L. adding, "You'll have fun with friends, but some times you'll have to work hard. It's not easy."

R.L. also balances a work study position in the special services office several hours a week. The OTP is among the very few programs in the United States for students with SD where the students may receive financial aid such as Pell Grants to fund program costs. It is thanks to former OTP director Linda Green—who passed away in the fall of 2007—that students are eligible for financial aid if they meet certain ability-to-benefit guidelines. Green approached state higher education officials with Certificate of Occupational Training checklists, and received approval for financial aid for most of the programs (special topics excluded). Most students also receive financial assistance from state vocational rehabilitation funds (see Chapter 18 for information on funding). Costs for the programs are relatively low, even for out-of-state residents, and some scholarship money is available if students receive at least a 2.5 GPA after their first semester.

The word is getting out about the effectiveness and efficiency of the OTP. This year, a student traveled all the way from Virginia to attend the program, and Texas, Colorado, California, Kansas, and Missouri, as well as New Mexico, are among the states represented by the student body. Denise McGhee, the program director, reinforces the message about the need for specialized vocational training for students with disabilities this way, "A program such as this is desperately needed because employment rates (for people with disabilities) are so low. Students need more training to become competitively employed."

FACTS & STATS

Name of program: Occupational Training Program at Eastern New Mexico University at Roswell, Roswell, New Mexico

Instructional focus: Vocational training in specific careers (auto body and paint, auto mechanics, child care, floral design, food service, nursing assistant, office skills, refrigeration and air conditioning management, sanitation/maintenance/grounds keeping attendant, veterinarian assistant, welding. Special topics include animal care taking and fashion merchandising

Living options: Residential

Level of support: moderate to low support

Level of inclusion: mixed (classes are specialized; internships and housing are inclusive)

Number of students: 70+

Admissions requirements: Vocational evaluation performed by ENMU staff, current psychological testing, ability to self-medicate and self-manage in the dormitories

Program staff and credentials: Teachers with training in specific vocational areas, support staff for providing accommodations (e.g., sign language interpretation), tutoring provided for all students if grades fall below a certain level

Tuition and fees at the time of press (housing included): $16,000 (in-state residents); $18,000 (out-of-state residents)

Day in the life: Students attend classes in their career area of interest and spend 13-18 hours per week on community-based practicums. Students have the option of living in campus residence halls or student apartments

Website: http://www.roswell.enmu.edu/special_services/occupational_training_program.php

Five Hundred Graduates Strong
The Threshold Program
Lesley University

Threshold is the holy see of nondegree postsecondary programs. It began serving students in 1981 and is widely recognized as the first comprehensive program for college students with significant disabilities in the United States. Threshold was the focus of the survey discussed in Chapter 1, and it can now claim to have more than five hundred graduates to back up its claims that PSE is an effective way to create positive adult outcomes for students with SD.

Professor Arlyn Roffman from Lesley University in Cambridge, Massachusetts, was the founding director of Threshold. While finishing her doctoral work, she got a call from a parent of a student with significant learning disabilities about the now defunct Para Educator Center, run by Judith Crane at New York University. The Para Educator Center was a commuter program that taught vocational skills to students with significant disabilities. In substance, this determined mother said, "I want you to go see the program at NYU, I want you to replicate the program at Lesley University, and I want my daughter to attend it."

Thus charged, Dr. Roffman went to see the program. She then came back to seek permission from the administration of Lesley, which she described as being "very entrepreneurial at the time," to start looking for funding. Lesley agreed to let Roffman set up a program for students with SD that would not only teach vocational skills, but also independent living skills in campus housing. Threshold was a pioneer on the Lesley campus as well, since it was a coed program while Lesley was still an all-women's college. The first group consisted of eighteen students (not all resident students, since Dr. Roffman was only able to secure ten beds in the campus dorms the first year), including the daughter of the woman who sparked the idea. In the next year, Threshold was at full enrollment, and has been so ever since.

The limited opportunities for students with SD in those early years were painfully apparent during the admissions process. "If we decided a student was not appropriate for Threshold and had to turn them down, people would literally cry, because there was nowhere else for them to go," said Dr. Roffman. Threshold has served as the inspiration for programs across the U.S., such as the Vocational Independence Program (VIP) at New York Institute of Technology, the Horizons Program in Birmingham, Alabama, and the PACE Program at National-Louis University in Illinois.

Helen MacDonald, Director of Admissions, shared a wealth of information on making a program thrive on a diverse urban campus for twenty-five years. The program admits twenty-five students per year. Originally aimed at students with nonverbal learning disabilities, the program now accepts students with a range of special needs. Applicants need to have basic academic skills (about 3rd to 6th grade reading level, math levels slightly lower), have the ability to complete homework independently, and be able to manage living in a dormitory with minimal supervision.

The program offers two major courses of study—Business Support Services and Early Childhood Education—and a host of instruction in independent living and transition skills, taught in the classroom and through internships. Students can attend the program for as long as four years. The two-year certificate program earns the students six college credits upon graduation and qualifies them to work as child care assistants or entry level employees in business. Some students benefit from another year of instruction to solidify independent living and vocational skills and participate in the Bridge Program after receiving their certificates. The students can move from the Certificate or the Bridge program to the Transition year program, where they are helped to find an apartment and a job, as well as taking a few additional courses for three more college credits. Many Threshold graduates still live and work in the Cambridge area, and they maintain an active alumni network, both in person and online.

My visit to Threshold underscored how typical an experience postsecondary education is for young people, regardless of the nature of their disability. The admissions packet is long and very comprehensive, to determine whether there is a good fit between the program demands and student abilities. So, by the time students arrive in Cambridge for an interview, they are closer than they realize to acceptance into the program. Apologizing for using an unprofessional expression, Helen described the look on their faces upon learning of their acceptance to the program. "They look happy, but there is what I call the 'Oh, crap' factor, too." The moment of joy is replaced by a moment of terror, realizing that this news means they will be leaving home and coming a whole lot closer to independence.

Helen showed me what she affectionately called "the mug shots" on the wall of the Threshold offices, taken of each entering class on moving-in day. By and large, cheerful expressions were covering signs of nervousness. They had good reason to be nervous. Helen described the usual freshmen trials: homesickness, concerns about the course work (too easy or too hard), roommate squabbles, and romantic dramas. In addition, the students need to learn to navigate the color-coded but labyrinthine Boston public transit system (affectionately called "the T") to travel to internships independently. (This skill was most impressive to me, since I rode the train into Cambridge, and needed a lot of pre-teaching from my brother-in-law to master the express train vs. regular service concept).

Parents of the new students are urged to resist the temptation to visit or to take their student off campus until Parents' Weekend in late October, to allow the students to get acclimated to campus and to their new schedules. The change in the students even in six weeks, Helen said, is amazing. She watches them proudly show their parents around campus, and even take them on "the T" to restaurants they have found while traveling to their internships.

Helen often sees former students on the Red Line of "the T," traveling to and from work or social occasions. These students have successfully navigated not just the complexities of public transportation in the area, but the complexities of college and independent living with a significant disability.

FACTS & STATS

Name of program: Threshold Program at Lesley University, Cambridge, Massachusetts

Instructional focus: Vocational (Business Services and Early Childhood Education) and transition/independent living

Living options: Residential program—students spend two years in the dormitory, and have the option of two additional years, including one where they rent their own apartment.

Supervision and support: Moderate to low (since classes are specialized, in-class support is assumed).

Level of inclusion: Specialized

Number of students: 50 (approximately 24 admitted per year)

Admissions requirements: Application and $50.00 fee. Educational evaluation, including academic achievement levels testing (see website for accepted tests—generally reading levels must be 3rd- 6th grade level with math levels somewhat lower), WAIS IQ testing, personality assessment (see website for specifics), three recommendations, and a personal interview

Program staff and credentials: (from the Threshold website) Threshold faculty consists of more than twenty highly qualified faculty members. Each has expertise in educating students with special needs, extensive experience, and an advanced degree in education or a field directly related to her/his role at Threshold.

Tuition and fees at the time of press: $48,800

Day in the life: Students take required coursework on the Lesley campus and participate in field placements related to their major. Students are taught to use the Massachusetts Transit system to travel to field placements. Students are eligible to join clubs on the Lesley University campus.

Website: http://www.lesley.edu/threshold/

Learning to Take Ownership
The College Internship Program
at the Berkshire Center

I recently read a quote that defined parenting as "the art of grace-fully giving ground." It's an excellent description of the ongoing, very dynamic relationship between parents and children, from the dependency of infancy through the acceptance of independence when one's children are no longer children.

Teaching independence is a challenging task with typical chil-dren—deciding how much to push them and how much to hold their hands. For parents raising young adults with significant disabilities, who may be less able, less aware, more impulsive, and more vulnerable than their peers, the level of difficulty rises exponentially. Parents struggle to figure out how to balance their young adult's safety with his or her desire to grow, knowing full well how hard it is for their son or daughter to un-derstand and navigate the world. How do parents "give ground," when the ground on which the young adult is standing is so uncertain?

Charles Houff, Clinical Director at the College Internship Pro-gram (CIP) at the Berkshire Center, called this assuming of adult roles by young adults with SD "taking ownership." "Many of our students come with a sense of entitlement," he said when we spoke at the central administration building in Lee, Massachusetts. The CIP is committed to ending that sense of entitlement, and building a sense of responsibility and self-management in their students, in all areas of their life. The controlling theme of the CIP, echoed at each of its four centers in California, Indiana, Florida, and Massachusetts, is "You were made for good purpose and you are inherently valuable." However, this theme does not mean that students sit around hearing how special they are; it means that the students must learn to accept their learning differences and learn how to accommodate and compensate independently, rather than to use their disability as an excuse.

Learning differences and neurological disabilities have effects that go far beyond academics. In response, the CIP is extremely comprehensive. Each of the program sites has an association with an outside postsecondary institution. The Berkshire Center in Lee, Massachusetts, partners with Berkshire Community College and the Mildred Elly Business School. It also provides in-house classes for all students and vocational training (called Career Skills Training and Employment Program, or C-STEP) for students who need more intensive support to pursue vocational goals. Some students have the academic capability to pursue an associate's degree program, while others are pursuing a certificate or earning credits that may be transferred after they complete the CIP. For every course the students take, they can receive tutoring or the support of a study group to meet the academic goals, monitored by the academic dean.

CIP also coordinates vocational internships and service learning opportunities, such as community volunteer work to give the students work and community experiences. Every week, as well, the students may sign up for a variety of social activities and day trips.

All students live in apartments within walking distance of the Berkshire Center. Under the guidance of residential staff, students learn shopping, banking and bill paying, meal preparation, cleaning, and minor home repair. Here, reports Program Director Gary Shaw, is truly where entitlement comes to an end.

Gary told the story of an irate parent who called the office, saying his son had just phoned to report that his toilet was backed up. Gary fielded the call and urged the parent to tell his son to call the office, and a member of the residential staff would come over to teach him to use the plunger.

The father was appalled.

"I'm paying all this money, and my son is going to have to fix his own toilet?" he demanded. Gary reminded the father that he was paying all this money so his son could learn to be independent.

"Sometimes, educating the parent is the biggest struggle," Gary said. However, parent input is not always negative. The CIP works with a parent advisory board to create policy and give feedback to the program staff on how well the program is meeting its goals. Based on the questionnaires given to graduates and their parents about their satisfaction, the CIP is meeting its goals quite well.

Instruction in self-management is given through formal groups and classes. The issues common to young adults with learning differences are addressed with refreshing directness. In "executive functioning" sessions, students are taught to monitor their personal organization, such as ensuring they have their bus passes, cell phones, and class materials, and to brainstorm strategies for making sure they stay organized. Charles Houff coordinates individual and group counseling for apartment mates, including meeting with the consulting psychiatrist as needed if a student needs medication, to ensure that the student knows what he is taking and why the medication is necessary.

One of the most necessary, but least enjoyed, groups for the students are the "reframing classes." Students with learning differences often have difficulty understanding their own strengths, weaknesses, and how to compensate for their difficulties. Three times a week, the students meet to discuss topics such as social skills, boundaries, relationships, and habits. These topics are uncomfortable for the students to discuss, because there is no hiding their deficiencies and their need to master the skills that other young adults seem to learn instinctively.

Instruction can happen informally, as well. As students become more comfortable with program staff, they begin to seek out advice and feedback on their own.

Gary told me the story of a young man who was delighted that a girl in his community college class had smiled at him when he sat next to her on the first day.

"So, she's my girlfriend now, right?" he asked Gary.

"Well, it could be that she's interested in being your girlfriend," Gary began his analysis. "But she might just have been being friendly. Maybe she's friendly, but might become interested in being your girlfriend some day. You'll need to see what happens over the next few weeks. But I think it's a little soon to assume that she wants to bear your children."

The Berkshire Center of the CIP also offers a program called Aspire, which is specifically targeted toward students with Asperger syndrome or high functioning autism. In the spring of 2007, the Aspire website proudly stated that the Aspire students had earned an average GPA in their college-level courses of 3.67. The most difficult issues that many of the Aspire students face are clearly not academic in nature. Paul Milenski, the program coordinator of the Aspire Program, described a typical situation for a college student with autism spectrum disorder who is intellectually able, but fails to make it through a degree program in college. Often, the student will stop going to class and hide in his dorm room, but will not have a good reason for doing so. Paul interprets this paralysis as fear of the future and fear of growing up. "They need this (program) as a prep school," Paul said.

FACTS & STATS

Name of program: College Internship Program at Berkshire Center, Lee Massachusetts/Aspire Program at Berkshire Center; The Brevard Center, Melbourne, Florida; The Berkley Center, Berkley, California; and the Bloomington Center, Bloomington, Indiana

Instructional focus: Academic and Transition/Independent living

Living Option: Residential program (students live in program apartments)

Supervision and support: High, moderate, and low available (tuition varies by level of support)

Level of inclusion: Mixed

Admissions requirements: Documented diagnosis of a learning difference such as Asperger syndrome, high-functioning autism, nonverbal learning disability, PDD-NOS, AD/HD, or dyslexia. Low average to high intelligence, emotional, behavioral, and psychological stability, high level of motivation to meet program goals. Potential to live and attend college or vocational program independently. Ages typically 18 to 25 years old

Classes and services offered by the Aspire program in association with the CIP include Theory of Mind class, where students are taught how to take another person's perspective, and Hidden Curriculum class, where they are taught social skills and subtleties that are easy for neurotypical students. Since people with autism spectrum disorders are visual and concrete learners, videos are made of the class activities, so the students can see themselves, both what they are doing correctly and incorrectly. The students also participate in "social mentoring," in which they are paired with a capable peer who models and helps the student with Asperger syndrome practice the skills learned in class.

Many students experience stress when they are addressing these issues for the first time. An Aspire student named Paul would often need to leave class halfway through, because of the stress. When I spoke to him in April, he was able to manage an entire class and was pleased about his participation on the Recreation Committee. Paul joined my

Staff and credentials: Certified staff for classroom instruction and psychological counseling, residential staff to oversee and provide instruction in life skills, college courses taught by professors at cooperating colleges and schools.

Tuition and fees: $38,500-$69,500 not including room and board and college/vocational courses. CIP is designated a "special school" under the Internal Revenue Service, so parents may be able to include costs as a medical deduction when filing their federal taxes. Some services (such as psychological services) may be covered by insurance.

A day in the life: Students live in program apartments with several roommates. Their daily schedules are based on their academic and vocational goals (i.e., working towards an associates degree, vocational certificate, or basic vocational preparation). Regular program classes and services, such as counseling, reframing, executive functioning, etc., are offered, as well as the opportunity to take classes at area colleges and business schools. Tutoring services are available.

Website: www.collegeinternshipprogram.com

discussion with Paul Milenski, appropriately and politely, when he had something to contribute. This young man told me, "I was nonverbal until I was four years old, but now I'm smart." What he meant, of course, was that now he could show his intelligence by confidently interacting with other people.

Other available services that address sensory and neurological effects of autism spectrum disorders are sensory integration therapy, hyperbaric oxygen therapy, neurofeedback training, and auditory integration therapy. Aspire prides itself on providing the most up-to-date and cutting edge therapy options to help its students become functional adults.

Through the comprehensive services and ongoing feedback, the students at the CIP and Aspire programs gain an understanding of how the world works and how they will be expected to behave outside of school in order to get what they want. Gary Shaw told one last story: "We had a student who was having trouble with a tutor at the college. This student called me and informed me, 'I want you to go to the college and straighten that tutor out.' I reminded him of the story, 'If you give a man a fish, you feed him for a day. If you teach a man to fish, you feed him for the rest of his life.' We won't do it for you." Gary did help the student more than usual that time, because it was the end of the semester. However, he called the student in for a meeting shortly afterwards, and the young man wrote a list of strategies for accessing his accommodations that he would use on the first day of the next semester.

The CIP and Aspire programs teach their students to fish for themselves.

Sharing the Gift of Music
The Berkshire Hills Music Academy

Kate greeted me cheerfully when I signed into the Berkshire Hills Music Academy (BHMA) in South Hadley, Massachusetts. She worked in the office and was accustomed to visitors.

"And what is it you do?" she asked.

"I'm a high school special education teacher," I said.

"And do you love it?!?" she exclaimed.

And I realized, "Yes, I do!"

Enthusiasm is contagious at the BHMA, as it only can be when the people at a school love what they do. "For people who love music, they have to do it. There's no choice, you simply must," said BHMA director Beth Hart. "It's no different for people with disabilities, and there needs to be a place for them, too. This is the most joyful place I've ever seen."

The academy has its roots in a weeklong summer music camp run by the Williams Syndrome Association. Begun in 1994, the camp was instrumental in proving the hypothesis that people with Williams syndrome, a genetic disorder that results in intellectual disabilities and specific medical problems, also have unusually strong verbal abilities and a great sensitivity to music. One of the founders of the camp and the BHMA, Dr. Howard Lenhoff, had noticed this sensitivity in his daughter Gloria, who, with extensive training, became an accomplished professional vocalist. People with Williams syndrome are not what are popularly called "idiot savants" (think of the movie *Rainman*) but, after comparing tests of verbal and musical ability in children with Williams syndrome, researcher Audrey Don found that those particular skills were near to normal levels, in spite of the children's IQ scores averaging only in the 50s. Don also did a "music interest survey," which revealed an almost universal passion for music in children with the syndrome. Teri Sforza, author of *The Strangest Song,* writes of Don's work:

> *After all was said and done, Don concluded that Williams wasn't a savant mystery, after all. Williams people were simply capti-vated by music, much more so than typical children. From the neuropsychologist's perspective, this made sense. Their hyper-responsiveness was probably connected to their hypersensitivity to sound, which led to extreme emotional responses. They had greater awareness of sound than regular kids, paid more atten-tion to music than regular kids, responded more passionately than regular kids. It didn't seem that they were, as a group, any more talented than regular kids; but it made sense that their passion for music might lead them to develop relatively good musical skills.* **When you have the interest, you have the pathway to develop skills**, *Don said* (Sforza, 2006—emphasis mine).

The BHMA, which opened in 2001 to a class of students gleaned from the Williams Syndrome Music Camp, decided to use the interest in music as a pathway to develop skills that would help young adults with SD become independent.

Although about 50 percent of the members of the current student body have Williams syndrome, the other 50 percent of the students have other cognitive issues. Their IQs range from 50 to over 100. The common factor is their great love of music. At the time of my visit, love of music was far more important than musical ability, but students interested in applying should have at least one year of formal musical training. Some students arrive with a high level of skill in several instruments.

The school was designed explicitly to be, according to its philoso-phy statement, "a nurturing and supportive environment" where music is central and a facilitating influence for learning independent living and functional academic skills. "There is magic in being with people like yourself, in an environment that doesn't question who you are," said Beth Hart.

Another characteristic of people with Williams syndrome is a high degree of empathy with others and a desire for positive social interactions, although sometimes they can be indiscriminate in their affection. As a result, applicants need to demonstrate a good social fit to the environment, and appropriate social skills training is ongoing while they are enrolled. Using the Circles Curriculum developed by Leslie Walker-Hirsch and Marklyn P. Champagne, students learn which people are in their closest social circle (family, boyfriend/girlfriend) and who is farther out, as well as the level of intimacy appropriate in each circle. The skills are practiced with characteristic enthusiasm. As I sat in the audience of the Friday afternoon "Variety Hour," but before the individual performances began, at least six of the students greeted me, introduced themselves appropriately, and shook my hand.

The school has dormitories and is on its own campus, but it is within easy reach of the five college groups in the Amherst area (University of Massachusetts, Hampshire College, Mount Holyoke College, Amherst College, and Smith College). BHMA students spend time on the Mount Holyoke campus, using the fitness facilities and participating in Best Buddies events, and Mount Holyoke students spend time at BHMA as work study employees. BHMA students travel frequently off campus to perform and to work in internships as music aides in nursing homes, childcare centers, and elementary schools. The students plan the performances from start to finish—choosing songs appropriate for the audience, deciding which equipment to bring, packing the vans—as well as rehearsing and performing.

To fulfill the requirements of the two-year certificate program, the students learn to cook, to manage money, and to improve their academic skills. They can learn basic office and grounds keeping skills by working on campus as well. According to Beth (speaking from her personal experience), every musician needs a "day gig," because the performing business is so uncertain, but a surprising number of BHMA graduates are working in the field as musicians and music therapy aides.

And, of course, there is the music. Students are able to study a variety of instruments, vocal music, and dance with private teachers. They are required to participate in the chorus ensemble to learn how to work musically in a large group. They have individual practice times in the school's practice rooms, which look out over the rolling hills of South Hadley. All of the students perform in a recital at the end of each semester, in addition to other scheduled performances throughout the school year.

The students had just returned from their spring break when I visited the campus, but they held their usual Friday afternoon Variety Hour. As the students milled about, chatting about their vacations, I watched them. Some individuals with SD have the habit of rocking while they sit, and I saw several students rocking while they were waiting. Not everyone was socializing—some students seemed rather withdrawn. That is, until the music started.

As Jeremy sat down at the piano to play a jazz improvisation, all of the students were drawn into the beat. Those who had been moving to their own rhythms synchronized their movements, and others began to tap their feet in time. I was overwhelmed by Jeremy's skill and his classmates' response to it. In all senses of the word, these students rock.

Each performance was followed by what Beth called "supportive comments and feedback" from the teachers who were present. The level of critique was advanced, using technical music terms, although the performance skills critique of a vocalist named Chris drew laughter when his teacher reminded him to "never show the audience your keister!" during a performance. The students were always reminded that performance was an interaction between the artist and the listener. A drummer named Devon was praised for moderating the volume of his drum solo to increase the comfort of listeners with auditory hypersensitivity due to Williams syndrome. (Many students stopped covering their ears as his performance progressed but a few commented that it was still too loud for them.) The audience also interacted with the performers, calling encouragement as they set up, and applauding enthusiastically when they finished. One of the performers was a very early level musician, playing *Edelweiss* on the piano. If anything, the applause after his performance was even louder than for the more polished performers, to support his progress.

The gifts the students have developed are meant to be shared with others, not just to be enjoyed by themselves, and they rise to this challenge in performance. However, they are expected to carry their weight in more practical ways, as well. During the tour of the school, with its cutting edge recording studio, grand pianos, and elegant practice rooms, Beth showed off what she called, "the most important room in the school." It was the student laundry room. There are no divas allowed here.

FACTS & STATS

Program: Berkshire Hills Music Academy, South Hadley, Massachusetts

Instructional focus: Vocational/technical (music) and transition/independent living

Living options: Residential, in dormitory setting

Supervision and support: High support, but students should be independent in self-care

Level of inclusion: Specialized

Admissions requirements: Between the ages of 18-30 years old, with a cognitive and/or learning disability with exhibited musical skills, effective verbal communication skills, basic self-care skills, ability to attend class independently, and stamina to manage a full day's schedule; must have health insurance, recommendations, audition recordings, and interview with applicant and family

Program staff and credentials: Music is taught by certified instructors in instrumental and vocal music

Cost: $61,000 per year (includes tuition and room and board)

Day in the life: A mix of academic and transition-type classes, group and individual music lessons, and individual practice time. Social activities are organized and students have access to the Mount Holyoke campus facilities

Website: www.berkshirehills.org

Becoming Part of a Greater World
Vista Vocational Program
and
Chapel Haven R.E.A.C.H. Program

A parent once said of her transition-aged daughter who had strong academic skills in spite of a significant intellectual disability, "Her academics are becoming a case of diminishing returns. She needs to learn how to be an adult."

Many students with significant disabilities who are included in general education classrooms for some or all of their public school careers must learn transition skills outside of the classroom. For many students, this means they spend some time after high school graduation learning skills such as cooking, cleaning, and budgeting that weren't taught at school. Or they may learn them in a group home or other residential setting after they leave home. Increasingly, however, students with SD have been enrolling in PSE programs designed to teach them these skills.

On a mid-summer trip to eastern Connecticut, I visited two programs that specialize in teaching young adults with a variety of neurological and cognitive disabilities how to be adults.

In addition for preparing their students for as independent a life as possible, both programs provide support that lasts well into adult-

hood, in the areas where help is still needed. For many young adults with SD, a system of ongoing support for work, socializing, or managing a household will be necessary beyond post-secondary education. For many, interdependence is the best of all possible worlds.

Vista Vocational Program, Westbrook, Connecticut

"We are a 'college model' without the college. The most important thing we teach is: the world is not about you; it is about you as part of the greater world." —Helen K. Bosch, Executive Director, Vista Vocational Program

At the time of this writing (2009) Vista Vocational is in its twentieth year of operation, providing young adults with SD an individualized and experience-based program to prepare them for living, playing, and working in the community. Helen K. Bosch has been the executive director of the program since 1991. Vista currently works with 170 people, although most of these people are graduates of the transitional program and are now part of the Outreach Program, where they purchase support services as needed.

The students have been diagnosed with a variety of neurological conditions: Asperger syndrome, learning or developmental disabilities, traumatic brain injuries, and mild to moderate intellectual disabilities. But they share certain commonalities, Helen told me.

"Our students often have deficits in social skills, social judgment, and executive functioning. They are developmentally younger than their chronological age and learn best through hands-on rather than classroom based-methods," she said.

The students progress at their own rate through a transition program that typically lasts from twenty-four months to four years. Vista is a year-round program and new students are admitted as places become available. Each student has an Individual Program Plan that is developed and reviewed every four months on a tri-mester system.

The students usually begin their program in The Residence—a beautiful, rambling house that has been converted into two-person dormitory rooms and shared bathrooms. This group living experience is crucial for learning impor-tant social skills.

"Negotiation, conflict resolution, problem solv-ing—these all happen in a group setting," said Helen. "Some programs will place students in community based- apartments as a first step, but I believe that to integrate as a first step is really isolating." By living together for the first two years of the program, the students are able to develop relationships with the staff and their peers that form a base of support for their eventual move into the community.

Unlike with the usual dorm experience, though, the students are responsible for cooking group meals and cleaning the dormitory. I toured the Residence during lunch, while the staff and students were enjoying baked ziti and salad in a family-style dining room, which also had comfortable furniture for visiting between activities. A number of students were hanging out before heading out for work, errands, or group discussions.

Students have individualized weekly schedules—which are as specific as need be for each student—that they carry with them in pockets or backpacks. They develop these schedules with their program manager. All aspects of life are represented—personal hygiene, shopping for supplies, chores, work, recreation, discussion groups, and exercise. If a student needs prompting to take medication or to use the bathroom regularly, it is noted on his or her schedule. Other self-organizer tools such as planners, calendars, and white boards are used as well.

It is not enough to teach life skills in isolation. The Vista program also teaches executive processing skills, which emphasize:

- goal setting (for example, I want to have my friends over to dinner on Saturday),
- planning (When should I invite them? What shall I serve? What ingredients do I need to get and when should I get them?), and
- monitoring, evaluating, and correcting behavior if needed (When do I need to start cooking? Are people enjoying themselves? How do I know and how can I help carry the conversation along?).

These competencies, in addition to skills, are taught using a three-sided model. Helen describes the model as follows:

The three "sides" to instruction are

1. experience—they learn skills by doing them with an instructor working alongside (e.g., meal planning for a week, then shopping and cooking the items);
2. small group discussion regarding the theory or concepts used in the experience (e.g., a class regarding nutrition); and
3. individual counseling about this issue (e.g., a student may set a personal goal to eat a certain way, may have food allergies, or just need to discuss why it is important to eat certain food groups).

Each group of staff on each side of the "triangle" communicates with each other to reinforce concepts being presented for the individual and for the group.

Vista has created a curriculum guide which contains a hierarchy of basic skills for independent living that helps staff monitor each student's progress. But, since skills are not enough, the guide also lists the underlying social and cognitive processes (such as goal setting and decision making) for each set of skills. Even doing laundry requires executive processing skills if you are going to have enough clean underwear to make it through the week. "We call these the 'doing' and the 'thinking' skills. Doing enhances one's ability to be independent, but doesn't guarantee it," Helen said.

Employment skills are taught in the community. Knowing that many students with SD may have limited work experiences and even more limited insight into their interests and abilities, Vista offers a readiness level in which students are exposed to three different work sites at a time over a trimester at places such as animal shelters, churches, offices, libraries, stores, and food preparation sites. After the students have exposure to many different types of work and have more insight into their interests, Vista can arrange a six-month-long internship at one community-based business to allow the student to receive more advanced training. When students are ready, they are helped to seek competitive employment in the community. Vista proudly reports that 90 percent of its Outreach Program members are employed in the community by approximately 140 employers. Vista has an in-house worksite called Vista Ventures which produces products such as natural dog treats for profit sales and also performs contract work.

As the students become more skilled in independent living, they move into the Vista Transition apartments in Guilford, Connecticut, a public bus ride away from the Residence and main Vista building. Still working with Program Counselors to build their skills, the students gain more experience in performing routines and planning for themselves. After successfully completing their time in the "Trans" apartment house, students graduate from the program and are eligible to become part of the Vista Outreach Program. Many students opt to make the Connecticut shore their permanent home. "The graduates aren't ready to finish learning," Helen explained, so the graduates can purchase individual teaching and other services they need on an as-needed basis.

I was able to meet with two Outreach Program members, Travis and Amelia, who were living in their own homes, working in the community, and juggling active social lives. They had graduated together from the program.

Travis spoke honestly about his rocky road to independence, struggling in high school and searching for the support that would help him launch into adulthood. Finally, he realized, "I couldn't be helped until I helped myself" and he became open to learning coping and social

FACTS & STATS

Name of program: Vista Vocational Center, Westbrook, Connecticut

Instructional focus: Transition/life skills

Living options: Residential program (dorm and apartments)

Supervision and support: starts very high, but is steadily reduced as students become more skilled

Level of inclusion: specialized

Number of students: Approximately 15-20 new students per year (rolling admissions)

Admissions requirements: Students must be at least 18 years old, have a neurological disability (autism spectrum disorders, learning, developmental, and/or intellectual disabilities), have basic ability for self-care and social judgment, not require 24-hour supervision, and have appropriate behavior to live in a dormitory and eventually a community setting

Staff and credentials: Each student is assigned to a Program Counselor who oversees his/her individualized program. Staff also includes job coaches, job developers, life skills instructors, and support counselors to support community, recreational, and residential life

Tuition and fees at the time of press: $59,000 a year for a twelve-month program (Entrance program); Outreach program is fee-for-service (e.g., participation in clubs, support paying bills, etc.)

A Day in the Life: Students in the Entrance program follow an individualized schedule of personal responsibilities, work and community experiences, and discussion groups. Later, students may have work internships. Outreach Members usually work in the community and set their own schedules for recreation and self-care.

Website: www.vistavocational.org

skills. He is now successfully employed at a restaurant and has a long-term girlfriend.

Amelia also spoke of these critical social skills, managing her emotions and asserting herself appropriately. She freely shared that she had experienced bullying due to her disability and says that she feels comfortable having a base of peer support through Vista. She is working at a retail store in clothing and returns. When I asked for her advice to high school students with SD who want to pursue postsecondary education, she said, "Tell them, things will happen, but it will take a little longer."

Both young people had volunteered to participate in a Diversity Program that visited local high schools and made presentations on what it was like to have a disability. Although the Westbrook community was welcoming of the Vista students, area teenagers frequently teased the students when they were out in the community. So Vista took a proactive educational approach. Travis and Amelia emphasized in their talks, "We're not different."

"It definitely helped," Travis reported. Amelia agreed, saying that she often recognized high school students from her talks when they came into the store where she works. "Now they say 'hi.'" A new generation of adults has been helped by this generation of students with SD.

After our interview, Amelia, Travis, and I shook hands, and they met a friend at his car in the Vista parking lot. Just like other twenty-somethings on a beautiful summer day, they headed out for some fun. The life of cheerful, confident young adults took a little longer for them, but it did happen.

Chapel Haven R.E.A.C.H. Program, New Haven, Connecticut

Located on a busy street in the vibrant city of New Haven, Connecticut, Chapel Haven has been offering education and support to adults with cognitive disabilities since 1972. Founded by parents with the foresight to know that they would not be around to care for their adult children forever, the program was one of the first postsecondary programs in the United States to focus on teaching independent living skills. Like the Vista Program, Chapel Haven has developed into an active community,

offering its members the chance to benefit from and contribute to the life of the city of New Haven.

"These students want to put the pieces of their lives together, just like anyone else," said Judy Lefkowitz, Head of Admissions and Vice President of Chapel Haven. The pieces of these lives are recognizable: life skills, continuing education, work, and social life.

For many students, the first step is the REACH (Residential Life Skills Educational) Program, a twenty-four month, year-round program that accepts a total of thirty students at a time. Students live on the cozy campus in apartments with a small group of roommates and staff available full time.

REACH students attend required life skills classes and are able to choose electives including art, digital photography, fitness, and music taught by Chapel Haven faculty. Students attend classes on the Chapel Haven campus from 9 a.m. to 3 p.m. Students can also take classes at nearby Gateway Community College and Southern Connecticut University after they have taken the introductory College Excellence and Master Student Curriculum, which are taught on campus. Both on and off campus, students learn quickly to get to class on time with all needed materials. "This is still school. Every moment is a teaching moment," Judy said.

Each student is assigned to a coordinating teacher who can provide one-to-one instruction and assessment. The students learn life skills in their apartments by rotating chores such as cooking, shopping, and cleaning with roommates. They gain more independence in monitoring their personal hygiene and health care. They learn to travel independently using the New Haven bus system. There is also time for fun—there are evening social activities in the student lounge and the Outreach Center, clubs for a variety of interests (including a large chapter of Best Buddies and several Special Olympics teams), and weekly opportunities to go out into the community to movies, events, and restaurants.

During their second full year on campus, students begin preparing for employment. Chapel Haven provides both job developers and job coaches for competitive and supportive employment situations, and Chapel Haven has many participating employers, including a local Naval base and Yale University. The REACH staff monitors each student's progress using an instrument called Expectations for Graduation.

When the students are able to demonstrate that they are ready for independent living in the community, they graduate and become Community Members, moving into their own apartments or condominiums in the New Haven area. If a student needs more time to gain skills, he can be referred to the Bridge Program for an additional year, where he will live in Chapel Haven-owned housing and receive ongoing instruction in life and employment skills. Some graduates join the Community Life Program (CLP) if they are not working or only working a few hours a week. CLP members volunteer in the New Haven community and participate in group activities with other CLP members. Other activities include exercise and nutrition instruction, discussion groups, and instruction in how to participate in community cultural offerings.

Chapel Haven also encourages entrepreneurial ventures among the students. Connie Brand, Associate Director of Admissions and

Marketing, showed me a consignment shop that a few graduates had begun and told me about a kosher kitchen that a student had operated a few years earlier. Chapel Haven teachers participated in training by the National Foundation for Teaching Entrepreneurship (N.F.T.E.) in

2002 to support students interested in opening their own small businesses.

Other graduates may work in the onsite Chapel Haven Café as interns or paid employees. Connie introduced me to Rich, the Café Manager, who manages the day-to-day and catering business of the Café (and offered me a complimentary drink). The Café was full of Chapel Haven graduates, all of whom introduced themselves and told me when they had graduated. One man came into the Café as we were talking, wearing a suit. He had to listen to his friends' good natured trash talk about the reasons he was dressed up, but it ended with handshakes and affectionate hugs all around.

The crowd of REACH students hanging out on campus looked much like any other crowd of college students—the occasional student in all black, lots of iPods, and cell phones of all varieties. Connie and I chatted with a recent graduate, now a Community Member, who had just returned from a Chapel Haven outing to ride a steam train. "I've never done anything like that before. I was surprised at how much I liked it!" she said. The world of Chapel Haven students and Community Members continues to grow into an ever greater world.

FACTS & STATS

· ·

Program: Chapel Haven, New Haven, Connecticut

Instructional focus: Transition/life skills

Supervision and support: High to moderate

Level of inclusion: Specialized

Number of students: 30 admitted per year; total of 220 students and community members

Admissions requirements: Students should be identified as having a developmental disability, have no major behavior problems, be able to function without one-to-one assistance, and have the potential to live in the community with support after the 24-month REACH program.

Staff and credentials: 120 staff people serving 220 students and Community Members; staff includes teachers, healthcare providers, support persons for apartments, community experiences, and work sites.

Tuition and fees: $53,000 a year for a year-round program (includes classes, life skills instruction, and room/board)

Day in the Life: Students in the REACH program are in life skills classes and electives from 9 a.m. to 3 p.m. five days a week. The remainder of the day is spent completing daily chores with the opportunity for recreation. Second-year students also spend time in the community at job exploration sites. Community Members set their own schedules for work, classes, and recreation.

Website: www.chapelhaven.org

"Energy is Anything That Causes a Change"
The Career and Community Studies Program
at The College of New Jersey

"In the long history of humankind …those who learned to collabo-rate and improvise most effectively have prevailed."
—Charles Darwin

The College of New Jersey is a picture postcard image of what a college should be—red brick buildings, white pillars, and manicured green grass—and the affection most of its students have for the school would be cliche if it were not so genuine. It seemed as though every other student I saw on a morning in late October was wearing a sweatshirt bearing the letters TCNJ.

"Honestly, it's almost too cute, but the students feel a real sense of connection to their cohort and the college," Professor Rebecca Daley told me as we met in her office to discuss the evolution of the Career and Community Studies (CCS) program. CCS offers a four-year program, which allows the students to become an integral part of the community at TCNJ. The program emphasizes a liberal education in order to improve the thinking of their students, as well as to prepare them for work by

offering campus and community internships. All CCS students are expected to audit one inclusive college class a semester. As well, CCS students are eligible to join college clubs and intramural sports teams. Professor Daley proudly reports that the campus chapter of Best Buddies is one of the largest in the country.

The CCS program admitted its first students in the fall of 2006. The program was developed through a grant given by Laura and Steve Riggio through the National Down Syndrome Society. The Riggio family hoped that their daughter would eventually be able to attend college through a specially developed program like CCS, but, sadly, Melissa died from complications of leukemia in the spring of 2008 before she could take advantage of these opportunities.

The Class of 2010 will be the first graduates from the CCS program, with a certificate in Career and Community Studies. In order to earn a certificate, students must complete 146 credit hours in specialized and inclusive classes to support development of academics, socialization, vocational skills (including on and off campus internships), and independent living.

The CCS program relies heavily on peer mentors, who are regularly enrolled TCNJ students. Mentors wear many hats. They accompany CCS students to inclusive classes and club meetings, if needed. They also attend mixed classes, like the Great Conversations class I will describe later in the chapter. In return, CCS students offer their perspective to their mentors, who are pursuing degrees in education and psychology. CCS students have given student teachers feedback on their lesson plans and provide chances for psychology students to gain real-life experience interacting with adults with disabilities.

Every day on campus begins with a CCS-specific class called Planning Forum. "The freshmen really need an hour a day in planning forum. The sophomores and juniors don't need that much time," said Professor Daley, as we went into the classroom. On the white board in front of the room was the daily agenda: planners, assignments, miscellaneous, and prepare for class. We arrived while the students were having an animated discussion (the miscellaneous step) about a Homecoming tailgate party they had attended that weekend. The gathering had been organized by the parents of one of the CCS students and had been well attended by CCS students and program mentors.

Parents have helped the program to evolve. "We asked TCNJ about residential options for the students, but we were only able to get approval for a day program," said Professor Daley. The parents stepped in to arrange off-campus housing in rented houses and apartments for their adult children. Now, students are able to participate in evening and weekend activities on campus, as well as having the experience of apartment living.

The sophomore and junior Planning Forum was lively and directed mostly by the students. One of the CCS faculty named Kelley reminded students individually about upcoming tests.

"Michael, you'll miss the review class, but still be there for the exam. Isn't that cool?" she joked with one young man.

"Kelley, you're killing me," Michael groaned.

The group discussed memory and test taking strategies, and helped one young woman by quizzing her on information for an upcoming test in her children's literature class. The sophomores and juniors then set off for their next class.

A course that CCS is justifiably proud of was created by Professor Stuart Carroll. Dr. Carroll teaches for both TCNJ and CCS. Initially, he was doubtful that students with developmental disabilities could benefit from college-level instruction, but he has become a staunch believer. He also listened carefully to the concerns of regularly enrolled undergraduates about the difficulty of interacting with students with SD, in particular the lack of common interests. One young woman expressed her frank displeasure about these interactions; "I'm tired of talking to retarded people about retarded things," were her exact words. Partially to counter these communication difficulties, Dr. Carroll created the Great Conversations class, which is attended by CCS students and their regularly enrolled student mentors.

"They (the CCS students) need to know stuff, so they can have conversations at the water cooler with everyone else," he said. The Great Conversations class is taught by experts in a variety of subjects—science, poetry, film, politics, religion—who lecture and discuss the subjects with the group for a period of several weeks. On the day I visited, Jim Messersmith, a professor of science education, was the guest lecturer on the subject of physics. He began by presenting the basic concepts of forces and energy (energy was defined as anything that causes a change), then challenged the group to raise him five inches off the floor while he sat in a child's wagon. He provided wooden boards and bricks. Initially a little hesitant, the CCS and TCNJ students were soon working together on the floor or calling instructions to create a ramp and pull the professor in his little red wagon up the required five inches.

He then had them experiment with dropping a light marble and a heavy weight. The question to answer: which would fall faster? He had the students generate the constants, such as keeping the two objects at the same height before dropping. When Mr. Messersmith held the objects at unequal heights, Phil called out, "It won't be fair. Nice try, though." Each CCS student then paired with a mentor to try out simple physics experiments—balancing a piece of cardstock shaped like a crayfish, running a marble through a loop—with varying amounts of success. Students were urged to remember the science facts in their solutions and to continue trying new approaches when their early attempts failed. "Science is messy," Mr. Messersmith reminded the group.

FACTS & STATS

Name of program: The Career and Community Studies Program, The College of New Jersey in Ewing, New Jersey

Instructional focus: Academic (vocational internships are available)

Living options: Commuter program. Several students live in nearby rented housing using parental support

Supervision and support: Medium to low

Level of inclusion: Mixed

Number of students: 8 admitted per year for a total of 32 students at any one time

Admissions requirements: 18-25 years old; New Jersey resident identified as having an intellectual disability; student conduct that demonstrates independence, motivation, and stability; a desire to continue one's education and have ability to benefit from a college-based program

Staff and credentials: Two full-time special education teachers, 9 part-time staff; inclusive and mixed courses taught by TCNJ faculty.

Fees: $10,000 per semester; summer term is $5,000

Day in the life: Students begin with a Planning Forum to organize for the day (after first year, this class may not be held every day), then attend program-specific and inclusive classes. Students participate in campus-based clubs and activities.

Website: www.tcnj.edu/~ccs

The class seemed an apt metaphor for the changing face of education for students with significant disabilities after high school. Start with facts and basic concepts, try out different ways of doing things, and keep trying when it gets messy. It takes energy on the part of parents, students, faculty, and staff to bring about a change.

A Spectrum of Support
College Options for Students with Autism Spectrum Disorder

"Some people need a real hands-on disability coordinator or a program specifically for students with Asperger's, and other students would not take part in that and really want to be anonymous on campus." —Jane Thierfeld-Brown, University of Connecticut (Good Morning America interview, 4/2/08)

Even among students with significant disabilities, those with autism spectrum disorders (ASD) are especially in need of specialized assistance if they are to succeed in higher education. To paraphrase an expression used in the autism community, "If you've met one person with autism, you've met...one person with autism." For example:

- Raji scored a perfect 800 on his math SAT, and his other scores on standardized tests were not far behind. But he is unable to maintain eye contact for more than a second and can't respond appropriately to small talk. He gets so panicked in large groups that he was allowed to pick up his high school diploma (with high honors) from the principal's office the day after graduation rather than attend the ceremony.

- Susie struggled through high school in spite of an IQ in the average range. She only managed to keep up with daily resource room support and constant tutoring and organizational help from her dedicated family. She acts far younger than her eighteen years, often dressing in sweat pants and bulky sweatshirts with colorful pictures on them; she doesn't like the jeans and tight tee shirts favored by her peers. She has terrific difficulty reading social cues, and is still inclined to pout and stamp her feet when she does not get her way. She even walks in an unusual manner. She did well enough in regular education classes to earn a high school diploma, but is delayed in every other way.

- C.J. has received intensive special education services all the way through school, mostly in special classes, although he has been included in electives. He has a one-to-one aide in his high school program, since he continues to need help to get his lunch, put on his jacket, and manage his needs in the bathroom. He is cheerful and good natured and is able to have simple conversations, although he frequently echoes other people's words. He no longer hits or bites when he is frustrated, but he still rocks and flaps his hands when he is nervous or excited. He is able to write his name and address and recognize a few coins, but his academic skills have not progressed beyond these basics.

All of these young people have disabilities that are on the autism spectrum, and these are only three examples of the variety of strengths, weaknesses, and characteristics of people with ASD. Unusual even within the scope of this book, students with Asperger syndrome or high functioning autism may meet (or exceed) the requirements for admission to a degree program, such as in the example of Raji given above. Every description of a person with ASD is going to be different and the college supports that will be needed to help the person grow and learn will be different, too. This chapter, then, will be unusual in that it will not describe a specific program, but a range of services and programs—a spectrum, so to speak—that are available to autistic or Asperger students who want to pursue PSE.

(Author's note: Although I have carefully kept to the use of "person first, disability second" terms throughout this book, there are self-advocates in the autism community who prefer that the terms autistic or Asperger syndrome come first. In this chapter, I will therefore alternate usage and ask for the reader's forbearance.)

Some people with ASD (especially those with Asperger syndrome) have average to superior intelligence. Academics can be the easiest and most rewarding part of their college experience, particularly if they are studying an area in which they have a passionate interest. With the increase of online degree programs, a student with ASD could conceivably earn several degrees without setting foot in a college classroom. For some students, like Raji, online courses might indeed be the best choice. But, as we have been discussing throughout, postsecondary education is more than just academics. Because people with ASD can have such devastating deficits in some areas of functioning, having normal to superior intelligence is a point of pride for them and their families. This makes it easy to fall into the "he has a 4.0—everything is fine" trap, when everything is really not fine. A Ph.D. is a terrific credential and a great honor, but is it an end in itself or a means to an end?

In order to make the most of their intelligence and their often prodigious skills, people with ASD need to master the other life skills that can be gained through PSE—how to work, how to be as independent as possible, how to advocate for their needs, and how to get along in the world.

Although Ryan is an extremely intelligent young man who has "been on the honor roll more times than I can count," he poignantly illustrates the struggles young people with autism spectrum disorders face in the social realm:

> *"I have difficulties understanding certain situations and knowing what is inappropriate or not. It has always been a challenge for me to make friends and actually keep them. I have difficulty understanding when someone has crossed the line and how to handle them. I have unconsciously pushed people away and I don't know why. I have been bullied, teased, manipulated, picked on, and treated like sh** by most people I have encountered....No one likes me, really. I can't trust anyone because I don't know if they are playing with my head or not. It's hard for me to know. And then, when they do something wrong, what do I do? What measures do I*

take? How can I fit in with the everyday world? I have not received any training for my disability." —Ryan, age 21

I spoke to one campus professional who told me about an autistic student on her campus who had earned excellent grades in every college math course he had ever taken. One day, she saw him standing on the side of the road, approaching the edge and backing away repeatedly. Recognizing that he was having some sort of problem, she approached him and asked him what was up. "I don't know how to cross the street," he confided. He does now, but if his academic performance had been used as evidence of his overall competence, he would still be standing on the side of the road.

For some autistic young adults, the academic demands of a regular college program will be too challenging due to overlapping learning or intellectual disabilities. Programs designed for students with intellectual disabilities and significant learning disabilities often serve autistic students with learning problems, as well. I am aware of students with ASD who have successfully attended many of the programs profiled in this section. Their autism is simply considered another characteristic as their individualized programs are designed and appropriate accommodations are made.

Fortunately, as autism spectrum disorders become more widely known and understood, higher education is responding with options for support to help these students benefit from all PSE has to offer. Depending upon his particular strengths and weaknesses, a student with ASD may need academic accommodations, instruction in independent living skills, and help to gain work experience. Virtually all students on the spectrum will benefit from structured social support and instruction. While colleges and universities are experienced and familiar with academic accommodations, these other supports may not be as readily available.

Begin with Person-Centered Planning

The first step in pinpointing the right type of postsecondary experience is to identify the needs of the autistic student.

For any student with SD who is planning for PSE, a person-centered planning meeting during high school is wise; for an autistic student, it is essential. Person-centered planning is based on the assumption that people with SD have goals and dreams, as well as situations they definitely want to avoid (nightmares). Person-centered planning involves gathering people who know and care about the student to discuss goals and dreams for the future. Because of the nature of their disabilities, students will probably need help from both paid and personal support people (family, friends, etc.) in order to realize these goals and dreams. There are models and checklists on the market to teach service providers and families how to run a person-centered planning meeting and create action plans.

Let's look in on a sample person-centered planning meeting to develop an action plan that deals with postsecondary education. (The student, family, and professionals are all composites.)

Robbie is 17 years old and finishing 10th grade in his local high school. He has been identified as having high functioning autism. He takes a mixture of general education and special education classes. He lives at home with his mom and younger sister. The following people bring information to a person-centered planning meeting for Robbie:

- Robbie's math teacher sees a student who is capable enough to earn a degree in mathematics. Robbie is as talented in advanced math as any student he has seen in seven years of teaching. Robbie's computer applications instructor agrees; Robbie is even able to give accurate instruction to other students when they fall behind in class.

- His special education teacher knows that Robbie does well in his math and computer classes, but knows that Robbie arrives on time and prepared with all of his materials and assignments for these classes because she spends at least 20 minutes a day one-on-one with Robbie helping him get organized. She also knows that he needs an enormous amount of help to understand what he reads and to write even short essays. He does not enjoy reading and writing tasks, and will avoid them when he can. Robbie will be receiving a certificate of attendance at graduation because he is not able to meet graduation requirements, except in math and computer science.

- Robbie's mother comes to the meeting a little chagrined; she has filled out an independence skills survey for her son in preparation for this meeting, and was shocked to discover how much she was doing for him. Once Robbie was able to dress himself, take a shower, and make his bed, she began to take it for granted that he was totally independent. She hadn't stopped to consider that she does practically everything else for him, and this realization worries her. As much as she loves her kids, she knows she won't be around for them forever, and both of the kids need to learn to live independently.

- Robbie's sister, Emily, could have told her mother about Robbie's lack of independence. At age 14, she's been cooking and helping with the housework for years. She knows her brother has trouble with fine motor tasks, but she resents the fact that she has to be more responsible at home than he is. However, Robbie isn't all bad—he is very helpful and patient when she needs assistance with any kind of math or technology tasks. Emily and her mother know better than anyone about Robbie's sensitivities—his rigid food and clothing choices, his fear of crowds and loud noises, and his need for routine and preparation for changes in routine.

- Robbie's guidance counselor sees him daily. He isn't scheduled to come to her office every day, but he comes in, sometimes confused and upset about social interactions, sometimes angry about the expectations of his teachers, sometimes just for reassurance or to talk with her about his interests in math and computers.

- Robbie's neighbor, Mr. Li, is an elderly widower who has been close to Robbie's family for years. He spends a few evenings a week with Robbie so his mom can go out, and the two are very close. He has learned a lot about computers from Robbie, and Mr. Li has the unusual ability to convince Robbie to try new things when no one else can.

- Last and most important, there is Robbie. He knows that he loves computers and math and might consider working in these areas in the future. He would like to study computers and math in college, if he didn't have to take any English or history courses. He isn't interested in getting a part-time job, although he likes having money to spend on computer games. He likes living at home, and has no plans to move out on his own. He doesn't have any friends his own age, and he doesn't want to leave Mr. Li. Although Robbie is eligible to receive special education services until he turns 21, he wants to graduate with his class in two years, when he is 19 years old.

Everyone at this meeting will have information critical to helping Robbie find a good match for PSE and beyond. The person-centered planning group decides to set the following goals and to meet again in three months to assess their progress.

- Robbie will begin sharing some of the household responsibilities with his mom and his sister. They will create a jobs chart, where they will take turns every week with chores such as vacuuming, doing dishes, cleaning the bathroom, etc. Robbie's mom agrees to pay Robbie an allowance of $10.00 a week, if he meets his responsibilities. This goal serves the dual purpose of increasing Robbie's independence and helping him make the connection between work and money.
- Robbie and his special education teacher will research community college options in the area to see what Robbie will need to do to enroll in math and computer courses as a continuing education student. Mr. Li will take Robbie to visit a local campus.
- Robbie's counselor will make a referral to a local autism support group, so Robbie can attend a social skills group geared toward teens with ASD.

Following a person-centered planning meeting, the needs and preferences of the student with ASD can be used to guide the choice of how and where to pursue PSE. Some students will be able to meet their goals with the academic supports of an Office of Disability Support Services at college and a personal circle of support, much like a typical college student. I will be describing the supports available to ASD students who need more specialized and frequent help to be successful.

Figuring out the appropriate PSE program for students with Asperger's syndrome can be especially difficult. Elizabeth F. Farrell writes in the *Chronicle of Higher Education* article "Aspergers Confounds Colleges": "Educating students with Aspergers can be particularly vexing because of the extreme inconsistency in their abilities. They often have an amazing aptitude for one specific subjects....In fact, Aspergers is also known as the 'little professor syndrome.'"

"I've had professors say to me that not only did the student read the textbook, but they could have written it," says Jane Thierfeld-Brown, director of student services at the University of Connecticut's law school. But some of those same students cannot write a coherent essay on their favorite subject (Farrell, 2004).

Farrell also writes about students who fail to read social cues, both in and out of the classroom, and the devastating effects social deficits have on the students as well as the immense drain on the already strained resources of Office of Disability Support Services staff when students with ASD need intensive help to succeed in college.

Fortunately, there are supports on college campuses geared toward helping students all along the autism spectrum find that help.

AHEAAD

Achieving in Higher Education with Autism and Developmental Disabilities (AHEADD) is a program that provides ASD students with the additional organizational, self-advocacy, and social supports that can make the difference between success and failure. Founder and director, Carolyn Komich Hare, began the organization by supporting one student at Carnegie Mellon University in 2002. This student, Valerie Kaplan, had outstanding academic credentials, but was failing in college due to social and organizational challenges. With Carolyn's help, Valerie not only earned a degree, but gained valuable skills in independent living and self-advocacy. A professor advised her to be open about her Asperger syndrome during a group project and ask her peers to be direct with her about what she needed to do for the project. She has found this transparency to be valuable in the workplace, too.

An article in the *New York Times* reported that Valerie was managing a Games Unlimited store as of November, 2006. She was still asking others to be direct with her: "Tell me flat out if I need to do something different," she says to her supervisor. Her career goal is to make video games or work for Dream Works (but only after *Shrek 3* is released—she wants to be surprised) (Moore, 2006).

AHEADD continues to support students with ASD at Carnegie Mellon, as well as the University of Pittsburgh and the Community College of Allegheny County.

"Our students are competitively admitted [to college] but in crisis," Hare said in a telephone interview. The organization is not affiliated specifically with the colleges, although it provides consulting to professors and administrators on how to help support students on the spectrum. Instead, AHEADD staff work directly with students to help them work effectively in their own college environment.

The goal of the organization is to have regional centers that can provide services to students at any college within their geographical area. In the fall of 2008, AHEADD opened centers in Albany, New York, Boston, Miami, Florida, Dallas, Texas, and the Washington, DC, metropolitan area.

The components of the AHEADD model are:

1. professional staff involvement (AHEADD staff)
2. developing a campus and community support network
3. using campus resources
4. peer mentoring

Enrolled students meet with the AHEADD staff twice a week for 30 to 90 minutes, first to address academic planning ("If they don't manage academically, they won't be around long enough for us to help them with their other issues," Carolyn says) and upcoming tests and assignments. They also receive guidance on managing the details of daily life, such as self-care, roommate relationships, making friends, and getting a job.

Peer mentors are volunteers who have been drawn to AHEADD's mission from a variety of backgrounds. Once a week, each AHEADD

FACTS & STATS

Program name: Achieving in Higher Education with Autism and Developmental Disabilities (AHEADD)

Locations in Albany, NY, Boston, MA, Miami, FL, Pittsburgh, PA, Dallas, TX, and Washington, DC

Instructional focus: Academic, but support is provided for social interactions and managing daily living skills

Living options: Students have the same living options as any other student on their campus of enrollment

Level of inclusion: Individually inclusive supports. Staff will work with students to find supports on campus

Tuition: $4200-$5700 per semester in addition to college tuition. Some scholarships are available

Website: www.aheadd.org

student and his or her mentor get together for typical college social activities. Once a month, all of the students and their mentors meet for a large group activity such as a potluck dinner or a picnic. Because of the organized nature of the interactions, the students on the spectrum can receive empathetic and supportive social guidance, without feeling the pressure to hide their social challenges. "The students just love it," reports Carolyn.

The College Program for Students with Asperger's Syndrome, Marshall University

Some students with ASD who are enrolled in a regular college program will need to meet with support people daily. These students could benefit from a program such as the one at Marshall University in Huntington, West Virginia. Marshall began a program to support high functioning autistic students and Asperger's syndrome students in 2002, initially supporting just one student.

Marc Ellison is the coordinator of the program at Marshall University. We met in the Old Main Building down the hall from the Autism Training Center that supports people with autism in West Virginia.

Marshall University entered the popular mind through the movie *We Are Marshall,* which tells the story of the tragic plane crash that killed almost all of the members of the 1970 Marshall University Thundering Herd football team, as well as several members of the coaching staff and many prominent fans. The day before my meeting with Marc Ellison, I came across the film on cable TV in my hotel room. It seemed an eerie coincidence, but also a good sign because the story tells of how the university football program overcame the tragedy through hard work and openness to new challenges.

"With the right supports...the sky is the limit" is the motto of the College Program for Students with Asperger's Syndrome. The program now supports twenty students, who are enrolled full time in degree programs at Marshall University and have made separate application for support from the College Program. Once accepted, the student with ASD is assigned to a graduate assistant who monitors his or her academic, social, and independent living needs. "We are peripheral support. We want the students to have as mainstream an experience as possible," Marc said. But the supports are individually tailored to the students' needs. Some students check in with their graduate assistant once a day; other students need help every two to three hours to make hour-to-hour plans to organize their study and leisure time

Before his first semester, the student with Asperger's syndrome and his family participate in an in-depth, person-centered planning meeting using PATH (Planning Alternative Tomorrows with Hope) and MAP (Making Action Plans) methods. (See Person-Centered Planning in the glossary.) At the meeting, goals are developed for the student and helpful strategies are listed. In addition, a student profile is developed to be shared with professors so effective strategies can be used in the classroom. The plan and strategies are reviewed with the student and family yearly, and updates are made as needed. The students are also registered with the Disability Services Office, but the program usually provides the students' academic accommodations (such as separate location or extra time for testing) in the Autism Training Center.

Although an emergency phone number is available after the Autism Training Center closes, the students are on their own overnight and on weekends, so a certain level of personal safety awareness and independence is needed for students to succeed in the program. The College Program is not afraid to be directive with students when needed. "Because people with Asperger's are dealing with anxiety and other issues related to their disability, they may not be able to overcome their issues enough to self-advocate. They also may not be able to see the point of socializing with their peers or changing habits," Marc told me, so program staff and graduate assistants help them to overcome these obstacles. However, students and their families are given the final say about course selections and room arrangements (single room versus living with a roommate). The College Program is also starting to develop initiatives to expose students to the world of work in preparation for the transition to life after college.

Marc and I discussed the university's climate towards students with autism and Asperger's syndrome. He told me that the campus is a community and that professors and students are willing to reach out to students who are out of the ordinary to help them succeed. We both wondered if this willingness might have been born out of the tragedy almost forty years ago, when students and staff learned the hard way that life often pushes you down unexpected and difficult paths, but if you are willing to keep walking, those paths could lead you to destinations you could not imagine before.

FACTS & STATS

Name of Program: The College Program for Students with Asperger's Syndrome, Marshall University, Huntington, Virginia

Instructional focus: Academic, degree-seeking students

Living options: Students have the same living options as any other student enrolled in Marshall University

Supervision and support: Low

Number of students: 20

Admissions requirements: Same as for Marshall University students; separate application required for the College Program

Staff and credentials: Graduate assistants assigned to support students; classes are taught by Marshall University professors

Cost: $3,200 a semester, in addition to tuition and fees for Marshall University

Day in the life: Students attend class based on individual schedule. Individualized plan of support is developed and followed based on students' needs

Website: www.marshall.edu/coe/atc/modelcollege.htm

Asperger's Syndrome Adult Transition Program (ASAT), New Haven, Connecticut

There are some students with ASD who could attempt college academics, but socialization skills or independent living competencies are bigger priorities. They may also have needs that require full time access to staff support. Scores on standardized tests—IQ or otherwise—cannot predict what type of program will be best.

I spoke with a young woman named Claire who earned a combined score of 1440 when she took her College Board exams. I shared that I had 1170 for a combined score, earning a 700 on my verbal exam, but not faring so well on my math. ("You got a 440," she told me immediately.

I deserved it, too.) Nevertheless, her difficulty managing her time and organizing her life got in the way of her success in a vocational training program for students with disabilities. After a transfer to a program focusing on independent living goals, she developed the insight to realize that success means very practical things. "You need to learn when to speak and when to shut up," she said honestly. "Don't expect things to always go your way. Things won't always be perfect. And if you have a bad day, don't take it out on everyone else." Claire is now working successfully at an internship in a government office and is living in a program apartment with minimal supervision. Her intelligence is being used well and she is working to learn how to manage her life.

Chapel Haven's Asperger's Syndrome Adult Transition (ASAT) Program in New Haven, Connecticut, and Chapel Haven West in Phoenix, Arizona, offer postsecondary experiences with a sustained focus on independent living skills, as well as opportunities for academic development.

Matt Kennedy is the supervisor of the New Haven ASAT program. The program is in session year-round and I visited in early August. Matt was dressed in well-worn jeans and a casual shirt, like a college student.

"We all do this on purpose," he said referring to the dress of the staff. "We want to blend in and look like fellow college students. We want to be discreet. If we are instructing a student about his behavior, we'll do it later or pull him off to the side. We don't want to call them out in front of everyone."

Judy Lefkowitz, director of admissions for Chapel Haven, had warned me before my visit that the ASAT students might be reluctant to talk with me, feeling that I might put them unduly on display. Coming through with Matt, though, seemed to give me additional credibility. For the first year of the two-year program, the students live in a small apartment building that also contains the program office. "It really helps the students at first to know that the staff is right there down the hallway. They can open the door to their apartments and see into the office," Matt told me. Each student has a private bedroom and shares the living room, bathroom, and kitchen space with roommates. Staff is on duty 24 hours a day.

The students learn independent living skills that they haven't already mastered, such as cooking and laundry, but all students have to prove their competency before they are allowed to work alone. This requirement annoys some ASAT students, but the staff is firm on this rule. In their second year, students live in an apartment building across the street from the main ASAT building.

Social communication competency is emphasized strongly. For students on the spectrum, these skills are more challenging than college level courses. "Some of our students have genius level IQs," Matt said. However, intellectual ability is not a predictor of success; social and personal competencies are much more important. With disarming honesty, one student told me about repeatedly failing in several college programs, before coming to ASAT.

Overcoming resistance to learning social and independent living skills is a major issue, I know from personal experience with students on the spectrum. How do the staff at ASAT overcome this opposition? Judy told me that the staff connects everything to each student's personal goals for employment and education. Fellow students and employees will expect you to smell clean, look clean, and act in ways that do not make others uncomfortable, she explained.

Working with students on the spectrum requires creative thinking. "You can't remake the core of the individual," said Judy, "but if they have a goal, such as competitive employment, they are going to have to conform some of their behavior to the norm." Judy told me a story of one student who would talk to himself when stressed out. When this young man was at his internship, this habit caused other employees to shy away from him. The staff finally fitted the young man with an ear piece normally used for hands-free cell phone communication. Now, everyone assumes he is talking to someone on the phone, and their comfort level with him has increased dramatically.

FACTS & STATS

Name of program: Asperger's Syndrome Adult Transition Program, New Haven, Connecticut

Instructional focus: Academic, life skills/transition

Living options: Students live in program apartments in New Haven

Supervision and support: High to medium

Level of inclusion: Mixed (academics are fully inclusive; residential is specialized)

Number of students: 16 total students, approximately 6-10 new students admitted per year

Admissions requirements: Application, psychological evaluation within 3 years, high school/college transcripts and IEP, speech and language evaluation, vocational evaluation if available, neurological evaluation if appropriate, advance deposit

Tuition: $80,000 per year (12-month program)

Staff: 24-hour residential support staff available; "point staff" can attend classes with students if necessary

Day in the life: Students live in off campus apartments with single bedrooms, take at least one course per semester at Southern Connecticut University, and participate in internships and job shadowing experiences. Daily practice in apartment maintenance, personal finances, cooking, and social interactions are provided

Website: www.chapelhaven.org (click on Asperger's Program)

All of the ASAT students enroll in at least one class per semester at University of Southern Connecticut in New Haven. These courses can be applied to a degree, if that is part of the student's plan, and also allow them to practice their social communication competencies. ASAT staff have even gone with students to class to provide indirect support, although they keep a very low profile and try to appear as if they are just other students in the class.

Trying to be sensitive to the students' efforts to maintain their privacy and to not stand out, I kept a low profile myself during my visit. I did compliment several students on T-shirts they were wearing that reflected their intelligence and ironic sense of humor. Matt approached a group of students waiting on the porch for transportation to the bank to ask if I could take an informal photo. A few students opted out and moved off the porch. I told the rest of the group to relax. "Just talk amongst yourselves," I said as I tried to frame the picture. Playing along with the irony, a few students began to chant softly, "We're talking among ourselves, just talking among ourselves." It's hard to frame a picture when you're laughing.

The humor continued as the students filled out forms giving permission for the photo to be printed in this book. I told one young man that he could leave one line blank unless he had a minor child with him. His response was, "Let me check," and he looked in his pockets. This same student saw me in the parking lot as I was leaving, addressed me by name, and expressed his pleasure in meeting me. The pleasure was truly all mine.

Working without a Net

Students with SD Attending College on Their Own

Students with SD have been attending college with the help of creative, individualized supports for many years. For example, Shawntell Strully and Sue Rubin, two women living with significant disabilities, attended college in the Western United States with the help of friends, house mates, and paid service providers. Sue was able to complete regular course requirements, given academic accommodations and a communication device; Shawntell was not, but was able to audit a number of courses and have many nonacademic experiences on campus. Both women lived away from home with support in off-campus arrangements.

Can a student with SD go to college without needing a special program to do so? Yes, it is possible, but attending college without a net, so to speak, requires a great deal of work, planning, and creativity.

First, let's separate "going to college" from "pursuing a degree." Many of the organized postsecondary programs for students with SD around the country are defined as nondegree programs. Several have arrangements at their own colleges or nearby colleges for students to earn college credits that can be applied towards a degree. Other programs support students in earning certificates. But participating in college classes, whether for credit or as an audit, does not have to end in a degree to benefit the student with SD.

In order to pursue a degree or certificate at a four-year college, community college, or vocational school, a student must meet certain requirements. These requirements can include:

1. A regular high school diploma or GED

   or

2. A minimum score on a pre-admission test, such as an Ability to Benefit test or Test of Adult Basic Education (TABE)
3. An interview with program officials
4. A vocational assessment
5. Other requirements set by the postsecondary institution, such as minimum grade point average (GPA) or two years study of a language other than English.

Students with SD who meet these qualifications can apply for regular admission to certificate programs and matriculation for degree programs. Effective self-advocacy and use of academic accommodations will be necessary for success, and I will discuss those issues later in this chapter. If a student with SD cannot meet the criteria for pursuing a degree or certificate, many colleges offer students the opportunity to take classes through divisions of continuing education.

Taking the Continuing Education Route

While programs for students with SD that coordinate services are appearing on campuses all over the country, they are more the exception than the rule. A parent researching college for a son or daughter with SD may realize with dismay that the nearest program is several states away. Even those living in states with several programs may find that the programs are too far away for easy driving or that the student does not meet the program qualifications. Often, programs that are funded by local education agencies (i.e., school districts) are not open to students who live outside the district. Sometimes the student may not qualify for the program, due to physical or behavioral disabilities. The program may be perfect, but the family may not be able to afford the price tag. Still other parents may look at the programs that are available and find them wanting. What postsecondary education options are open to students with significant disabilities in these cases?

Many communities in the U.S. have access to community colleges or adult vocational programs (e.g., BOCES or an educational collaborative; see glossary), which provide educational and training services to adults of all ages. In the area of New York where I live and work, nearly 40 percent of graduating seniors begin or complete their PSE at community colleges. Others attend trade schools for specialized training in cosmetology, auto mechanics, health careers, etc. These institutions serve a wide student body and are tremendous resources for nontraditional students to further their education.

Every fall, I receive mailings from the local community college and BOCES programs, informing me of continuing education classes held on campus and at various community sites. The classes are usually short in duration (a few weeks, at most), on a variety of topics, and open, with very few restrictions, to anyone who is able to pay the fee for the course. These classes may be a good starting place for a student with SD, and might even be a source of lifelong education as the student enters adulthood. There are, however, options for a typical, on-campus experience for students with SD as well at community colleges, vocational schools, and four-year colleges.

Say a student with significant disabilities wants to attend a local college (two- or four-year) as a day student. The first step is to find out the college's policy on nonmatriculated or nontraditional students. Many colleges have courses available that do not have prerequisites (such as pre-testing or previous course work) and ways to take courses that would not require full participation in academic work (such as auditing). If so, any student who registers, pays the course fee (often reduced for auditing students), and appears for class at the scheduled time can participate in a single course. But, if a student with SD wants a fuller college experience, there are ways to create one.

Creating Individual Supports for College

On Campus Outreach (OCO) through the University of Maryland's Department of Special Education published a fact sheet in May of 2001 that suggested the following steps for students with SD who want to attend college using what the OCO terms "individual supports." Each step will be elaborated below.

1. Meet with the student to identify goals.
2. Determine the college of choice.
3. Identify partners and potential support resources.
4. Meet with disability support service personnel at the college.
5. Identify classes the student wishes to take.
6. If possible, meet with the teacher(s) of the course before the start of the semester.

Step 1 (Identify Goals)

Identifying goals for an individualized PSE experience is a step that can be taken at any time in the student's K-12 career. The student may have a particular career goal in mind, he may have certain interests or skills (computers, world history, etc.) that he may wish to explore, or he may just enjoy the experience of school. Any of these goals are good ones for pursuing PSE.

I would caution against the vague goal of "Well, everyone else is going to college, so he should, too." While many college freshmen enroll as "undeclared," they are not allowed to maintain this status forever, and even when they are undecided about their final goal, colleges keep them busy taking liberal arts courses that form the foundation of every major. Even if the goal for a student with SD is not to earn a degree or certificate, she undoubtedly has areas of strength or areas that need improvement, and these areas should be used to focus the reasons for going to college. Remember, postsecondary education is not an end in itself, and college does not and should not last forever.

Here are a few samples of goals for PSE for students with SD:

Julianna

- Julianna's area of career interest is early childhood education. She would like to audit four courses at the college level relating to early childhood education.
- She would like to have an internship or service hours working with young children.
- She would like to improve her reading and writing skills.
- She needs to gain experience in negotiating the campus by herself, making purchases independently, advocating for her

academic accommodations, and in traveling to and from campus by herself.

Sharon

- Sharon enjoys physical activity and needs to gain experience in a variety of jobs in order to determine her skills and preferences. Sharon uses a few basic signs ("yes," "no," "hungry," "drink") but is not able to communicate her preferences in an extended way.
- Sharon's support team would like her to participate in a college-level exercise or fitness class. They have decided to start with yoga, because the teacher has experience working with students who have disabilities and Sharon is good at imitating movement. The quiet, soothing atmosphere is a good fit for Sharon.
- Sharon is eligible for job coaching, transportation, and life skills training through an adult agency. The agency arranges for Sharon to work in a small office in the building next door to the fitness center two days a week on the same days as the yoga class. The team discusses goals with Sharon and she answers "yes" to learning to walk from her class to her work place alone, learning to use a shredder in the office, and learning to buy a soda from a vending machine for her break. She says "no" to the idea of a swimming class and working in the locker room.

Michael

- Michael is 19 years old and still eligible for IDEA services through his school district. He does not have a career goal yet. He is able to communicate with a computerized communication device, but is reluctant to use it to talk with people he does not know well. He needs to learn to self-advocate, since he has physical disabilities that require him to have help to move his wheelchair, eat, dress, and manage bathroom needs. He is concerned about taking a college-level course, because his reading skills are minimal (his communication device uses pictures and symbols).
- Michael and his speech therapist decide on a goal to use his communication device to participate in an introductory communication class at a local college.

- Michael will participate in classroom activities, such as conversations and using appropriate body language (eye contact, nodding to encourage a conversation partner, both of which he is able to do) and give two short speeches during the semester, which he will prepare with his speech therapist. A speech-language pathology graduate student will attend class with Michael to fulfill the grad student's field requirement hours.
- The grad student will also accompany Michael to the Student Union every day he is on campus. Michael will use his device to order something at the coffee shop.

Step 2 (Choose a College)

Location. Determining the college of choice often follows the old real estate axiom of location, location, location. Students with SD who are enrolling in classes with nontraditional or continuing education status will probably not be eligible for campus housing like a regularly enrolled student and will commute to school from home daily. In some cases, it is possible to arrange off-campus housing for a student with SD, either in an individually rented or purchased house or apartment with individual supports or in housing arranged and staffed by a local adult agency. The student then travels from her local housing to campus every day. Be forewarned that arranging these options can take a long time and a tremendous amount of coordination, and that either the student or a local caseworker will have to do all of the onsite coordinating of college services. If a parent or family member is the primary coordinator, the student with SD will need to attend a college near home.

Transportation. Transportation to and from campus may be a consideration, too. A school district may be able to provide transportation to campus as a service for a student between the ages of 18 and 21 provided she still qualifies for services under IDEA, but this service is not guaranteed and not necessarily the most desirable option, anyway. My students actually laughed when I asked them, "Do you think anyone rides a school bus to college classes?" They knew that public school buses aren't used on college campuses. As well, school district transportation departments operate on a fixed schedule that could limit the course options available to the student and will definitely limit the social options.

Private transportation with a friend or family member, public transportation like buses, taxis, or trains (following travel training), or specialized transportation through an adult agency may be better choices. Students with the luxury of several colleges to choose from in their area may choose a school on a bus or subway line that is easy for them to get to.

Other Factors. Consider the intangibles of the college environment, too. Every campus has a distinct "culture." Will the student with SD feel comfortable at the chosen school? Colleges with a strong community service culture and colleges that have human service or education programs may be more welcoming to students with disabilities. Other factors that may affect whether or not the student feels comfortable on a particular campus may include: whether there are comfortable places for commuter students to "hang out," how large the typical class is, or how noisy the campus is.

Step 3 (Find Partners for Support)

Partners to support a student with SD are available on every campus but not as the "one-stop shopping" model available under IDEA. Even if a student with SD is still eligible for services under IDEA, the local education agency may not be providing all of her supports if the student is pursuing educational goals on a college campus. Schools are required to provide "free and appropriate educational services" and are prepared to provide services for students with SD through their usual channels until the student reaches age 21 or graduates with a diploma, whichever comes first.

An individually supported postsecondary program will likely be considered something beyond the district's full responsibility for providing "appropriate education." As a result, a student with SD attending a local college with individualized supports may be able to receive some, but not all services from her school district. Transportation services were mentioned previously. Some districts have also continued to provide related services such as speech or occupational therapy (although these may be provided at the school rather than the college), paid for textbooks or fees, or provided tutoring or classroom support to students.

When seeking services from the local school district, always consider the fact that this is a college experience. Even if the district is generous enough to pay for and to coordinate everything, the inevitable move toward independence and individual responsibility will be delayed, rather than encouraged for both the student with SD and her family. If the student's postsecondary experience is too much like high school, it runs the risk of setting the student apart as someone who is not capable, which is just what a college experience is trying to disprove. Just because a student can receive services from her school district doesn't mean she should, if the services work against the student's ultimate goal of a self-determined life.

So, what other options exist for support on campus? Supports for students with disabilities can be found by looking at the services available to all students on campus. All students can seek help from the faculty and assistants in the classroom or during office hours. Many campuses also have academic support centers (such as a writing center) to provide tutoring or other academic services to students who need them, and students can advertise and pay for additional tutoring from peers. Computer labs and libraries are staffed with people whose job it is to help all students locate needed resources. Other students can provide informal or "natural" support; anyone can hold a door open for a student with a mobility problem or answer a question on course work or due dates for another student. Often, college students are willing and able to help each other, recognizing that they need help at times, too.

Other supports for students with SD can be sought from local agencies for people with disabilities. ARC or vocational rehabilitation services may be sources of individualized campus supports, such as tutoring, supervision, transportation, or travel training. See Chapter 18 for more information on vocational rehabilitation.

Step 4 (Meet with Disability Support Services on Campus)

Students with a variety of disabilities can obtain academic accommodations in their classes with the help of what is often called the Office of Disability Support Services (ODSS) on campus. Students with SD should meet with the ODSS staff before the start of classes to disclose their disability and request needed academic accommodations for any courses they will be taking on campus (credit or audit).

Accommodations. The ODSS will make sure the student's disability and need for those specific accommodations is properly documented (usually by looking at recent psychological or educational testing and give her a letter to share with her teachers showing that this requirement has been met. (See the appendix for more information about how to request accommodations.) The student is then responsible for sharing the information with the teachers involved. The ODSS will help advocate for the student if the professor balks at allowing the accommodations, but the office will not take care of making sure the professor knows what the student needs.

Academic accommodations (also called academic adjustments) that must be provided to a student with a disability are defined in this statement from the Office of Civil Rights:

The appropriate academic adjustment must be determined based on your disability and individual needs. Academic adjustments may include auxiliary aids and modifications to academic requirements as are necessary to ensure equal educational opportunity. Examples of such adjustments are arranging for priority registration; reducing a course load; substituting one course for another; providing note takers, recording devices, sign language interpreters, extended time for testing, and, if telephones are provided in dorm rooms, a TTY in your dorm room; and equipping school computers with screen reading, voice recognition, or other adaptive software or hardware.

In providing an academic adjustment, your post secondary school is not required to lower or effect substantial modifications to essential requirements. For example, although your school may be required to provide extended testing time, it is not required to change the substantive content of the test. In addition, your post secondary school does not have to make modifications that would fundamentally alter the nature of a service, program, or activity or would result in undue financial or administrative burdens. Finally, your post secondary school does not have to provide personal attendants, individually prescribed devices, readers for personal use or study, or other devices or services of a personal nature, such as tutoring or typing.

The key word in accommodations is "reasonable." Accommodations must allow all students to have access to educational programs, but not necessarily to do everything that would assure success. This distinction is a major change from accommodations that are allowed under IDEA.

For example, when a high school student of mine has the accommodation of a reader for tests, that reader is a live person (a teacher or teacher assistant). When a student is working with a live reader, she can ask for questions to be clarified, as long as "hints" are not being given to the correct answer. The live readers—who often know the student well—can also give encouragement when she is starting to lose heart or remind her to use the resources available to her. This same student may show up for the first test in a college course, expecting someone to read, clarify, and encourage her through the test, and may instead be handed an audiotape recording of the test or be shown how to use reading software on a computer that will read (in a computerized voice) a scanned copy of the test. The accommodation has been met—the test is being read aloud—but the student will have a far different experience of the accommodation in college.

The college is not required to modify the course or program content (something that also happens frequently in high school) even if the student with SD is auditing the course. In some individually supported situations, the student with SD is allowed to sit in the classroom and absorb what she can, often with disappointing results. Rather than just allowing the student to be a minimal participant, modifications such as shorter papers, simplified reading, or mastering fewer objectives can be made to the material. However, these modifications must be made by a support person rather than the professor, although the professor can play a role if he or she wishes. For example, a professor at Hobart William Smith College in Geneva, New York, graciously accepted and corrected a short history paper written by an auditing student through the College Experience Program (Ontario County ARC). The program staff had modified the assignment and helped the student complete it. This young man was actively engaging with the material, although not at the same level as students seeking credit, and was learning the information much more thoroughly than if he was just sitting in the room.

In-class Support People. Colleges usually allow support people in the classroom with the student, but will not pay for or arrange this support, unless the support person is also providing other accommodations (e.g., note taking, sign language interpretation). Contact the ODSS at the college before the beginning of the class to make sure a support person will be allowed. Sometimes, a fellow student can be hired to be a personal attendant or in-class support person.

A word of caution—think long and hard before reflexively hiring a support person to go to class with a college student with SD just because she has had support in class in high school. An unintended consequence of a one-to-one support person is creating the impression that the student is not able to communicate for herself. Well-meaning peers and professors may direct comments toward the support person instead of the student. Students who have significant physical disabilities, uncontrolled seizures, communication needs, or behavioral control problems should really be the only automatic exceptions, due to health and safety needs. Even in these cases, an attendant might be able to wait outside the room during the class or be seated a row or two behind the student in the room to give her some space. A privately arranged signal (e.g., a hand gesture for an attendant seated in the room, a text message to an attendant in the hall) can alert the attendant that the student with SD needs to leave the room to use the restroom or for a break. Since college students are usually free to come and go during class as needed, a break will probably not be unduly disruptive.

Consider whether having a support person in the classroom is really needed for the health and safety of the student and everyone else in the room, or is just a "security blanket" for the student with SD in case something goes wrong. The student with SD needs to take maximum responsibility for her classroom behavior and academic requirements.

Behavioral Challenges. What about students with behavioral control problems that might be distracting in the classroom? For some students, requesting the accommodation of priority seating (perhaps near an exit, with a "safety zone" around the student) might solve the problem. Other students may find it too difficult to be very quiet and still for the duration of a lecture, and would do better in a class that incorporated movement or was more tolerant of noise (i.e., fitness, cooking, computer work, art).

Sue Rubin, the college student mentioned at the opening of the chapter, has difficulty controlling vocalizations. It is grueling for her to be silent and still for a two-hour lecture, but necessary for her to meet the requirements of her degree in history. During the class filmed for her documentary *Autism Is a World*, her note taker/interpreter can be heard encouraging Sue in her efforts to control her vocalizations and movement, so that the lecture can be heard. It is tempting for advocates for students with SD to expect professors and classmates to be tolerant of such distractions. But, remember that the student with SD may not be the only student in the room with a disability. A student who wears hearing aids or a student with AD/HD may be negatively affected by these noises, and the rights of these students must be respected as well.

Aggressive behaviors (hitting, hair pulling, etc.) must be controlled at all costs. If a student with SD has these behaviors, extremely careful planning must be done to avoid having disruptive behaviors surface in class or on campus. Other students would be disciplined or dismissed for attacking other students or having a public tantrum, and students with SD are no different, even if allowances were made for these behaviors in high school. In the case of a student with challenging behaviors, a slow and well thought-out introduction to campus life may help point out areas of difficulty and allow time for her to learn appropriate behavior.

Step 5 (Choose Courses)

Keeping these realities in mind, the student with SD can begin choosing courses. Again, student goals should drive the choices. Students may want to improve their reading, writing, or math skills or pursue an area of interest or strength. If a student has a specific career goal, she can choose courses that will lead to a certificate or that will build skills in that particular area.

Don't overlook the value of taking courses in an area that has traditionally been a weak one for the student, such as writing or math. While setting a student up for frustration or failure isn't good, avoiding a particular skill or topic because the student doesn't like it or does not do it well will not correct the problem. I regularly require students who have profound reading disabilities to read aloud, because practice is the only way they will improve their skills. It is boring and frustrating, but it works. Complaints that a subject is hard or boring might indicate that the student with SD needs work in that subject.

Other things to keep in mind when choosing courses, especially if the student is taking them for credit:

- Does the class last too long for the student to maintain focus? (e.g., a 3-hour class versus a 50-minute class).
- Can the student keep up with the pace of writing and other assignments? Consider asking for a syllabus to see what's required.
- Is the size of class important (huge lecture hall vs. more intimate round-table approach)?
- What are the teacher's characteristics that may increase or decrease the student's chances of success? (Some professors

have accents that may be hard for the student to understand, may lecture without visuals, etc.)

Step 6 (Speak to the Faculty Member Teaching the Course)

Communication with faculty is critical. The student may very well be the first person with a significant disability the professor or teacher has ever met. I recommend that the student make a simple, well thought-out introduction of herself and her needs, taking responsibility for herself and her learning. For example, a fairly articulate student may identify herself as having Down Syndrome, which in her case means she learns more slowly than other college students and she will need extra time and reading services for tests and copies of class notes. A student with more difficulty speaking may present an individualized fact sheet, which identifies her disability and accommodations.

It is best to make the introductions before the first day of class. This type of introduction will most likely reassure the professor that the student's participation in the class is not only manageable but desirable. This attitude on the part of the professor will filter down to the members of the class, and the experience for everyone will be much more successful. Staff from the Office of Disability Support Services may have other advice on how to approach this meeting in a positive way and help the student practice the introduction.

. . . .

Individualized Supports in Action— A Real-Life Example

A young woman I will call Connie and her mother followed many of these steps in creating an individualized college experience at a community college near their home. Connie had left high school without a diploma but still had several years of eligibility for special education services under IDEA. Her parents advocated for her to receive postsecondary services outside the walls of her high school, and her district agreed.

Connie's experience at the college began through a specialized office skills program that was coordinated by a local agency serving adults with disabilities. After completing the one-year business skills certificate program, Connie decided that she wanted to continue her college education.

Her mother writes:

*The (business skills) program director discussed Connie's pro-
posed program with the person in the Office of Student Counseling who worked with students with disabilities, and he was
receptive to the idea (of Connie taking courses), so we met with
him to discuss how it would work. This was new territory for
everyone, and there were no precedents or guideposts. We agreed
on two courses for Connie, a remedial writing course,which was
a prerequisite for many other courses (and which I wanted her to
take in order to improve her writing skills) and a political science
course, which was Connie's choice. The political science course
was one of the more difficult courses offered but the professor had
lectured to the (business skills) students and had taken a real
shine to Connie. We agreed she would audit that course to remove
the pressure of grades and tests. The counselor was comfortable
with what we proposed and approved her program. He told us as
we were leaving that Connie was the first student with an intellectual disability who had ever attended the community college.
He was eager to see how it would work.*

Connie took the required placement tests, attended orientation,
and began attending classes on her own. She worked with a private
tutor (paid for by her local school district) and used test accommodations. Throughout her college experience, she learned to travel to the
campus, find her way to classes, and use a cell phone. Connie has taken
a combination of audit and credit courses, pursuing her interests in
political science and community service.

Her mother credits much of Connie's success to the welcoming
climate of the community college and the presence of specialized programs on campus that familiarized the faculty with higher education
for students with SD. Reflecting on the experience as her daughter's
college career draws to a close, she writes:

*At the outset, we said we wanted her to have the college experience,
develop better skills, broaden her perspective, and enrich her life.
I think we attained that. We were not focused on attaining a certificate or degree, or in following a scripted program that may or
may not have met her interests....She has now spent 4 years at (the
community college) and we've talked about the fact that it will be
time to look for a job at the end of this semester. She accepts that*

and is ready to move on. What the future holds is anyone's guess, but I'm guessing we will be forging new territory there as well. The college experience has given her confidence and increased skills, as well as a much broader outlook on life. I have watched her mature into a wonderful young woman.

Isn't that what all parents want from a college education for their child? Individually supported experiences can create more chances for other parents to see the same growth and maturity for their child with SD.

FACTS & STATS

Name of program: Individually designed PSE experience

Location of classes, tuition/fees, and supports: Vary based on the needs of the student

Supervision and support: low to high, depending on student's needs; all extra supervision and support must be arranged for by the student or family

Level of inclusion: Inclusive

Admissions requirements: Depend on the college chosen

Living options: On campus housing is at the discretion of the college if a student is not attending full-time and pursuing a degree. Students have arranged for off campus housing using individualized supports.

Part 3

Making It So—
**Advice for Students,
Their Parents,
and Secondary Education
Professionals**

So You Want to Go to College
Advice to Students

First, congratulations on having a goal—wanting to continue your education after high school. You may be looking at going to a typical college, a trade school, or a special transition program. To make things easier to read, I have called all of these options "college."

This chapter has a list of suggestions to help you make your goal a reality. These suggestions are based on many conversations with students with disabilities who are in college right now and the teachers and program staff who are helping them. You can start using some of the ideas today. You can use other ideas if you have an interview at a college. (Many colleges want to talk to students who are applying for admission. This helps them

decide if their school is the right one for you.) You can also use some ideas once you are in a college to help you get the supports you need.

1. What is your disability?

Know your disability. Practice telling people about it in ways that they can understand. Telling people about your disability is called *disclosure.*
For example:
- "I have learning disabilities in reading, writing, and math."
- "I have Down syndrome."
- "I have mild mental retardation and I use a walker to get around."

If there are terms to describe your disability that you do not like, use other terms that mean the same thing.
- Intellectual disability, cognitive impairment, or developmental disability are other words for mental retardation.
- Learning difference means the same as learning disability.
- Some people with a learning disability in reading call it dyslexia.
- Some people with a learning disability in math call it dyscalculia (dis-cal-CUE-lee-ah).
- For emotional disturbance or mental illness, you can use the words that your doctor uses. For example: depression, bipolar disorder, or obsessive-compulsive disorder.
- Autism spectrum disorder means the same thing as autism. There are different types of autism spectrum disorders. For example: Asperger syndrome or PDD-NOS. Check with your parents or an advisor to decide which term best describes your disability.

2. How does your disability affect your life?

Be able to describe how your disability affects your ability to learn, to work, or to manage on your own.
- "My disability makes it difficult to learn a lot of new information quickly. I need extra time to learn."
- "Because of my AD/HD, it is hard for me to concentrate when it is too noisy. Also, I find it hard to finish my work without reminders."

- "My Asperger syndrome makes it hard for me to understand what to do in social situations and to work with others."
- "Because I have a physical disability, I need help to dress and to use the restroom independently."

3. What helps you do your best in school?

Know what helps you to do the things you need to do. These kinds of help are called *accommodations and modifications.*

- "I can understand when people read to me, but I don't understand when I read to myself."
- "I need to write my answers in the test booklet."
- "I use a computer with voice recognition software to write assignments for school."
- "I need extra time to complete assignments and tests."
- "I did different work in my high school classes than my classmates did. When I audit your class, my peer tutor will help me."

You may already know about being a self-advocate. If so, good for you. If not, start practicing now. You can practice with your parents, teachers, guidance counselor, or even a friend.

IMPORTANT TERMS TO KNOW

- **Accommodations** only change how you learn and how you show what you have learned. For example, you might use reading software to read the same book as other students.

- **Modifications** change what you learn, even though you may learn in the same class as other students. For example, you might read one book instead of five books in a semester or you might read an easier book than the other students.

- To disclose your disability and to ask for accommodations or modifications is called **self-advocacy or being a self-advocate.** You will need to learn how to be a good self-advocate to succeed in college.

You may feel embarrassed or sad about talking about your disability. You may never have done it before, and like all new things, it can be uncomfortable at first. Talk to someone you trust about your feelings.

Try to find good examples of adults with disabilities. Go on-line to sites like www.specialolympics.org or www.YouTube.com to find videos of adults with disabilities leading active lives. You may also want to find a state self-advocacy group (go to www.selfadvocacyonline.org). Adult self-advocates are the experts in living life with a disability and they may have good advice for you.

If you haven't started already, start attending your IEP meetings at school (you should have at least one meeting a year). At the meetings, work with your teachers and parents on picking your goals for the future. Attending meetings is a good way to start learning about self-advocacy. You can practice telling people about your plans for the future and what you need to get there.

4. Are you ready for college?

Start acting like a student who is planning to go to college. Going to college means you are going to have to be responsible for yourself and be ready to work hard. Answer the questions below with "yes" or "no." Now is the time to be very honest with yourself.

YES NO

☐ ☐ Are you in school on time every day, unless you are sick or there's an emergency?

☐ ☐ Are you doing your school work and homework regularly?

☐ ☐ Are you doing as much of the work as possible by yourself?

☐ ☐ Are you exploring careers, whether through work study, volunteering, home economics or business classes, or part-time work?

☐ ☐ Are you involved with school activities or in the community (youth groups, teams, clubs, etc.)?

☐ ☐ Are you taking any general education classes? Are you participating in classes as much as you can?

☐ ☐ Do you stay out of trouble? (Remember, I said to be honest!)

☐ ☐ Do you know how to use popular technology (computer, cell phone, iPod, personal organizers) not just for fun but to help you learn things and be independent?

☐ ☐ Have you talked to your parents, teachers, and counselors about wanting to go to college?

☐ ☐ Are you reading regularly or listening to recorded books?

☐ ☐ Do you follow current events by reading the paper or watching the news every day?

☐ ☐ Are you as independent as you can be at home and at school?

If you answered "no" to any of the questions above, do something in that area starting today. For example:

- Meet with your guidance counselor to ask about taking another class or to ask about college.
- Go to the library to get a book or a recorded book.
- Watch the news.
- Use the computer to look up college information rather than using I.M. or checking your email. (Check out one of the websites listed in the resources section.)
- Get an alarm clock and learn how to set it.
- Ask your parents to teach you how to cook and do laundry.

5. What are you doing outside of school?

Get involved. This advice is in every book for college-bound students. Joining clubs, playing on sports teams, having a part-time job, volunteering in your community—these are all good ways to develop your interests and your social skills.

Getting involved will get you thinking about what you would like to do for work or for fun when you finish school. It can also help you make friends, and point out new skills you might want to learn. Also, college applications have places to list the activities you have done in high school.

6. Do you have a good attitude?

Like most teenagers, you've heard a lot about attitudes but let me explain what I mean. I have a sticker on my plan book that says "Attitudes are the real disability." I thought the world was to blame when people with disabilities could not reach their goals. I thought the world had an attitude problem.

The world sometimes is not fair to people with disabilities. People may have been mean to you or underestimated you because of your disability. They may have teased you for being different or talked to you like you were a baby. The world has gotten more informed and more understanding about disabilities, but there is still a long way to go. Everyone who cares about the rights of people with disabilities needs to play a part in teaching society how to treat people with disabilities with the same dignity and respect as everyone else.

Attitudes That Will Hold You Down

But let's look at the other side of "attitudes." See if you know this guy.

A student with disabilities (let's call him Adam) walks into his guidance counselor's office in the spring of his junior year of high school and asks about the upcoming college fair. The counselor knows that Adam has a disability but she doesn't know that there are ways for students with Adam's disability to go to college. So, she tries to talk to Adam about job training, since she knows that he did well in his technology class. She also tries to talk to him about his attendance (not good) and his discipline record (also not good).

Adam gets mad because the counselor is "underestimating" him and not being supportive. He stalks out of her office. For the rest of his life, even if he eventually goes on to college, he blames the school and everyone who works there for not supporting him in his goals. Later, he'll start blaming staff from adult agencies, the government, his employers—whoever does not give him what he wants. He will always say: *They never did anything to help me!*

Who are "they"? Everyone talks about "them" quite a bit. It's as if people believe that a whole army is out there trying to keep other people down. As a teacher, I have often been labeled as one of "them." This usually happens when I tell a student something he doesn't want to hear. Or it happens when I tell a parent she can't have something she wants for her kid. I am trying to be honest but not to keep people down.

I think if people believe that the mysterious group called "they" are out to get them, it explains why failure isn't their fault. After all, you can't fight against "them," can you? ("They" must be pretty busy!)

Here's an example of another kind of attitude:

Karen is very cute and social. Because of her disability, she is a lot smaller than other people her age. She is funny and has some good skills, but she's learned to use her disability to get praise for doing ordinary things. If she opens her locker or passes a test, everyone at school, including the principal, makes a huge fuss over her. They think it's just great that "she is able to do what everyone else does, in spite of her disability." If they don't fuss, she gets upset. And she gets upset when she is corrected for doing something wrong. Karen has also learned to use her disability to get away with things. Do you think Karen has any plans to improve herself or become more independent? Probably not, since she gets a big fuss just for getting through the day and she is able to use her disability to get everything she wants.

I cringe when I see someone with disabilities being praised or treated like a hero for doing ordinary things. Sure, it's great when someone with disabilities does something really well (play sports, sing, or help in their community). They deserve as much recognition as anyone else. But doing your best is not an amazing achievement. This attitude makes people with disabilities expect to be treated like a hero for doing what everyone else does. When they don't get treated like a hero, they stop trying to get better at doing things.

Attitudes That Help You Grow

Here are some do's and don'ts about attitudes.

- Don't be angry or constantly blame other people. Do use your energy to meet your goals.
- Don't expect praise for every little thing you do. Do your best anyway, even if no one notices.
- Don't use your disability to avoid responsibility. Do things for yourself as much as you can.
- Don't have a bad or stuck-up attitude. This will hold you back, more than any disability ever will. Do be positive and listen to other people.
- If you catch yourself talking about "them," stop. That attitude won't get you anywhere you really want to be.

I put up a slogan on my board at school sometimes when I catch my students blaming the world because things are going wrong for them. The slogan is "No victims." If life isn't going your way, you are not powerless. There is almost always something you can do to improve the situation.

Changing Other Peoples' Attitudes

What if people try to tell you that you can't go to college because of your disability? It's probably because they haven't heard of it happening before. Think back to Adam. His counselor had never heard of students with his disability going on to college. Professionals don't know everything, and you can forgive them for not knowing that students with disabilities can attend college. When they were in college, it probably didn't happen. So, try telling them!

Adam could have told his counselor what he knew about college for students with his disability. He could even have taken this book to her office and asked again for information about the college fair. If someone tells you that you can't go to college, first listen to the reasons why.

Adam did need to improve his attendance and his behavior. Karen needs to improve, too, although she doesn't want to hear it. You may hear some things about yourself that you don't want to hear. Maybe you need to get organized. Maybe you need to do more for yourself. It may be hard to hear, but it will help you reach your goal.

Maybe you are already acting like a college-bound student, working hard and behaving well in school, but the people at school still do not support you in your goals. If this happens, smile politely, thank them, and leave the office. Find someone else to help you—another guidance counselor, another teacher, your parents, or a case manager from an adult agency.

If you are really serious about going to college, it's up to you to make it happen. Don't spend your life blaming someone else for not helping you to meet your own goal. You're not a victim, so don't act like one. Don't forget either that a lot of people have helped you to get to this point. Don't get full of yourself and think you're perfect. There is plenty of room in everyone for growth and improvement.

- -

7. Can you be flexible in your dreams?

College is a chance for you to create something brand new in your education. Take some time to dream about your future:

- Do you want to start training for a specific job?
- Do you love a certain subject, and want to take lots of classes in that subject?

- Do you want to join clubs and go to social events?
- Do you want to live away from home? (For many students, this is the whole point of college.)

Now that you have taken the time to dream up what you want, hear this: *No one's college dream turns out exactly the way they dreamed it.*

Did you know that some colleges will only let half of the students who apply come to their school? Even people with a high school diploma, great grades, and high test scores sometimes can't get into their dream schools. Those lucky people who do get in will find out that dreaming of college and really going to col-lege are not the same thing. It will be that way for you, too. Now that I've said that clearly, let's talk about how to be flexible.

First, look at the choices that are open to you. In high school, you may have gone to a special school or your local high school. You may have taken all special classes, all general education classes, or a mixture of both. You don't have to choose the same kind of program in college. Make a list of three colleges that seem to have what you want. Find out more about these programs (online or call for information).

If these first three choices don't work out—maybe because they cost too much or you don't get into the program—don't give up. Keep trying to find a college program even if it takes a while to find one that has what you want. It may be completely different from your dream, but it could be a great choice for you.

8. How can you put your best foot forward?

It is a good idea to visit the programs and colleges that you want to attend before you apply. Some programs will require an interview when you apply. If you are going to a college that does not have a special program for students with disabilities, make an appointment at Office of Disability Support Services to talk about accommodations.

If you have a meeting on campus, give this meeting a lot of thought and preparation before you go. Your first impression will be very important. Here are some tips:

- Dress well. You don't have to wear a prom dress or tuxedo, but dressing nicely is a way of showing that you think this meeting is important. Be sure to shower, shave, and wash your hair, too. If you think people won't notice as long as your clothes are nice, they will—and it will work against your chances.
- Make eye contact and shake hands properly. Practice introducing yourself clearly.
- Act as grown up as you can. Admissions officials will understand if you are nervous, but keep the silly jokes, the giggling, and any roughhousing under control. You want to look like a college student.
- Be ready to tell about your disability and your accommodations (#1-3).
- Have a list of questions about the school or the program. For example, what happens during the day? What classes can you take?
- Ask to have part of the interview or tour without your parents. This can be tricky, because you don't want to hurt your parents' feelings. But you need a chance to show that you are comfortable without them sitting right next to you. After all, you are the one going to college, not them! Talk to your parents before the interview or meeting and tell them that you need to speak for yourself. Maybe they can even excuse themselves during the tour so you can show the admissions people that you can take care of yourself.
- Be absolutely honest about what you can do for yourself and what you have done in the past. Don't say that you had the lead in the school musical if you were only in the chorus. Don't say that you played football every game of the season if you only got a few minutes of play in the last two games. The truth will come out, and it makes you look bad. Especially don't exaggerate about your independent living skills. Making a sandwich is not being "a great cook." And staying home alone for an hour is not the same as spending a weekend by yourself.

9. Do You Know Your Rights and Responsibilities?

Thanks to a law called The Americans with Disabilities Act (ADA), it is against the law to discriminate against people with disabilities. That means you have the right to benefit from the same services and opportunities as anyone else. Just by looking around your community, you probably have seen some of these changes that make buildings and services more accessible (maybe you use some of these accommodations yourself):

- ramps, elevators, and automatic door openers on buildings (although some older buildings are not required to have them)
- wheelchair lifts on public buses
- service animals in restaurants or stores that ordinarily do not allow pets.

The ADA also requires other kinds of access for people with disabilities. This includes access to education. If you have a disability that affects your ability to learn, you can ask for academic accommodations to allow you to learn the information in your classes and to allow you to show what you know about a subject. You might already use some of these accommodations in school:

- a reader for tests
- copies of notes
- extra time to complete tests
- a separate location for tests
- special computer technology to help with reading and writing
- a sign language interpreter
- materials provided in large print or Braille

You can ask for these accommodations in college, too.

Here's where the responsibility comes in: in order to get the accommodations that you need in college, you have to tell people that you need them. Remember, this process is called disclosure. You will need to share information about your disability with the people who can help you get accommodations at the college. (This is often called the Office of Disability Support Services or ODSS.) Usually, you will need to show them the results of testing that shows you have weaknesses in certain skills. You might also need letters from a doctor showing that you have other disabilities (such as AD/HD, bipolar disorder, etc.) in order to ask for accommodations.

If the ODSS decides that you have enough proof for accommodations, they will give you the information you need to ask for the accommodations from your teachers. You will need to go to the teachers yourself to ask for the accommodations you need. You will probably be nervous the first time you talk to a college teacher. Practice with a friend or someone from the ODSS office so you know what to say. Try to talk to the teacher at least a week before classes start.

The law says that accommodations have to be "reasonable." This means the supports can't cost the college too much money, be too much work, or go against what the college feels is very important. Here are some examples:

- Maybe you had an aide in high school to help you with your work or help you get your lunch or use the bathroom. A college will not hire someone to help you during the day, because that would cost too much. Special programs specifically for students with disabilities won't hire an aide either. If you need the help of an aide, you will need to hire someone to help you.

- Your high school might let you stay after school every day for help with your homework. A college teacher does not have to stay after class every day to help you with your assignments, because that isn't work these teachers are expected to do. You will also have to do your own work in a special program for students with disabilities. If you need accommodations that the college does not consider reasonable, you will need to do without them or arrange them for yourself.

- Colleges and programs decide how students will earn a degree or certificate. Accommodations can't interfere with meeting these goals. For example, you may not have had to take certain courses in high school, like math or French, because of your disability. But if you want to earn a degree in business or international relations, math or speaking another language are required skills. The college does not have to change the rule because of your disability.

What if you aren't able to get the accommodations you need, even though you can prove that you need them and they are reasonable? You can try following your college's grievance procedure. A grievance is just a formal way to make a complaint that you are being discriminated against because you have a disability. Be sure you keep a record of what you have tried to do to solve the problem. (Keep copies of letters or emails or a record of phone conversations or meetings.) An accurate record will help if you need to file a grievance.

. . . .

10. How are your time management skills?

Learn to use your time: When I asked current college students with disabilities about the most important skills they used in college, most answered "managing my time." You won't be changing classes at the bell in college and people will be checking up on you a whole lot less to make sure you are where you need to be. Get or make a good, clear copy of your schedule and keep it with you until you've learned it. Get a watch and work on telling time. (If you can't tell time, get a watch with an alarm that will signal you at important times during the day.) Whether you realize it or not, a lot of people—parents, teachers, and friends—have done a lot for you, reminding you about when to go where you need to go. Now, it's time for you to take over this skill.

Managing time is more than just following a daily schedule. It is also about planning ahead and allowing enough time to get things done. This type of managing will help you plan out how to complete a paper or a project so you do not miss the due date. It can also help you with day-to-day planning. Say you are running low on deodorant. Somewhere in your schedule you need to make time to get to the store to buy some more. Otherwise you may have no deodorant to wear when you go out with friends to the movies on the weekend.

You may envy your friends who do not have disabilities because they might just graduate from high school, go straight to college, earn a degree, and get a good job. Your path might not be so easy. One college graduate with a disability that I spoke to had this advice: "Tell the students that things will happen for them; it just may take a little longer." You may need more time to learn how to do things on your own or learn job skills. You may need to do things differently. That's okay. The important thing is that you are doing what you need to do to get where you want to be in life.

Once you start taking over control of your future and your daily life, you will realize how much your family and teachers did for you over the years. Be sure to say, "Thank you."

You're welcome—now, get going on your future.

Touching the Future
The Secondary Teacher's Role in Facilitating PSE

"What happens to them later on?" I have been asked this question many times in my career, about what the future holds for my students and others who have similar disabilities. What people are asking, of course, is will my students be able to work, to live independently, to have a traditionally "good" quality of life? Will postsecondary education be a part of that life?

I usually answered, in all honesty, that many of their options were limited. Some students came from families with limited finances and serious family problems, but many more simply did not have the skills they needed to succeed. All the more reason for educators to encourage students with significant disabilities and their families to pursue PSE options that will enable the students to gain the skills and experiences they need to change these limiting patterns. Education is a great equalizing factor, and fortunately, it is more within our control than any of the others.

There are factors we can't control. The recent testing hysteria in the United States, fueled by the No Child Left Behind Act, has devastated special education. Even children in elementary schools are aware of "the tests" and the consequences of not passing them. More and more students with relatively mild disabilities are being shut out of traditional high school diplomas because of their inability to pass the standardized tests required for even the lowest tier of "regular diplomas." These students wind up on track for certificates of attendance or other special education credentials (such as an IEP diploma) alongside their peers with significant disabilities. In my opinion, very few students with disabilities in any district should be receiving these alternative credentials.

In the past in some states, the IEP diploma was a formal recognition of the achievement of students with significant disabilities at the end of their school career. It used to represent individual achievement, and it honored students who had painstakingly met their goals, learned many skills, and participated in a variety of educational experiences. Now it has lost this status. Now more than ever before, if a student is placed on IEP diploma track for graduation, it represents failure—primarily failure to pass the state tests.

This failure devastates individual students and negatively affects special education classrooms, too. Students in my special classes now have reading levels ranging from pre-primer to high school—previously, the span was far narrower. It is a planning nightmare to try to reach all of these students at their various levels and really improve their skills.

In the past, students who did not want to take college preparation classes, high stakes tests and all, were encouraged to enroll in vocational education programs. For many students who struggled in academic classrooms, vocational education (also called Career and Technical Education or CTE) was a godsend—hands-on learning, an opportunity to learn marketable skills, and structured building of necessary "soft skills" that employers wanted. The options for CTE are shrinking. Ironically, access to CTE programs in high school is limited due to increasing academic requirements for graduation. Vocational education programs have also had to bolster their academic components to meet state education requirements. The academic requirements for vocational education are also keeping out students with SD.

Special educators can do something about these trends, one classroom and one student at a time. In spite of my state's increased testing requirements, I believe that my success as a teacher is not dependent on my ability to "get my students through the test." (I once got a round of applause at a department meeting by saying that out loud.) I view the individualized nature of my students' educational programs to be an advantage. It gives me a chance to teach them what they really need to know, so they can be the ones in charge of "what happens to them later on." Here are some of the principles I use in my own classroom to use the current state of American special education to prepare my students for futures that I hope will increasingly include PSE and success in the future as contributing citizens.

1. Make Your Students Educated and Knowledgeable about the World

Students with SD are able to learn many more things than was ever before thought possible. In the past, I have had students who were experts on baking, computer technology, history, Soduku, animals, sports, etc. They can learn facts, practice applications of those facts, and can teach those facts to others. Particularly when it comes to technology (cell phones, iPods, computer games, flash drives), I turn to them first to teach me what I need to know. I don't need to learn the theory—just tell me what to click. My students easily oblige.

Basic skills and facts don't have to, and should not be, neglected in high school special education programs. Educated people should have a working knowledge of academic topics, including historical and scientific information, and students with SD should have this knowledge, as well. Some students with SD will spend their high school years gaining academic skills in full inclusion settings, and others will spend time in separate settings. Whatever the student's placement, the goal of the educators should be to make the student with SD as well rounded as possible. Developing a wider world view will give students with SD a better basis for work at the PSE level.

Time spent developing academic skills is not time taken away from functional skills. Academic skills support life skills. Math instruction supports money skills and measurement used in cooking. Health class can support a student's understanding of good nutrition and regular medical exams. Every transition component has specific vocabulary that students may learn across the curriculum. (For example, income/expenses may be discussed in math class, communication terms in English class.) Reading and writing skills support independence at home, at work, and in the community.

2. Make Your Students Competent in Areas beyond Academics

I don't mean to suggest that academic instruction is all that students with SD need for future success. Special education teachers in particular can't afford to neglect nonacademic areas, because our students have such difficulty with incidental learning. Many special education programs allow for community-based instruction (shopping, using public transportation) and work study opportunities, and the skills learned in these settings will be invaluable in PSE and beyond.

Even if your current program does not allow for teaching community-based or employment skills, social skills are no doubt a daily part of your curriculum. Whether through formal training or using "teachable moments" when students run into conflicts, every teacher teaches the skills for social success. Take a long view with these skills. Behaviors and conversations that are "cute" or at least tolerable in a young child with SD often become intolerable and limiting when that child grows up. Have the expectation, early and often, that your high school students—regardless of their disability—will behave like the young adults that they are. Your own interactions with them are critical. For example, an eighteen-year-old student should be called Josh, not Joshie. Use the same tone of voice and vocabulary you would use with other teenagers.

Teach your students old-fashioned manners. If they use appropriate language and common courtesies, others will be more willing to help them and they will be more pleasant to be with. Especially for students who need major support for academic work, for physical care, or to perform everyday tasks, they have a responsibility to be "help-able." A "please" or "thank you" to whomever is providing the assistance should be mandatory.

Self-advocacy skills can be practiced every day, throughout the school environment. Special educators have been trained to help students, to anticipate difficulties, and to make tasks simpler. Sometimes, we do this too well! I know it is time to pull back when I see students turning around to look for me before attempting to do something on their own. Urge the students to try tasks by themselves first, and if necessary let them take the responsibility to ask you for help. Emphasize asking for help appropriately, however the student is able to do so. We can often serve our students best by holding back.

3. Be Practical about Educational Requirements You Can't Control

It's always bad news when your principal stops you with a smile on his face at 7:30 in the morning.

This time the news was about Regents Exams, which are New York state high school tests. Up until a few years ago, my students were exempt from state testing, due to the fact that they were not included in general academic classes. The core classes (English, math, social studies, and science) that I taught were considered "pre-Regents" level, and thus not subject to a state test, as long as I did my own testing. My students were not delayed enough to qualify for the New York State Alternative Assessment, and too academically delayed to pass the Regents Exams. They were what we called "the gray area" kids, and for about five years, there was no appropriate assessment for them. Now, the state had tightened the guidelines, and the students were no longer exempt.

The long and the short of the story is—they survived. In New York state, because my students are eligible to receive an IEP diploma and have enough safety nets in place, they manage to stay on track for graduation in spite of the tests. Written assessments are here to stay, at least for the foreseeable future, and students with SD must learn to deal with this reality.

I scrutinize the tests for skills with long-term value—reading comprehension, writing a business letter, problem solving—and teach those skills thoroughly. There are other benefits, too. My students need to keep track of their testing schedule in January and June, making sure to show up on time, which is good practice for time management. They have a greater appreciation now for their test accommodations.

The biggest benefit is that my students learn the very critical lesson that, sometimes, they will simply have to do things they would rather not do in order to reach a goal. Graduation requires taking state tests. If a few long and stressful testing sessions in high school teach this lesson, that will be good enough for me. I can't change state testing requirements, so I do my best to use them to my advantage in the classroom.

Make sure you stay current on graduation requirements for your students. There are states that are liberal in their graduation requirements. Other states are extremely test driven. If your state is one of them, your students may work tremendously hard for "only" a certificate of attendance. Always remember, though, that college is still possible.

But avoid smiling principals first thing in the morning.

· ·

4. Require IEP Participation, Teach about Disabilities, and Teach Disability Law

Back in the old days, a student with special needs could spend 18 years in public school special education programs and not know she had a disability, let alone what the disability was, how it affected her learning, and what helped her perform better. Parents would tell me confidently, "She's always been treated like she's any other kid. She doesn't think of herself as disabled. I don't think she even knows she has a disability."

Trust me, she knows.

But disability was a forbidden topic, even in special education classrooms. Maybe if we all just hoped enough, worked hard enough, praised the kid enough, and told her she could be anything she wanted to be, the disability would go away, or, at least, stop mattering. It didn't—and we let far too many students go out into the world not knowing what they needed to know about their disabilities and how to advocate for their needs.

Annual review meetings with the IEP team are one place for students to learn more about their disabilities and academic accommodations. My students are very intimidated by meetings. Meetings have traditionally meant they were in trouble or the school had bad news to report, and both the students and their parents are often reluctant to attend routine annual reviews. The IEP team (me, included) always encouraged the students and their parents to attend, but encouragement alone didn't yield good results.

So, using a time honored teacher trick, I decided to hit the students in the grade book. My students are now graded on their preparation for and participation in their annual review meeting. If they are "sick" (or really sick) on the day of the meeting, they must write an essay that outlines the information they would have presented at the meeting. Most students, obviously, find it easier to attend the meeting.

We start the process with questions about each student's future goals (including employment, independent living, community involvement, and, of course, plans for postsecondary education), present skill levels, and areas in need of improvement. Then, we discuss new goals for the next school year, and each student writes or dictates a summary we call a "cheat sheet." I explain that everyone goes into important meetings with notes, and they should as well. They practice reading their cheat sheet aloud and have the chance to review the draft of their IEP before the meeting. We role play meetings and discuss the roles of everyone at the meeting before the big day.

A friend and former school psychologist who watched my students at their meetings over the years once commented, "If your students can do this for their meetings, *every* student receiving special education services should be able to do this for their meetings." The students, their parents, and I have all gained from their active involvement, and meetings have lost much of the intimidation factor for everyone involved.

"Oh, meetings are no big deal," the upperclassmen assure the nervous freshmen every spring.

I have always had the luxury of a flexible curriculum in my special class and I teach IEP and transition planning as a unit every spring. If you are working in a more inclusive model, you may have to be creative in finding other times to meet with your students to make sure they are involved in the process. For more ideas on how to include your students in their IEP preparation and meetings, check out the online resources for student-led IEP meetings.

Another unit I have recently included in my curriculum is disability law. The first objective is to define disability. I watched my students carefully as I outlined the definitions of learning and intellectual disabilities. Tense at first, they slowly relaxed as I reinforced that neither definition included the words "dumb" or "lazy." We discussed the differences between IDEA and the ADA. We talked about reasonable and unreasonable accommodations, and I asked them to think about the academic accommodations they really needed to succeed. I compared the accommodations to using the stairs versus using an elevator.

"We all prefer to take the elevator, but most of us can climb the stairs even if we don't like to do it. But what if you were using a wheelchair? Then the elevator is a necessary accommodation." They got it.

Students need to learn how their disability affects their learning, and what accommodations bridge the gap. Do they need a reader or a scribe? Do they need extra time on tests? Do they need directions rephrased or simplified? Require that they ask for the accommodations they need in an appropriate and polite way: "Could you read this paragraph for me?" "Can you check my project as I go along to make sure I'm following the directions?"

Do an honest assessment of their independent work and study habits. How well do your students know how to work? Can they initiate tasks, carry through, and complete them without one-on-one help? One instructor in the Transition Program at Middlesex Community College in Bedford, Massachusetts, encouraged teaching students strategy use—not just what to do, but how to do it independently. Since the Transition Program teaches entry level business skills, such as data entry, students must learn to keep their place in paperwork by using a ruler or sticky notes. Look at the tasks the students are performing and the amount of help you must provide to get them started, keep them working, and bring projects to quality completion. Teach them how to monitor their own progress, perhaps by using a checklist or a list of questions. Fade your assistance back, steadily and consciously. Someday soon, they will need to do all of this without your help.

I asked several college directors for other specific things that I as a secondary special education teacher needed to do to better prepare my students for higher education. Their advice follows:

- Students need to monitor their progress toward their own goals, to see their own progress, and to speak for and advocate for themselves.
- Start teaching the hidden curriculum of college skills—how do you act in the classroom and in the coffee shop, how do you read a room as you enter it?
- Believe they are going to go to college; give them a vision that college is for them. Organize social interactions with students without disabilities (for example, study partners, buddies for involvement in clubs and school events).
- Encourage parents to send their kids to camp or on school trips and to spend time away from home as soon as possible.
- Mirror college design in courses. For example, use a syllabus to outline the semester and list when assignments are due.

5. Always Plan for the Future, Including PSE and Employment

Postsecondary education will remain in the realm of dreams for students with significant disabilities and their parents if they have no idea how to make it a reality. That's where the guidance of secondary education professionals becomes critical.

I was almost totally unaware of both the benefits and the possibility of PSE for students with SD until very recently. For years, I did not know enough to be able to mention PSE as a viable option for my students. Awareness is an important first step. Check out the websites and other resources at the end of this book. Then, you can encourage parents and students to begin investigating options, too.

Once you begin looking at your students with SD as college bound and with goals beyond college for working and living in the community, you will probably begin changing what you teach. Think of the skills you needed to get through a day on campus—following a schedule, using the library, socializing, studying, navigating the campus, etc. Consider the skills you need now to manage on your own. Use these lists to develop transition goals and start teaching them.

In the initial thrill of learning about the possibilities, parents, students, and their teachers may lose sight of where this adventure may end. College is only the beginning of a person's adult life. Begin the conversation about future goals and how PSE might nurture those goals.

6. Become the Local Expert on PSE Options for Adults with SD

Postsecondary education is not just college. It is lifelong learning. Lifelong learning is given lip service in secondary education; sadly, very few secondary professionals really help their students plan for education beyond college. Researchers are beginning to discover, however, that engaging in intellectual challenges in adulthood is very good for our brains. Adults with SD are no different. If we expand our definition of PSE to include adult education, we find even more opportunities for accessing these benefits for our students. The "post graduate" experience can take as many forms as the students who wish to pursue them. A secondary special education teacher can help a student and her family shape this vision.

First, you must become the authority on what is available to your students once high school comes to an end. After all, you have the inside information on your students and your community. Consider the following questions:

- Where is your nearest college or university? Are there extension sites within easy reach?
- Is there public transportation available to these places (buses, subways, specialized transport for people with disabilities)?
- What are the economic resources of the families you work with? Can they afford the costs of postsecondary education?
- Have you looked at all of the options for adult education in your community?

Not every community is within easy reach of a four-year college or university, but many have access to community colleges, business schools, and technical schools. Community colleges have what is called "open admissions," which means that College Board testing is not required for admissions. Students without a traditional diploma can take certain courses, although they may not be able to matriculate directly in a degree or certificate program.

Consider all other adult education options. Our local community college, Board of Cooperative Education Services (BOCES), and even our school district offer a variety of adult education classes—computer skills, cooking, yoga and fitness, etc.—to people in the community. Your city or county recreation department may offer adult education classes as well. There are few admission requirements, the courses are affordable, locations are convenient, and there is little pressure for grades or performance.

ThinkCollege.net recommends that adults with SD also explore private instruction in specialized areas. Private lessons are available in art, music, dance, karate, gymnastics, personal fitness, etc., and these lessons can be paid for using personal funds, including those provided by trusts.

There are even resources available to help adults with SD to become more independent and organized. Anne Ford in her book *On Their Own* urges parents to also consider a new type of personal instruction called life coaching. Ford writes:

> *My first question was the most obvious and basic of all: 'What is life coaching?'*
>
> *Casey (Dixon, a life coach working in Pennsylvania) defined it as a partnership between a client and a coach that helps the client move toward goals and take actions that will enable them to become the person they want to be in a more focused and rapid way than they would be able to on their own* (Ford, 2004).

In a sense, a life coach works with a client to create an IEP completely of their own choosing. Life coaches help their clients decide on specific actions to take toward their goal. For example, if an adult with SD wants to buy his own home, the coach would help him create a plan to achieve this goal and break down the task into specific steps. Life coaching is expensive (Ford writes that prices can range from $250-500 a month), but can be an efficient way to help achieve personal goals. Help to reach personal independence goals can be provided in other ways, too. Students who meet the eligibility requirements of their local ARC might be able to learn similar skills through adult services or life skills classes.

Many students with SD come from economically and educationally disadvantaged families. The student with SD may be the first in his or her family to finish high school, never mind being the first to continue beyond high school. For families who lack money, transportation, or awareness, educating a student with SD beyond high school may never be considered. What resources are available for these students?

Free opportunities to improve basic academic skills are available in most communities. Literacy Volunteers of America can work with students over the age of 18 to improve reading skills. Adults with SD have also formed and joined book clubs in order to improve their reading as well as to enjoy literature. Adult students who have earned IEP diplomas or certificates can go to local GED classes if they test within certain grade levels in reading and math. For students who are below those levels, Adult Basic Education (ABE) classes may be a possibility to help them improve basic academic skills. (Search online or in local directories for GED programs and ABE services.)

Secondary special education professionals who are frustrated by a lack of PSE possibilities in their communities can approach their school districts for permission to start their own programs for students with SD in association with available colleges and adult education programs. I have visited a few such programs; they are a significant improvement over an extended stay in high school for students with SD. These programs allow for more age appropriate experiences—socializing with other young adults, work experience, community based instruction, etc.—and are an affordable option for families when they are funded through IDEA. However, programs that accept IDEA funding must follow IDEA regulations that can limit the benefits of postsecondary education, including regulations which can limit enrollment (students must live in certain school districts), dictate educational requirements (such as physical education and instruction in IEP goals), insist on constant supervision (when students should be developing independence), and create paperwork headaches for teachers.

Local ARCs and other Office of Mental Retardation and Developmental Disabilities (OMR-DD) service providers have opened programs associated with local colleges. Tuition and fees can be covered by these agencies if the student qualifies. New York state has instituted a program called Options for People Through Services (OPTS), which can help people with SD access a variety of agency services that could support them in a local college program.

Some students with SD really want to have the experience of studying away from home. Job Corps is a national organization that provides young people between the ages of 16 and 24 who are financially eligible the opportunity to improve academic and vocational skills at no cost to their families. Dormitory style living arrangements are available with dining halls and recreational offerings. Job Corps will accept students with IEP diplomas or certificates or who have dropped out of school without any credentials and is prepared to offer accommodations for learning and cognitive disabilities. Students must be free of behavioral problems, have good self-care skills, basic academic skills, and must be willing and able to learn work skills. Many vocational training options are available at centers across the United States. (See www.dol.jobcorps.gov.) Students are expected to study for a period of eight months to two years, are helped to find a job upon graduation, and are offered ongoing guidance and counseling for the first eighteen months on their own.

Christa McAuliffe, the teacher astronaut who died in the explosion of the space shuttle Challenger, once said, "I touch the future—I teach." Our responsibility to our students is not just to deliver them safely to high school graduation. Secondary professionals can touch the future of students with significant disabilities by opening the doors to educational opportunities they never thought possible.

Time to Face the Music

Parents' Roles in Building Competence for PSE

If you can teach the skill, teach it. If you can't teach the skill, adapt it. If you can't adapt it, figure out a way around it.... If you can't figure out a way around it, teach the neurotypicals to deal with it (C. Sicile-Kira, 2006).

The decision has been made. Perhaps committed to paper on a transition plan, perhaps a family discussion, perhaps it is just assumed in your family, but the decision for your child with significant disabilities has been made—he will be going to college. Now is the time to start getting him prepared to strike out on his own.

Ideally, preparing children for independence unfolds throughout childhood. From the first time your baby squirms out of your sheltering arms, to the "Me do it" stage in toddlerhood, on and on through the teenage years, typical children insist on taking matters into their own hands. There is reluctance sometimes—more in some children and parents than others—but most major issues are resolved and typical young adults are able to manage on their own by their early twenties.

They learn to live and work independently, only needing guidance from their parents at key milestones such as buying a first car, getting married, or becoming parents themselves.

Although there are exceptions to the rule, this process of becoming independent is not smooth for young adults with SD. A significant disability affects more than just academic development; it will affect the individual in all aspects of life. In fact, even for someone whose intellect is highly superior, a disability that impairs social skills or the ability to perform activities of daily living can be incredibly debilitating unless the skill deficits are addressed.

I have an unapologetic bias on issues of independence for young adults with SD. It is absolutely essential that they learn to manage activities of daily living on their own. I believe that unless maximum independence and positive interdependence is gained, whatever else learned in school is useless. There are people with SD who have physical and cognitive needs that require unavoidable, ongoing assistance from others. While these situations should be acknowledged and assistance capably provided without judgment or ill will, I believe that if a person can possibly learn self-care skills, he should.

I believe in teaching independence so strongly because I have witnessed the consequences when I have caved in and stopping insisting upon it. A student I'll call Emma had good independent toileting skills when she came to my class. She could transfer to and from the toilet from her wheelchair and manage dressing and undressing with no help, except for a spotter during the transfer. It was hard work and she did not like the routine, but she could do it on her own. Then, we included Emma in an art class. She would arrive late to the class every day, because she always needed to use the toilet before class and the routine took her a long time. She had an advocate who argued that Emma had a "right" to get to art class at the same time as the other students. She should be lifted on and off the toilet and helped to dress, so she could get to class on time. The advocate was someone I was reluctant to offend.

After several weeks of debate, I gave in: the advocate won, and, I believe, Emma ultimately lost. Her self-care skills in the bathroom started to decline immediately, and by the end of the year, they were completely gone. Her future choices for work, socializing, and independent living became severely limited, because she would always need a paid attendant to help her in the bathroom, wherever she went. I still feel badly when I think about how I failed her, even though she passed art.

Adolescents with significant disabilities are frequently passive participants in their own lives. Often, this passivity is called learned helplessness. Learned helplessness is traditionally attributed to persistent failure—a child with disabilities struggles endlessly to learn skills and fails over and over again, and so becomes afraid to try anything new. This theory contains some truth—children with SD often have to work very hard to learn to dress, to tie their shoes, and to do many other life skills, and the effort may become discouraging. But learned helplessness is not that simple and it is not the whole story.

I have watched the interaction of many parents and children over the years. In many cases, the parents regarded their child as less capable or much younger than he really was because of his disability. The child figured out quickly that it was easier to let Mom or Dad do the hard stuff. I don't think this happened because the parents were incompetent. Finding the balance between helping and independence is difficult for all parents, and parents of children with SD have it even tougher. The parents have to protect their child from a world that doesn't understand him, poses real threats, or goes too fast, and overprotection becomes a habit even when the child is ready for more independence. Often the kid isn't complaining and life is easy.

What Does Your Adult Child Need to Learn?

How do you go about changing expectations that have been set too low? If the goal for your adult child is for him to attend post-secondary education and then live as independently as possible, you must start assessing his level of independence well before high school graduation.

Try enlisting the help of a trusted and honest observer—a teacher, a neighbor, a friend, a grandparent—to help you figure out if you are giving the right level of support. Give the person carte blanche to tell you the whole ugly truth. I have had parents ask me in amazement how I "got" Johnny or Sue to act so well. Often, I was able to give the parents a few simple ideas that they could try to get their child to comply at home, and I appreciated the chance to help. I'm sensitive to the fact that for the parents of my students, this child is often the first adolescent with disabilities they have ever known. I have known many disabled adolescents, and I have lots of tricks I can share.

There are times when all that is needed for growth to happen is for parents and professionals to simply stop helping. I cannot count the times that I handed kids the telephone, the money, or whatever was needed to accomplish a task, said, "Go for it"—and they did. I would spend the next day and a half kicking myself for not expecting them to demonstrate their competency earlier. Parents and teachers often reach this point after becoming tired, frustrated, or distracted. How much growth would we see in these young adults if we consciously held back in the first place? We may have to watch a brief (or not so brief) struggle while they figured out what to do, but we will avoid that smothering behavior they find so annoying and that holds them back from becoming adults.

Fostering other independence skills may need a systematic, planned approach. Just stopping your assistance may not spur your adolescent with SD to learn independence. You can just stop doing his laundry, preparing the meals, or pestering him to shower and shave, but this approach may backfire. We all know that teenagers have an enormous tolerance for dirty laundry, dirty selves, and for eating junk food rather than cooking. Stopping assistance completely will also backfire if your teenager simply does not know how to care for himself, and just becomes frustrated when he can't meet his own needs.

There are resources that outline step by step how to teach new skills, and, even more importantly, how to motivate the young adult with SD to change his behavior. Two great resources I have found are *Incentives for Change: Motivating People with Autism Spectrum Disorders to Learn and Gain Independence* (Lara Delmolino and Sandra L. Harris, Woodbine House, 2004) and *Steps to Independence: Teaching Everyday Skills to Children with Special Needs* (Bruce L. Baker, Alan J. Brightman, et al., Paul H. Brookes Publishing, 2004).

Skills for College

What independent living skills will a future college student need? Using the analogy of packing the equipment for a trip up a remote mountain, what tools will he need to manage on his own? Some items to have in this metaphorical backpack are:

- tools for self-care (hygiene, laundry, taking medicine)
- tools for self-advocacy (knowing what he needs, asking for help appropriately)

- tools to travel alone (driving, walking safely, riding public transportation)
- tools to stay organized and manage time (using a planner, telling time)
- tools to relax and have fun (calming down when upset, spending time with others)
- tools to stay safe (information about drugs and alcohol, locking doors, securing belongings)
- tools to stay in touch (cell phones and email)
- tools to manage financial resources (able to handle money, get cash from an ATM)

Self-care skills, such as independent eating, toileting, dressing, and managing personal hygiene, should come first. If your adult child has a physical or cognitive disability that precludes complete independence in any of these areas, does he participate as much as he can? Does he ask for the needed assistance appropriately? Will he tolerate help from several different caregivers? Does he make himself easy and pleasant to help by using courtesy? Even if complete independence is not possible, look for ways to maximize his involvement. If the individual skills have been mastered, consult the excellent information in *Steps to Independence* (Baker et al., 2004) on establishing routines and self-monitoring.

Sex Education

As an important area of self-care, your adult child needs to be prepared to deal with sex and intimacy. He also needs an understanding of sexual violence. People with significant disabilities are extremely vulnerable to sexual abuse and exploitation. Although abuse remains an awful reality, I think the special needs community has done well in addressing the issue openly. Young adults with SD, particularly young women, need this information and assertiveness training to protect themselves.

But sexual awareness should not stop there. Young adults with SD have consensual sexual relationships and they need the same preparation for a healthy and satisfying sex life that any other teenager needs. If your child with SD is going away to a residential PSE program, make the assumption that he or she is going to have the opportunity to have sex (commuter students should also be prepared). Young men should learn how to use condoms appropriately, and know that they should use them in every sexual encounter. Young women should have their first gynecological exam and get advice about appropriate birth control options. Then, they need instruction in how to use the methods correctly (e.g., taking the pill every day, using a spermicidal foam or jelly in a diaphragm).

In her book *Couples with Intellectual Disabilities Talk about Living and Loving,* Karin Melberg Schwier interviews fifteen couples about their intimate relationships. Many of the women had unplanned pregnancies in their late teens, presumably because no one had assumed they would consider having sex or need to know how to protect themselves. Several of the people interviewed had undergone surgical sterilization, some without their consent. Others were successfully meeting the challenge of raising young children. The decision to undergo a tubal ligation or a vasectomy is not one to take lightly, particularly in young adulthood, although some young adults with SD have decided that surgery is their best option. The best protection for an individual needs to be considered with the advice of an informed doctor. For a good discussion of the issues and teaching materials and activities, you might want to consult *Teaching Children with Down Syndrome about Their Bodies, Boundaries, and Sexuality,* by Terri Couwenhoven (Woodbine House, 2007).

Alcohol and Drug Use

Your adult child, like all young adults, will be able to purchase and drink alcohol legally at age 21. He may also encounter situations in which he is tempted to drink before he is of legal age. Ideally, you will take the time to explicitly teach your child about responsible alcohol usage before the temptation and opportunity to try it arise.

If your adult child is taking certain medications and/or alcohol will negatively affect his condition, he also needs to know that information and what to do in situations where others are drinking. A plain soft drink can masquerade as a mixed drink, and he need not call attention to the fact that he is choosing not to drink.

Before your child begins a PSE program, consider finding out what the staff's attitude is toward alcohol use to ensure it meshes with family values. Once while I was visiting a program, a group of students was planning a vacation trip to a beach resort. They were going to be escorted by agency staff people, but frankly asked the director of the program to tell the staff that they wanted to be able to visit the bar. The young women were all of age, and the request was approved.

A supervisor from the same program told me, "They need to learn responsible drinking, too, and better that they learn the consequences of overdoing it while we are still here to hold their heads in front of the toilet the next day."

Illegal drug use needs to be discussed in terms your adult child can understand. Make sure he understands the effects on his body, as well as the very real possibility of being arrested for buying and using drugs. As well, make sure he knows not to share his prescription medication (particularly medicines such as Ritalin or pain killers) with other people and not to take anything not prescribed for him.

Social Skills

Social competence skills are critical, and will elicit the strongest reaction from others, both negative and positive. Rick Lavoie describes "zero order skills" as skills that are only noticed when they are not present in an individual (Lavoie, 2005). Appropriate eye contact—neither too much nor too little—during a conversation is an example of a zero order skill. We only notice it when a person does not use it appropriately. Don't forget to note your child's ability to use these skills and to plan to address them. Otherwise, his social interactions may be compromised from the beginning because other people are feeling uncomfortable.

Social competence can be taught and practiced in a variety of ways and in a multitude of settings. Social competence among individuals with SD can make the difference between people being "nice" to them and people really being their friends.

Different types of encounters and interactions can be taught and practiced over time with social rehearsal. Social rehearsal sounds fancy, but it is a technique you have been using with your adult child since he was a baby.

"Say 'bye-bye, Daddy.'"

"Say 'please.'"

"Say 'thank you.'"

It is putting the language of social interaction and information sharing into a child's mouth. For an adult child, you just have to put in different information. You can pre-rehearse all kinds of situations:

- college admission interviews,
- phoning for doctor's appointments,

- approaching a professor for needed accommodations,
- asking a roommate to pick up his side of the room.

This kind of practice can reduce your child's anxiety about new situations and put him in control.

Create accommodations for your child to use when negotiating social situations at home. For example, for an adult child who has trouble remembering information, create a binder with information about his medical information, names and numbers of doctors, etc. A practice script can be included, if that will be helpful. If your adult child cannot read, pictures or symbols can be used instead to maximize his independence.

Teach Your Child to Handle His Own Problems

Begin teaching your teenager to handle small problems on his own. Parents must monitor their own reactions to the minor crises that their adolescent with SD faces on a daily basis if they want to encourage him to be resilient and to advocate for himself. I have had parents call me, close to hysteria or to filing a lawsuit, because their son or daughter came home crying. The upsets were over low grades, an argument with a friend, or other teenage stresses. Other classic parental overreactions happened when their child was disciplined for a violation of a school rule.

Start by being honest with yourself: how do you *really* react in these situations? If you call the school to insist upon an immediate conference to address every tiny issue rather than talking with your child and urging him to come up with a plan of action, you are depriving him of a chance to learn how to deal with stress. Teenagers are highly emotional creatures—sometimes they cry and curse as a release. They are prone to feeling that the world is coming to an end. Good thing they have parents to tell them that it is not!

When my students are upset, I remind them to use the "one week" rule—will you or anyone else remember or care about this in a week? Most crises, especially social dramas, will pass or at least seem far less important than they do today. The one week rule really works; most issues are resolved within that time, with no intervention other than patience and encouragement. If not, then it's probably a problem that warrants a conference or some kind of action. Certainly, there are exceptions to this rule (bullying or harassment, for example), but if your child's health and safety are not in jeopardy, try waiting a week to see what happens. Often, the situation will resolve itself. Even if it doesn't, resist rushing in to fix the issue for your child. Postsecondary programs and support staff will expect him to manage his own issues or approach them directly for help.

Parents often tell me that they don't want their child treated any differently than any other child. Not wanting to burst anyone's bubble, but your child with SD can and does violate school rules and mouth off to authority figures. Do you want him treated differently when that happens? I have seen otherwise supportive parents back-peddle over discipline and insist that their child could not possibly have done anything wrong, or that another child convinced him to violate the rule. Other parents blame their child's disability—"He has AD/HD and couldn't stop himself." Be very, very careful of using this excuse. Even if the child is very impulsive, and this contributed to him swearing at the teacher or punching the locker, the behavior should have a consequence. It won't fix the impulsiveness, but it will teach him that his behavior affects other people and their opinion about him, and that he must be accountable when he messes up. People forgive a lot when someone takes responsibility for his behavior and tries to make amends.

Taking responsibility for managing your own life is just another name for self- advocacy. Although throughout this chapter, I have used the term independence over and over, I fully recognize that I rely on other people to help me get things done. I don't grow all of my own food—I buy most of it. I don't sew my own clothing—I buy it. I don't fix my own car...and so on. I have to know what I need, how to get it, who to call, etc.

Pamela Groupe Groves explains interdependence in her essay "Growing Up with FAS/E" and gives steps that parents can take to build their child's self-advocacy:

- Name both their problems and their strengths.
- Help children learn how to identify sources of help.
- Let the children speak for themselves and take the risk of doing things on their own.
- Help build social confidence and skills throughout life by providing a variety of opportunities for children to interact with people of different ages and backgrounds and to act independently (Kleinfeld, Morse, and Wescott, 2000).

Prepare Your Child to Live Away from Home

If you and your child are considering a PSE program with a residential component, don't overlook the need for advance practice. Self-care, self-advocacy, and personal responsibility look different away from home. Your child will need to be able to adjust to a group living situation, sharing common areas (including bathrooms and showers), eat food that is prepared differently, etc. Especially if your child has sensory sensitivities, this controlled practice is critical. No place else is going to smell or feel exactly like home!

Try out your child's adjustment abilities by arranging extended sleepovers with friends or family, allowing him to go on class trips, or sending him to sleep away camp (all with minimal phone calls to you). This practice is less about learning skills and more about the emotional and psychological readiness for your adult child to leave the nest. It's also a time to test your own readiness to let him go and trust he will manage without you.

Independent living and self-care skills make young people safer and immensely increase their options for inclusive work, housing, and socialization. Some parents have it backwards. I have been accused by some parents of not doing enough to include their students with SD in school activities or challenge them at school or work training. These same parents think nothing of packing their teenager's lunch, holding their son's hand while crossing the street, or waking their adult child in the morning, rather than teaching him to use an alarm clock.

Guardianship

Now, we need to discuss the question of guardianship. Say you've done all the right things—taught basic health care, worked hard on money, tried to build social skills, etc. What if you have done all of this planning and practice with your teenager and you still have doubts that he will be able to make responsible and safe decisions about life in all of its complexities? Maybe the information isn't sticking. Maybe he is just too impulsive or just doesn't get it. Whatever the reason, your child's legal majority is coming and you are losing sleep over it.

When a person reaches the age of 18 in this country, he or she is a legal adult. For individuals with SD who may have struggled to be viewed as capable and equal in humanity, this matter-of-fact episode is momentous. It also indicates an equally momentous change in status. Once a person turns 18, he can have free rein within the law to make decisions for himself, regardless of what his family members, friends, or support people think about those decisions.

To get an idea of the decisions your child will be able to make for himself as an adult, ask yourself the following questions as they apply to your teenager:

- What if your daughter decides to date or even to marry someone you don't approve of (a man or another woman)?
- What if your son decides to spend all of his savings on a trip rather than save for a car or a deposit on an apartment?
- What if your daughter decides not to have her wisdom teeth removed?
- What if your son decides to stop taking his AD/HD medication or to stop seeing his counselor?
- What if your daughter decides to leave the program you just worked so hard to get her into? What if she decides to change programs and to try another postsecondary option?
- What if your daughter decides to rent an apartment in a bad neighborhood?
- What if your son decides to quit his job and collect government support?
- What if your child doesn't understand what he needs to do to maintain eligibility for government benefits such as a Medicaid and does something to make himself ineligible?
- What if your daughter decides not to use birth control even though she is sexually active with multiple partners?

These are issues you need to talk about frankly with your adult child and other family members. You may be fortunate to have a responsible adult child who you can trust to make good decisions or an adult child who may be quite content to have you involved in his decisions even after the age of 18, even seeking your advice for decisions. But he will be the one with the power if there is a disagreement between the two of you.

It is important to remember that education is not a cure for disability. Some adults with SD will never achieve complete independence for a variety of reasons and this is not a failure. The point of higher education is not to develop rugged individualists, but individuals who have learned how to live in a larger world. But they don't have to live there alone.

Individuals living with cognitive problems that severely affect their judgment or ability to be safe may need ongoing support. In her essay "What the Wisdom of Practice Teaches Us" in *Fantastic Antone Grows Up* about the challenges facing adults with fetal alcohol syndrome, editor Judith Kleinfeld writes:

> *Once an effective external structure is in place, beware of pulling it up in a misguided belief that supervision is no longer needed. The most tragic problems [my note: arrests for violent crimes, descent into drug abuse and alcoholism] I have come across, working with the families in this book over several years, took place because effective supervision was withdrawn....Other families have learned a similar lesson: Supervision is a bearing wall. Do not tear it down* (Kleinfeld, Morse, and Wescott, 2000).

Teresa Kellerman adds in her essay "Broken Beaks and Wobbly Wings":

> *We also need to work on selling the importance of these interventions to the "system" so that our birdies get the support they need to fly, even if it means flying with them to support them when they start to veer off course or take a dip too low* (Kleinfeld, Morse, and Wescott, 2000).

Some families decide that full guardianship is the best way to provide the support their adult child with SD needs. If you are considering guardianship, research the process in your state (guidelines and costs vary somewhat). In general, guardianship will be granted after a hearing on your adult child's competence. He will need to have the representation of a lawyer separate from your own in order to represent his interests, and even under full guardianship, your adult child (called the ward) will retain certain rights. The appointed guardian, even if the guardian is a family member, now works for the court and will probably need to make regular reports to make sure the ward's interests are being served. All rights not given specifically to the guardian are retained by the ward. Generally speaking, the ward retains all rights that are allowed to all people under the United States Constitution and the constitution of his home state. Unless the guardianships state otherwise, the ward will retain the right to marry, to have children, and to keep his own information private, even from the guardian. Some states will not allow the ward to vote.

Full guardianship is not the only option to protect a vulnerable person. The ARC and other advocacy organizations for adults with developmental disabilities urge families to consider alternatives to full guardianship whenever possible. Full guardianship requires that the ward be found incompetent and unable to make critical decisions about his or her own life.

Other options families may want to consider are:

- **Limited guardianship:** In limited guardianship, a court appoints a guardian only over the portion of a person's life where he is not competent to make decisions for himself (e.g., financial transactions), but the person retains all rights not specifically given to the guardian. This can also be accomplished by appointing a guardian of the estate (to manage assets and payments) while allowing the person with SD to maintain his personal rights (instead of having a guardian of the person).
- **Power of attorney:** The adult with SD can authorize a parent or other person to handle areas of his life that he does not feel equipped to handle, such as legal issues or finances. This permission is given by the adult to a person of his choosing, not taken away from him due to a ruling of incompetence. The adult can revoke or transfer this power of attorney when he chooses.
- **Health care proxy:** Similar to power of attorney, but the young adult gives the proxy the right to make medical decisions on his behalf if he is unable to do so (e.g., if incapacitated due to a seizure, diabetic emergency, or in a coma).

It is important to note that both power of attorney and health care proxy documents are often used by nondisabled adults to protect their health or assets should they become ill.

Other options that can provide oversight or structure for areas that your child just "doesn't get" can be arranged. A representative payee can receive an individual's SSI or SSDI checks, deposit them into the individual's account, and help the individual manage the money. Other families set up a joint checking account with both a parent's name and the adult child's name on the account, so both people have legal access to the bank information. Parents can give their adult child a debit or credit card with a set limit to avoid overspending. A special needs trust, monitored by a trustee, can provide financial security while still allowing a young adult with SD to maintain his eligibility for government disability benefits like SSI and Medicaid.

Even if these supports are not enough and you decide that full guardianship is the only way to provide security for your adult child with SD, guardianship is not set in stone. As your adult child becomes more mature and able to make responsible decisions, you may petition the court to terminate guardianship altogether or reduce guardianship to limited guardianship for areas where he may still have trouble. It is important to note, too, that your adult child maintains the right to petition the court to have guardianship terminated if he feels it is no longer necessary.

Independence and competence in life management is never 100 percent for anyone. We all live in a state of interdependence with family and friends. We all hire professionals to do for us what we cannot or do not want to do for ourselves, be it fixing the plumbing or filling out income tax returns. So do not hold back from pursuing postsecondary education for your adult child until he is fully competent. Most programs and support services teach these skills as part of their mission. Your adult child may also learn skills best when he is out on his own at college. But remember the "you are your child's first teacher" maxim? You, as a parent, have a crucial role to play in helping your adult child become as independent as possible.

The Buck Stops Here
The Fine Art of Financing

One of the biggest hurdles facing families of students with significant disabilities who want to attend a postsecondary education program is money. College is getting more expensive every year for all students, and includes more than just tuition—fees, housing, materials, and books also contribute to the cost. The Princeton Review projected that for 2009, total average costs for a private college are $34,132 annually and total average costs for a public college (in state) are $14,333 annually. Some of the specialized and comprehensive special programs I have profiled in this book can also cost well over $30,000 a year. For all but the wealthiest of families, these can be disheartening figures. "It sucks," one parent told me bluntly. "It's not just white collar families that have kids with disabilities."

Most families rely on financial aid packages to help meet the cost of college educations for their typical children. Students with significant disabilities who have a traditional diploma or a GED, or who can earn the minimum score set by the college on an Ability to Benefit test can apply just like any other students for federal financial aid by filling out the Free Application for Federal Student Aid (FAFSA). Colleges then determine how much money in the form of grants, loans, and scholarships a student can receive based on their expected family contribution (EFC). They can then use this money to pay for higher education.

According to the Americans with Disabilities Act (ADA), if a student with a disability meets the qualifications to be admitted to a college program (e.g., high school diploma, minimum GPA, and College Board scores), she is eligible to receive financial aid based on financial need, just as any other student would be. I will not try to repeat the excellent information on financial assistance that already exists for this type of student. High school guidance counselors have a lot of experience with the typical financial aid application process. There are also books, websites, and college and private financial counselors that can help families through the process.

For students with SD who do not have these academic credentials, the financial picture is much more complicated. If a student is still eligible for IDEA funding, some school districts will be able to help defray postsecondary education costs. But for our purposes, I will assume that many students are no longer eligible for IDEA funding or want a different PSE experience than their district provides. Instead, I will focus this chapter on the ways that students with SD and their families can find ways to help pay for the specialized and individualized options we have been discussing so far.

Sources of funding

College funding typically comes from four sources:
1. scholarships or grants (which do not need to be paid back),
2. loans (which need to be paid back in the future by the borrower),
3. personal earnings or savings, and
4. parental assistance.

Scholarships and Grants

In August of 2008, President George W. Bush signed into law the Higher Education Opportunity Act. This law will allow students with intellectual disabilities to become eligible for selected educational grants from the federal government, including:

1. Pell Grants and Educational Opportunity Grants, which are federal grant monies for students who demonstrate financial need, and
2. the Federal Work Study Program, which allows students to take jobs on campus and earn additional college money.

At the time of this writing, the specifics of this law have not been tested. According to a press release from the National Down Syndrome Society, students with intellectual disabilities could apply these funds to "programs that have been designed for them in higher education"—which leaves unanswered the question of whether funds can be applied to private programs not directly affiliated with a college.

The passage of this law is a tremendous first step in the government's acknowledgment that people with SD have much to gain from continuing their education beyond high school.

There is some additional "free money" available for students with SD. Recognizing that their fees are often out of reach for middle class families, some private nondegree programs may have limited financial assistance for students who have been admitted to their programs. These programs raise funds through a foundation that can disperse them to students in financial need. Ask what is available early in the application process. Be warned, though, that this assistance will not cover the entire cost of such programs.

Organizations for people with disabilities have begun to offer scholarships for postsecondary education that can be applied towards tuition. The National Down Syndrome Society is one of them, awarding several $1,000 scholarships a year to young adults with Down Syndrome who wish to attend a variety of PSE options. Scholarships are limited and students must apply early. Similarly, the Autism Society of America offers $1,000 scholarships through the CVS/All Kids Can scholarship program. As postsecondary education becomes a more common option for students with significant disabilities, hopefully other organizations will follow suit.

Funds for Job Training

If the PSE goals of a student with significant disabilities are directly related to a career goal (such as auto mechanics, computers, certified nurse's aide, etc.), there are federal and state funds that can pay for training. State vocational rehabilitation funds may be used to pay for tuition or materials. Vocational and Educational Services for Individuals with Disabilities (VESID) in New York State, for example, can provide as much as $3,000 a semester to students with SD who are pursuing postsecondary education programs that will equip them to work in a particular vocational area.

Vocational rehabilitation services are available throughout the United States; once an individual has applied for VR in one state, the benefits will follow her to other states, as well. Students can apply for VR services during their junior or senior year of high school. A VR counselor can help a student access funds by helping her create a clear vocational goal.

Every state has at least one agency in charge of vocational rehabilitation to help people with disabilities seek and maintain employment. A complete list of websites by state can be found at www.abledata.com. Look under the resources tab for a link to the vocational rehabilitation page. Most students and families who are making use of this book will be found eligible for services under vocational rehabilitation (VR).

Because VR services depend on government funding, the extent of services can vary and there can be waiting lists for services. People with the most significant disabilities are usually served first. Students with SD should plan to apply for VR services one year before leaving public education. VR counselors can also provide guidance on how a person can work while maintaining eligibility for government benefits through SSI and how to navigate government work incentive programs, such as Ticket to Work programs.

Anyone who is looking for training related to a job—whether or not they have a disability—can go to their local One-Stop Career Center. One Stop Career Centers offer information on jobs available in the community, as well as training and assistance in job-seeking skills (writing a resume, interviewing for a job). One-Stop centers can help job seekers obtain an Individual Training Account. These are vouchers that can be used to purchase a slot in a career-related training program at a program listed on each state's Eligible Training Provider list. A quick glance at the Eligible Training Provider list for my area listed all the local colleges, many vocational training programs, and even a reading improvement program that served both children and adults. The vouchers are given at the discretion of the One-Stop Centers, and are dependent upon available funds, but for young adults with SD who have a clear and viable career goal, this funding option can be attempted.

"Free money" will only go so far. Even for regularly enrolled students, financial aid packages are based on the information contained on the FAFSA application that results in a figure called the Estimated Family Contribution (EFC). The EFC indicates how much the student and the student's family can be expected to contribute to the costs of higher education. Grants and scholarships, though a great help, may only total a few thousand dollars a year even if the family cannot contribute a great deal of money. The rest of this chapter will deal with how to fill in the gaps in college funding.

Loans

Many college students seek financing through student loan programs. If a student with SD is employed, he or she can apply directly for a student loan. Otherwise, parents may need to co-sign a loan. Some parents really resist the idea of their child accumulating any student debt, which I have never understood. Certainly, it's not a good idea for students to bury themselves in debt, but repaying a loan is a way to establish a credit rating and to coax a slow-to-launch graduate to get a job! Loans are a fact of life when adults want to buy a house, a car, or even own a credit card. If you want your adult child with a disability to have these advantages, taking out a reasonable student loan (which she helps to repay) may be a good decision.

Using Student Funds

Students can help finance their education, too. Work study programs have helped students pay for college expenses for years. Through work study, college students can earn up to a certain dollar amount (e.g., $3,000 a year) as an employee of the college that can be applied toward their expenses. Often, students are able to work in campus offices, dining halls, libraries, etc. Depending on your student's situation, she may be able to apply for work study funds. However, young people with SD, like their peers without disabilities, can apply any earnings from part time, full time, and summer employment toward college expenses.

A common form of earnings for people with SD who are over 18 years old and have never been employed is Supplemental Security

Income (SSI). Individuals receiving SSI and Medicaid health coverage are restricted in the amount of savings or resources they may own themselves—usually less than $2,000. Students who have saved money carefully for PSE or received financing from family members may find themselves having to forgo the savings in order to receive SSI and health coverage—a catch-22 situation for many people. Fortunately, the Social Security Administration will allow SSI recipients who want to use their resources to improve their employability to develop a Plan for Achieving Self Support (PASS) in order to temporarily "set aside" their savings or resources that will help them get further education and work training.

For example, say a woman with SD receives an inheritance of $5,000 from Great Aunt Mary, who wants to encourage her to continue her education. The young woman would no longer be eligible to receive SSI or Medicaid, unless she developed a PASS that would allow her to continue receiving benefits as long as her inheritance is going to pay for postsecondary education or another designated purpose related to employment or personal independence. PASS plans have a set time frame and the person must be meeting certain milestones in order to continue to qualify for the program. A Social Security benefits counselor can help an individual with SD to develop a PASS. SSI funds can also be used to pay for PSE directly if the person with SD does not need the money for living expenses.

The Social Security Administration has created new regulations for people receiving SSI or SSDI that allow them to work while still receiving their supplemental checks and government sponsored health insurance. If a young adult with SD is receiving these benefits, she should have a conversation with a benefits counselor about the Ticket to Work program and how it applies in her case. The additional money earned at work can be used to help pay college expenses.

ARE SSI RECIPIENTS ELIGIBLE FOR SCHOLARSHIPS AND GRANTS?

According to information from the Social Security Administration, grants a student receives for study do not count against SSI benefits as long as the grant is used for educational expenses (tuition, fees, etc.) and not living expenses (room, board, etc.).

Using Parent Funds

Parents are a major source of funding for PSE for all of their children, not just those with special needs. Financial aid packages are determined using the Expected Family Contribution (EFC), which is based on family income and savings. Parents often begin saving for their child's education through 529 plans (specific for college saving), IRAs (Individual Retirement Accounts), trust funds, and traditional savings accounts.

Most states operate something called a 529 plan to encourage parents to save for their children's college expenses. Savings are invested by the plan in hopes of earning interest, but like 401k plans and IRAs, the funds fluctuate with the stock market and you can actually end up losing money. 529 plans are free from federal taxes during the savings period and funds can be withdrawn without federal taxes if the money is used for qualified higher education expenses (tuition, fees, books, room and board) for a designated beneficiary (child, step-child, grandchild, etc.) at an eligible educational institution. States will allow parents to deduct their contributions to a child's 529 plan from their state income taxes. Be sure to speak with a financial advisor while setting up a college savings payment plan, since laws change frequently.

Traditional and Roth IRA funds are usually opened for people to save for retirement; they are subject to penalties and/or taxes if the owner withdraws them before age 59½. However, the money may be used without penalty for higher education expenses. For Roth IRAs, the money must be left in the fund for at least five years before withdrawal. The limiting factor in both of these options is that the funds can only be used at an eligible educational institution, which will eliminate some private, specialized programs for students with SD, but will include community colleges, public and private four-year institutions, and many vocational/technical schools.

Families have used trust funds to plan for the needs of children with disabilities for years. Most parents are familiar with special needs trusts, which can be used to help with their adult child's financial needs after their death. However, trust funds are another way that parents of students with SD can save for college. Trust funds can be used to cover a variety of expenses, without burdening the adult with SD with assets over $2,000. Irrevocable trusts have more flexibility than trusts that can be revoked. In an irrevocable trust, the person setting up the fund officially gives up ownership of the money (although he or she may still receive interest payments) to the trust; the advantage here is that the trust cannot be counted as an asset of the young adult with a disability. A trustee is named and has control over dispersing the money. The funds can be used to pay for higher education expenses and any other expenses listed in the trust ahead of time. A financial advisor or attorney who specializes in trusts should be consulted to set up the terms and conditions.

Parents can also save money in traditional savings accounts and Certificates of Deposit. The money should not be saved in the adult child's account if she needs to apply for SSI and Medicaid benefits.

Getting Professional Advice

An accountant or financial advisor may be able to give you guidance about other ways to make PSE expenses affordable. It would also be wise to consult an SSI benefits counselor to make certain that any financial decisions will not affect your adult child's eligibility for SSI or Medicaid.

Some expenses related to a specialized PSE program for students with disabilities may be deductible or may be eligible for reimbursement from health insurance. Generally, educational expenses are deductible from federal taxes as a medical expense if the main reason a child or adult dependent is attending the school is to receive medical care in the form of special education for a diagnosed medical condition (documentation will probably be needed for this). Keep in mind that only the portion of your medical expenses that exceeds 7.5% of your adjusted gross income is deductible. For example, if your AGI is $50,000, the first $3750 (7.5%) of your medical expenses are not deductible; only the amount above that level is.

Creating funding options takes time, and it is the least sexy part of the college process for parents. Ideally, the planning and saving process can be done systematically over the years leading up to college. But don't despair if you are only just beginning to consider college for your child with SD in her senior year of high school. Many specialized programs allow students to enroll up to age 25, and adults of any age can enroll in college or vocational programs. Perhaps the student can begin the process slowly by auditing a course at a local community college while funding is being arranged. The investment of money as well as effort will be worthwhile in the long run.

The Nuts and Bolts of College Admissions
How to Start

Among the saddest conversations I have are with parents who have lost hopes for higher education for their children.

"I know that he is not college material," they will say. It has been a tremendous relief for me to let them know that all avenues to higher education are not closed, simply because their child was not able to meet the requirements for admission to a traditional four-year degree program.

If you have made it this far in your reading, you know that other options exist and you are probably serious about taking on the challenges of guiding your son or daughter with SD through the process of finding and applying for postsecondary education and supporting him or her during the college years. To be successful, you will *need* to be serious—understanding disability law, finding and coordinating financing for higher education, and the scary process of letting go of the careful control you have had over the life of your child with a disability are all serious issues. It can be done, and you can do it, too.

First Steps

In earlier chapters, we discussed using questions such as the ones below to guide transition planning for your child:

1. What does my adult child want to do?
2. What does he need to learn to have a satisfying life?
3. How can these goals best be achieved?

While the questions are simple, the answers may not be. Not for the first time, you may find your desires at odds with those of your soon-to-be adult child. He may be ready to sign on to a program you feel is completely beyond his ability level and way across the country to boot. He might also be the reluctant one, fearful of moving out into the world and wanting to stay in the safety of familiar routines, while you may see that he is in need of more.

What does he want to do? Your child may not know—teenagers and young adults with SD often do not have the life experience to make an informed decision. But you may know, just from watching him at school over the years, that he truly enjoys and benefits from the educational setting. That may be all the information you need to begin planning for PSE.

Your child may also have a definite plan. He may want to earn a degree or certificate in a specific area of study (if so, see the information below). He might want to study a topic that fascinates him. He may also want to learn job skills or improve his independent living skills. If he is truly dying for independence, you may decide to take a chance and begin investigating programs that have a residential component, keeping in mind his ability level and your own concerns about safety.

On the other hand, he might be adamantly against going on for more education, learning job skills, or becoming more independent. If so, you will need to tease out why. Is he truly not ready or interested, but could be in a year or so? Perhaps delaying enrollment would be a wise decision. Is this reluctance his usual reaction to new challenges or due to a lack of motivation? You may need to push him, in this case. A few parents have simply filled out the paperwork and told their adult child the decision was made for him. (You alone can decide whether the ensuing family battle is worth going about enrollment this way.)

Probably your child will fall somewhere between these two extremes, perhaps even from one conversation to another! In these early discussions, parents need to balance what their child wants to do and what their child needs to do, while not closing off any avenues for post-secondary education yet. Aren't you glad you started early?

High School Is Ending and the Times Are a Changin'!

High school is almost as much about parents and families as it is about students. Remember the last high school graduation you attended? You probably congratulated the parents as much as you congratulated the young graduates. Finishing high school is a group effort—parents, teachers, and students all share in the achievement. Most high school students, even the independent ones, still live at home and are involved with the routines of their family. Parents are informed if their student is failing or getting into trouble. Parents have practically unlimited access to their child's information.

As the parent of a student with SD, you have probably been more involved in your student's high school career than a typical parent. You are probably very familiar with the laws and procedures that assured your child the right to an appropriate education since preschool. You have attended many meetings and participated in writing many IEPs for your child. You are used to communicating with a small group of people who keep you apprised of your child's progress and behavior in school—the good, the bad, and the ugly. It's all about to change drastically. Transition author and parent Jo Ann Simons has this advice:

> Turning 21 or 22, or getting a diploma—whatever point your state has determined is the end of free public education—is the beginning of the rest of your life. Everything will change. Nothing will be the same, but believe me, you will survive. . . . The biggest difference between the years your child is in school and adulthood is that your child is not "entitled" to services. There is no national or state law that entitles your child or your family to any assistance because your child has (a significant disability)....So, what's a family to do? Prepare, prepare, and act (Simons, 2004).

As you begin planning for the future for your student with SD, it is critical that you clearly understand how the education system that met his needs through high school is going to change once he moves into higher education. IDEA is the law that has protected your child's right to education for many years. But IDEA protection does not last forever, and the public school district that has paid for and coordinated services for your child for many years may not play much of a role in his PSE experience.

Be absolutely certain how long your child will be eligible for educational services under IDEA. States differ in how long they consider students eligible, although your state should provide coverage until at least age 21. Often, students with SD attend typical high schools and watch their peers go through graduation and leave school at age 18 or 19. Students with SD may be grouped with their same-age peers, and may get graduation information and senior privileges at 18 or 19 as well.

Find out your school district's policy on graduation. Students with SD may be allowed to "walk" with their peers at the graduation ceremony in cap and gown at the end of what would have been considered their twelfth grade year, receive a certificate of attendance, and still return to school the following fall, a good option if your student needs another year or two to prepare for PSE options. However, some districts will not allow students to participate in graduation ceremonies unless they are receiving a diploma. Your student may need to delay receiving his diploma if he is going to continue attending school beyond twelfth grade and not participate in graduation until he is ready to receive his diploma. You must find out the policy of your school district, preferably before what would be considered your child's "senior year."

If your child is still eligible for IDEA services but is ready to pursue PSE options, you and the district may be able to work out a "dual enrollment" situation with a local college or technical school. In dual enrollment, the student with SD is still considered to be a high school student who is taking PSE classes. The district may be able to help with expenses such as tuition, books, and transportation. If you are looking into this option and want to pursue an individually supported model, carefully review the information in Chapter Fourteen on creating college options with high school supports. Some school districts are willing to pay tuition for specialized nondegree programs as well, but your child must still be eligible for IDEA coverage.

Once IDEA protection ends, many systems parents take for granted come to an end as well. Let's start with the IEP, which has governed your child's education up to this point.

I have heard parents and professionals confidently say, "Well, the IEP will follow him to college." An IEP is a very specialized, individualized, and comprehensive plan. It lists the student's current abilities, classroom management needs, modifications to the educational program, behavioral strategies that are effective, transportation requirements, transition information—almost everything but the color of the child's eyes! It also has an expiration date. IEPs must be reviewed and revised yearly, for as long as the student is covered under IDEA. However, once the student graduates or ages out, there is no more IEP. No matter what anyone tells you, a student's IEP will not follow him to college.

Part of the IEP lists academic accommodations for the classroom and for testing. These accommodations could follow a student to college. I understand that some hopeful parents and students show up at the DSS office with a current copy of the student's IEP, thinking this documentation will be enough to get needed accommodations for college. Most of the time, it will not be enough. Prior to requesting accommodations for a college or certificate program, find out what type of documentation is required to request accommodations. Often the documentation needed will be copies of test results and letters from a qualified professional specifically requesting certain accommodations (a reader for tests, note taking services). (See the appendix for tips for securing accommodations from the Office of Disability Services.)

I'm sure you're thinking, "Wait, what about the ADA and Section 504? Aren't those laws that entitle my child to attend college and get specialized services?" The ADA and Section 504 are antidiscrimination laws, and although they may protect an individual's right to needed accommodations in college, *entitlement* is not in the language of either law.

Some parents are shocked to find out that under the ADA their child may not even meet the criteria for having a certain disability. Students with SD often have more than one condition, and not all of them may be considered disabilities. Under the ADA a disability must significantly limit a major life activity (working, learning, walking, etc.) or the person must have a history of or be regarded as having a disability. If medication for AD/HD controls the symptoms and the symptoms do not interfere with major life activities, under the ADA the AD/HD might not be considered a disability, unless a person was discriminated against because of his past history or someone else's prejudices about AD/HD. Some conditions that are considered disabilities under IDEA, such as emotional or behavioral disturbance, do not have an equivalent under ADA, although psychiatric disorders such as depression or obsessive-compulsive disorder might be severe enough to be considered a disability. Accommodations that were given in high school without much trouble might not be considered "reasonable" in college or technical school, and may not be granted.

Finding the Right Path to Higher Education

Now that you have done the preparation, the search for an appropriate postsecondary situation can begin. Begin by gathering information. Consult the websites of the programs listed in Part 2 or websites in the Resources section at the end of the book. If you contact programs directly, they will be able to send you their information packets, which will list admissions requirements and descriptions of program components. If you decide that the best option for your child is an inclusive individually supported situation, begin gathering information from the colleges or programs your child is interested in attending.

What credentials are available to students with SD? A major point of postsecondary education is to complete a prescribed course of study that attests that a student has learned certain skills and studied certain information. In a typical college situation, this course of study ends in a degree. Start your research by becoming familiar with the types of programs your student with SD can pursue after high school. The following are options that are available to students with SD at the postsecondary level and important information to know about who can be admitted and what is needed to earn the ending certification.

1. Associate's and Bachelor's Degree Programs

These options are what most of us think of when we speak of college. While most associate's and bachelor's degree candidates are admitted after earning a high school diploma or GED, students can be admitted to associate's and bachelor's degree programs without a traditional diploma if they are able to earn a minimum score on an Ability to Benefit test. An Ability to Benefit test is a test of reading, writing, and mathematics that shows that a student has the basic skills to do college-level work. Students who earn the minimum score set by the college on an approved Ability to Benefit test can begin the course work for a degree.

Students in these programs are eligible to apply for federal financial aid. In order to earn a bachelor's or associate's degree, all students

must meet all of the set criteria for a degree (complete all course work and earn passing grades). Students with disabilities are eligible for academic accommodations if they can provide documentation that they need the accommodations.

2. Certificate Programs

Earning a certificate is a way to increase knowledge in a specific field and increase earning potential in that field. Certificates are offered through community colleges and trade schools, and, less frequently, through four-year schools. Certificate programs provide focused training for a specific career path, such as certified nursing assistant, child care, office skills, automotive repair, culinary arts, etc. Certificate programs may require applicants to have a high school diploma or GED for admission, but some programs will accept students without a traditional diploma if the student is able to earn a minimum score on basic skills testing (reading, writing, mathematics).

Earning a certificate often takes less time than earning a degree (programs can last from a period of weeks to two years). All students must complete all of the set criteria for the certificate (often including state level tests) and students with disabilities are eligible for accommodations if they can provide documentation.

3. Auditing or Continuing Education Options

Most colleges and universities will allow students to take courses without receiving credit for them. This option is called auditing a  course. Often, there are no prerequisites such as testing for the courses, although colleges differ on their requirements. Course fees are usually reduced for students who are auditing.

Audited courses may not be counted toward a degree, but some students with significant disabilities have audited courses and then retaken them at another time for credit. A student with SD could also take just one course a semester for credit, even if he is not able to meet the requirements for admission to a degree program. A student with an interest in computers or history could take a course in those subjects for personal interest or to improve his existing skills. Colleges may list information about class audits under continuing education or adult education. Accommodations are available for eligible students.

4. Non-degree Programs

Many of the programs profiled in Part 2 of this book fit into this category. Non-degree programs offer a variety of educational options for students with significant disabilities. They may focus on transition instruction, academic classes (separate or inclusive), or vocational experience in the form of internships, and may or may not include residential options.

As the name implies, the programs have curricula and goals, but do not culminate in an associate's or bachelor's degree. Admissions criteria are often based on academic achievement levels, IQ scores, and social and independent living competencies. Each program has a list of criteria in its print and online admissions information. Students are required to meet certain goals and learn certain competencies in order to earn their final certificates from these programs, but goals can be individualized.

Testing, Testing: Pre-admission Assessments for Degree-Seeking Students

A student who wants to pursue a degree or certificate from a college or technical school may need to take standardized tests if that is what is expected of other degree-seeking students. These tests may include the SAT (Scholastic Achievement Test) and/or the ACT. If a student is applying for admission to a degree or certificate program without a standard diploma or GED, he may need to take a college approved Ability to Benefit Test (see above) and earn a minimum score.

Students who have disabilities are entitled to ask for accommodations when taking these tests. Accommodations that may be granted include:

- Extended time
- Use of a calculator on sections of the test that don't directly measure computational skills
- Use of a reader on sections of the test that don't directly measure reading skills
- Administration in a small-group setting to minimize distractions
- Writing answers directly in the test booklet rather than bubbling them in on the answer sheet

Getting accommodations for standardized admissions tests is far more complicated than requesting accommodations for school or even state-mandated testing in high school. The bar is set much higher for college placement tests. The student must not only have a disability that requires accommodating, he must also submit a Student Eligibility Form and copies of documentation supporting the needed accommodations. The documentation itself must meet seven required guidelines and state the functional limitation of the disability.

I asked a good friend, Laurie Finch, a guidance counselor who has guided several students through the process of requesting accommodations for the SAT and ACT, to review the process with me. The website (www.collegeboard.com) is clear, but is as long and detailed as the U.S. tax code. Students who are applying for accommodations should work with their guidance counselor or special education director to complete the needed paperwork and to gather documentation.

In our conversation, I asked Laurie if the application process was good preparation for future accommodations requests. She replied, "Absolutely. It more accurately reflects what they will be facing in college." Because the process is so complicated and application for accommodations must be made well in advance of the actual test date, she urges students to begin gathering documentation in their sophomore year of high school, or earlier if the student is planning to take the Preliminary Scholastic Aptitude Test (PSAT). She also cautioned that many more students have been refused accommodations over the last several years, because the College Board and ACT administration have tightened their guidelines for granting accommodations.

A student with SD who is seeking admission to a degree program that requires SAT and ACT testing should be prepared for the possibility that his request for some or all accommodations may be refused. If so, he should be ready to take the admissions tests in the same room and following the same procedures as the rest of his graduating class.

There are colleges that do not require standardized tests, such as the SAT or ACT, for admission to a degree-granting program. See a list of these schools at www.fairtest.org.

Even if the student is refused accommodations for admissions tests, he may still be eligible for academic accommodations for his degree program. See the section below on how to gather the needed documentation to request these accommodations.

Pre-admissions Testing for Nondegree Programs

If your student is seeking admission to a program designed to support students with significant disabilities, he will not need to take typical college admissions tests, such as the SAT and ACT. A student who is designing an inclusive individualized supports experience by choosing specific courses will not need typical college testing if the courses will

not be applied toward a degree. He may, however, need to take placement tests in English and math, if that is needed for requested courses.
But before you breathe a sigh of relief, other types of testing may be
required for admission. By starting the process of admissions early, you
can make arrangements for the necessary testing to be done.

Admissions requirements and documentation needed for accommodations vary from school to school. Specialized private programs
usually list admissions requirements on their websites. An example is
shown below for the Transition Program at Middlesex Community College, a two-year business skills program in Bedford, Massachusetts:

1. A completed Transition Program application
2. A completed Middlesex Community College Application for
   Admission
3. A high school transcript and a copy of most recent IEP
4. Three letters of recommendation on forms provided by the
   program, one of which must be completed by a Special Needs
   or Resource Room teacher; two other recommendations on
   specified forms can be from guidance counselor, teachers,
   employers, etc.
5. IQ results—preferred test: WAIS-R
6. Individualized Diagnostic Reading and Math Test results
   (preferred tests: Woodcock Johnson or Stanford Achievement with all subtest scores and grade equivalents in the
   written report)
7. A Diagnostic Interview by a certified Psychologist or a Projec-
   tive Psychological Test (e.g., Thematic Apperception Test).
   Reports must be no more than 2 years old.

Programs with specific tests listed in their admissions information
will usually refuse to accept alternate tests.

As part of their free and appropriate public education, most students with SD receive updated psychological testing approximately
every three years. If the student is planning to apply to certain private
programs, his parents or teacher should make a list of the specific tests
the program requires and begin the process of having the testing completed. Another good reason to start the planning process early!

If the student with SD is planning to attend PSE, this goal should
be noted on each of his high school level IEPs in the transition plan
section. Transition plans include Long Term Adult Outcomes (LTAO),

which are individualized goals for adult life, and a Coordinated Set of Activities, which are steps towards reaching those goal.

Postsecondary education is one of the LTAOs that must be addressed on the IEP. Even if the student chooses not to pursue postsecondary education, a statement indicating that this is the student's wish should be recorded on the transition plan. One of the coordinated sets of activities for PSE could be for the student to meet with the school psychologist to have the required testing completed before graduation or to practice listing his academic accommodations.

School psychologists routinely perform IQ and achievement testing, as well as other tests that might be required by a private program. Make a copy of the requirements for admission and share it with the school psychologist to make sure the testing is done in the right time frame. Programs vary on how recently the testing must be performed (usually no more than two years before the time of application).

Depending upon your school district, you may not be able to get all of the required testing done by the school psychologist, but it is worth asking to have the required testing done, in connection with your student's transition plan. If not, you may need to make arrangements to have the testing done privately. Your school district should be able to provide you with a list of psychologists who can do educational testing. Some of these private practitioners charge fees on a sliding scale. Other costs for testing may be covered by your health insurance or if your child is eligible for SSI/Medicaid. Vocational rehabilitation agencies may also be able to pay for required testing and assessments, especially vocational assessments that might be needed for admission to a technical certificate program. (See Chapter 18 for more information on vocational rehabilitation.)

Getting to Know You: Visits and Interviews

Perhaps the most important step in the application process is campus visits. Before even beginning the needed paperwork to apply to PSE programs, take the time to see programs in action. If your student wants to take classes at a local college, take a day to walk around the campus. Visit the Disability Services office to get information. Buy a cup of coffee at the student center. Get a feel for the campus and your student's comfort level there.

Visiting specialized programs will require an appointment in advance, but visits can be arranged by contacting the programs. Helen K. Bosch, director of the Vista Vocational Program in Westbrook, Connecticut, compiled a list of twelve questions in the book *Many Shades of Success* that parents can bring with them to help gather information. Some programs will require a student interview or an extended assessment while the student stays on campus. This process will also inform your decision—your child will need to be able to speak for himself and manage on his own for a few days.

Read through Chapter 15 with your child to prepare him for a campus visit. It would be helpful to role play an interview, perhaps even videotaping it so he can see and hear his own performance. Demonstrate how to answer questions in complete sentences, rather than one-word answers (e.g., "Yes, I do" rather than just "Yes").

- Where did you go to high school?
- How did you hear about our school or program?
- What are some reasons you want to go to college?
- What activities or clubs have you been involved with in high school?

If your child typically uses Social Stories to prepare for new events, it would be very helpful to write a Social Story about the college visit and interview process. If he has an augmentative communication device, make sure it is programmed with the vocabulary he will need for the interview.

You will also learn how well your nerves hold up under the strain of not being able to speak for or do things for your child! Just as he is coming out of the experience beaming and confident, you may learn that you are the one with the separation anxiety!

Because of limited space in postsecondary programs for students with SD, consider helping your child apply to more than one school, if this is at all possible. It is also important to have a fall back plan if he does not get into a program at all. This plan can include education (tutoring, adult education programs), employment (working part-time or volunteering), and continuing development in independent living skills. How to create a viable plan "B" is a good life skill for your adult child, and for you, too. Life will never be quite the same, it is a different world, and yes, you will survive.

And They're Off!
Supporting Your Student during the College Years

You are suddenly faced with the eerie silence that descends when one of your children is not in the house. Perhaps your son or daughter is coming home in a few hours from a nearby college. Perhaps he or she won't be home for several months if you have just left the dormitory or student apartments. In either case, life as you have previously known it with your child has just changed in a dramatic way.

You are justified if your first reaction is relief. The college admissions process for a student with significant disabilities is even more arduous than the admissions process for a typical student. While the paperwork and meetings are not over forever, you do get a break for a while.

You are also justified if you are near panic. Even if your son or daughter is living at home, you have now been relegated to a supporting role. Any problems or issues that arise will not be yours to solve. Due to college privacy rules, unless you are your child's guardian, you may not be informed of problems with grades or behavior until your student fails or is told not to return to school.

Specialized programs will also try to keep your involvement limited. You will not be consulted or informed about your child's daily activities—and a few programs will even ask you to sign a waiver, allowing her to make certain decisions, even if you *are* her guardian. It is all part of the letting go process: a challenging time for all parents and their college student, whether or not the student has a disability.

From the Parents

When I asked parents of currently enrolled college students and recent graduates with significant disabilities about how to support a son or daughter in college, the theme that kept emerging was that the greatest support they could give was...less support. A few of their comments follow:

> *"Looking back, it was such a total leap of faith. Sometimes I still can't believe that we let her go all the way across the country to*

this program! However, it has worked out incredibly well. We've been fortunate with the program and with our daughter, who has demonstrated reserves of strength and stick-to-it-ness that I never knew she had….I'm so proud of her and proud of us (my husband and myself) for having faith it would work out."
—Mother of a 21-year-old daughter, current student

"Letting go is difficult, especially for the special-needs parent. You need to have confidence in the program you have chosen and let them handle the crisis. Don't be available all the time by cell phone or email. Try whenever possible to get them to work out their problem or crisis with the program's staff…. The natural inclination is for parents to want to care for their child. You have to actively encourage independence and self- determination."
—Mother of a 24-year-old son, already graduated

"Understand the great force of survival present in all humans. It may be very emotionally painful to let go, and your child will show fear when you let go, but after a while, he or she will start going in an area that has been muted up to this point. It was wise of you to be protective of your child during their early difficult years, but now it is most helpful to let them/force them to fend a little for themselves."
—Father of a 24-year- old son, already graduated.

"I knew it was going to be hard for me to let go, so I found the right people and challenged them to pry her [my daughter] out of my hands! This is the transition to independence, so you can't be too involved if it's going to work.

"When you spend so much time helping a young adult with a disability move to adulthood, it's easy to get lost in the transition. I realized that over my life I had been thinking ahead to how I could facilitate most of her transitions, and her moving toward independence was another challenge. However, it's a little weird helping your child "reject" you as other children do when they are coming of age. We had become very close, but I could hear the frustration in her voice when I would be talking too much, when she would shut down and wait for me to leave."
—Mother of a 25-year-old daughter, already graduated

Parents emphasized the need to consciously move back and allow their college- age student to become independent. While this goal is more naturally accomplished when the student is away from home, other parents made space for the independence for an adult child living at home.

Supporting independence requires a shift in relationships: you were the caretaker and now you are the coach. If you have ever watched a coach on the sidelines of a game, you see how hard this role can be. Working with this analogy, the coach can only advise, not play the game. Ultimately, the players are the ones who must do what it takes to affect the outcome of the game. The coach, no matter how good her advice, cannot run out on the field and do it for an individual player.

No One to Sue!

Under IDEA, families and students with disabilities have many rights. You may have exercised these rights to the fullest by taking important issues to an impartial hearing or even to court to make certain your school district respected them. You may have breathed a sigh of relief when your child crossed the stage at graduation, hoping you would never have to see some of those administrators across the table from you again. (I don't think I am telling tales out of school to say that the feeling was probably mutual!) Many parents feel proud of these advocacy efforts, particularly when their child with SD got great benefit from them.

Once your child enters the world of postsecondary education, IDEA no longer applies. The Americans with Disabilities Act (ADA) and Section 504 of the Rehabilitation Act provide some protections, but as I have said before, these are anti-discrimination laws, and colleges and universities are not required to go beyond basic compliance to these laws. As Jo Ann Simons writes:

> The biggest difference between the years your child is in school and adulthood is that your child is no longer "entitled" to services. There is no national or state law that entitles your child or your family to any assistance because your child has Down syndrome (or any other significant disability). There may not be any lawyers to hire or advocates to line up (Simon, 2004).

There is also a difference in attitude at the postsecondary level. In the course of one conversation with a college-level support coordinator,

I mentioned the challenge of managing all of the legal requirements of IDEA and the difficulty my district has sometimes had with litigious parents. I asked if litigious families were a challenge at her level and she seemed almost startled by the question. Paraphrasing her response, she told me, "We don't deal with that dynamic. In fact, since we are providing the support because we believe in the ability of these students to be in college, we would consider the possibility of legal action a lack of respect. I don't think we would accept a student if we felt the family would be litigious." In other words, in public school, the environment and professionals need to assure the progress and success of the student, while in postsecondary education, the student needs to do what it takes to progress and be successful given a reasonable chance.

Postsecondary study is a privilege, not a right, and the legal requirements are much less at this level. Parents who have historically gone into school conflicts with all guns blazing will need to rethink their approach. Postsecondary programs and services often have waiting lists, and a student who is troublesome or has a troublesome family may even be asked to leave. One admissions officer even told me, "If I have a choice between a student with a demanding parent, and a student with a parent who will be reasonable and work with us, I know which student I'm going to admit." Keep this reality in mind.

* *

What You Can Still Do

Don't assume, however, that once your child crosses the threshold of the admissions building, you must just throw her to the lions. You are coming in with a deep understanding of your child and a long history of knowing what works and what doesn't work for her. Bring that knowledge to bear when you are advising your child or giving input to program staff who are seeking it.

Marc Ellison from Marshall University advocates a thorough planning meeting with the student, her parents, and support staff before the start of a student's first semester. This meeting is the forum to discuss goals, accommodations, strategies for learning, and how and with whom information about the student will be shared. Remember, your adult child will have the final say as to how much information is given to you if she is her own guardian. "Some students tell us, 'You can share anything with my folks.' Others say, 'Talk to me first before you say anything to my parents,'" Marc said. College support people must respect these requests from students due to privacy laws. Express your desire to stay informed to your adult child and to the support people at the meeting, but be ready to concede this point.

Continue being vigilant about how much support your college student needs to be successful. Sometimes when a student is using accommodations and supports and is being quite successful, the student assumes that she doesn't need the accommodation anymore. Some students really want to start fresh when they reach college and are eager to try things on their own.

Program staff may overestimate a student's ability to manage certain aspects of her life because she seems so confident (although most programs do a thorough orientation and require students to demonstrate their skills before allowing them to assume responsibility). These assumptions can be dangerous. Similar to a person who has an illness controlled by medication, just feeling good or doing well doesn't mean that the medicine isn't needed anymore. Success could be evidence that the medicine is doing its job. Fading supports slowly, or agreeing to taking one test without accommodations and then reviewing the results is a much better strategy for determining whether support is still needed. You may all be surprised that supports that were once critical are no longer needed or can be reduced.

If at First You Don't Succeed...What to Do When It's Not Working

Over- or underestimating the level of support a student needs for a successful PSE experience will not result in good outcomes, no matter how much everyone may want it to succeed. Whatever model a student may choose—inclusive, mixed, or specialized—if she tries a program and finds it wanting, she has the same option as any other student who discovers that her dream college is not all it's cracked up to be: transfer to another program.

Some sources have reported that as many as 60 percent of college students transfer to a different school before earning a bachelor's degree. The rates are not as high for students with SD, but some do change schools. Claire, the student mentioned in Chapter Thirteen, began her PSE experience at a vocational program designed for students with SD. But she soon found that the program's expectations for independence were too high for her to manage, while the introductory vocational courses did not challenge her enough. She transferred after one year to another program that has more of an independent living focus and finds it a much better fit. I have communicated with several parents whose adult children transferred from an inclusive individually supported model to a specialized model and vice versa, as a consequence of evolving goals and needs.

Peggy, a parent on an online PSE forum called "The Choice for Everyone" through the ThinkCollege website, writes about the challenges her son faced trying to find a good "fit":

> Our son graduated from high school at age 19 and was very capable of attending community college with support. What we found was that support combined with his immaturity fostered his belief that only the "norm" can succeed. We then tried vocational job-supported programs…which led our son down a path of no hope.…[After finding the Taft college program], he is able to live in a dorm (independently), manage a budget, attend classes (both segregated and mainstreamed), work, and, most importantly, establish friendships. He's also learning to accept himself for the great person that he is. Basically, at the age of 23, he was able to move away to college.…What works so well in the Taft program is that it integrates education, vocation, and independent living into one inclusive program integrated on the main college campus. Before Taft, it seemed that we could only pursue one of these three options (education, vocational training, independent living) and be supported" (Forum post, 8/8/07).

Monitoring Mental and Physical Health

College can bring a whole new level of stress, both mental and physical, to all students. Suddenly, the student with SD is having to assume far more responsibility. Be alert to how she is managing these new physical, emotional, academic, and psychological demands.

If your child is commuting, you will have the chance to observe her regularly. Keeping an eye on her appetite, sleep patterns, and any noticeable weight loss or gain can give you an idea of how she is coping. Are you seeing signs of emotional stress—crying, bouts of anger, an increase in nervous habits?

If your child is living away from home, listen closely during phone calls and take seriously any reports from staff that might indicate she is not dealing well with stress. She may be sad, much quieter than usual, angry, uncooperative, etc. You know what is "normal" for your adult child. If something doesn't seem right, check into it further.

Dennis McGuire and Brian Chicoine have written an excellent book entitled *Mental Wellness in Adults with Down Syndrome* that provides information about the manifestation of mental illness in people with this condition. The information is useful across disability classifications, including a checklist of common warning signs of depression including:

1. Sadness or unhappiness
2. Apathy and loss of interest/participation in activities, including withdrawal from family and friends
3. Slowing down of activities
4. Loss of energy or feeling of fatigue

McGuire and Chicoine also write about learned helplessness as a contributing factor to depression:

Learned helplessness can occur when a person has limited experience solving her own problems or standing up for herself. As a result, when faced with a major challenge such as the physical and emotional turmoil of the teen years, she tends to shut down and withdraw into a state of helplessness rather than meet or deal with the challenge (McGuire and Chicoine, 2006).

Suddenly having to advocate for herself or independently work out day-to-day problems can be overwhelming for a student with SD. If parents are aware of this dynamic with their college-aged child, they can recognize the signs of stress early and encourage her to seek appropriate treatment. Parents can be prepared with information about counseling services on campus (look for these on the campus website or through the Health Services Office) or urge their child to speak to helpful program staff.

If your adult child is already dealing with the challenge of mental illness before entering college, emphasize to her the importance of taking her medicine, attending therapy, and caring for her physical health (getting enough sleep and exercise, watching her diet) while she is in college. Poorly managed mental illness can derail anyone's college plans, and students with SD are no exception.

"My Own Voice"—Suggestions from Current Students

What do current college students have to say about the support they need and want from their families?

"When I was in high school, my mom was so involved. Now, she is less involved. Now I have my own voice. When I moved into my apartment, it took my mom an hour to leave and then she sat in the parking lot and cried!"
—Adrienne, age 23

"One thing parents should do is let them (their son or daughter) go. Spread their wings. Take risks. Life is about risks."
—William, age 24

"My mom has helped out by handling the paperwork for DVR (Department of Vocational Rehabilitation) and paying for classes."
—Carrie, age 22

"My mom helped me get my own bank account that I keep track of. I budget my own spending money. Parents should not yell or do everything for their kids."—Tsambika, age 22.

"I live in my own apartment. My family hugs me when I come home."—Rick, age 23

As you can see, these students are aware that they need the emotional and practical support of their parents during this time of transition. But they want and need their parents to see them as the competent young adults they are becoming.

Advice from the Trenches: Postsecondary Professionals Speak

Professionals are your allies in the process of letting go. The professionals you may encounter in postsecondary education may be program directors or staff, Disability Support Staff, psychologists, counselors, or professors. I asked several professionals—Helen K. Bosch of Vista Vocational Program, Judy Lefkowitz of Chapel Haven, Dr. Marty Boman of the Kelly Autism Program at Western Kentucky University, and Dr. Stuart Carroll of The College of New Jersey—for their advice to parents who are preparing for their adult children to attend college. I have quoted their advice in the section below, without accreditation. My own thoughts follow.

- *"The most successful students have parents that can acknowledge that they might be afraid (of letting go), but they are giving the gift of trust. And it is a gift."*
- *"The best possible support for students coming in are the families that have allowed their child to have some 'rope' and to get a few bruises. These are the students who make the best transitions."*

Young adults with SD are continuously reminded of the things they cannot do or cannot do easily. For these young people, having their parents tacitly signal that they do have the ability to take on the challenge of college and preparation for the community is extremely significant.

Even if they are putting on a brave front, the students are probably nervous in the first few weeks or months, too. A parent who acknowledges those concerns, shares his or her own worries, but follows it all with a declaration of confidence in the young adult's ability to cope will be giving a great gift indeed.

- *"Do not put safety above all else. The only way to be totally safe is to not have a life."*
- *"Helicopter parents need to back off. Allow your kid to fail sometimes."*

I recently read an editorial in our local newspaper about school children being warned of the dangers of a time-honored playground entertainment. Dodgeball? Running with sticks? Riding on bicycle handlebars? No—hula hoops.

I wish I were kidding.

Overprotective parenting is by no means limited to the parents of kids with special needs. It is an effort to control parental anxiety. Obviously, it is wise to teach safety and to monitor children's activities to avoid danger. The responsibility continues into adolescence when the consequences are more serious than a skinned knee or a bump on the head. But, referring to the above example, risk can be found anywhere if you look hard enough.

Yes, it is risky to allow a young man with significant disabilities to travel alone on a city bus or subway. Yes, it is risky to allow a young woman with SD to take a job that promises to be difficult for her. Yes, it is risky to allow a young man with limited math skills to manage a debit card. Yes, it is risky to allow a young woman who is so naive to go out with her girlfriends shopping or to have a boyfriend. But what are the consequences of safety at all costs? The young adults have to stay home unless someone transports them and have limited, if any, opportunities to work, no control over their money, and limited opportunities to expand their relationships or to have satisfying relationships. Consider the risks of those future scenarios before pronouncing new experiences too risky.

Kristen D. Holtz, Amanda K. Ziegert, and Cynthia D. Baker, authors of *Life Journey through Autism: A Guide for Transition to Adulthood,* had this to say about the process parents must go through when deciding how much freedom to allow their adult child with SD to have.

> *Identify the level of "risk" with which you are comfortable and then work to maximize independence within that framework. (For example, while you may be uncomfortable with him crossing the supermarket parking lot without close supervision, he may not need the same intensity of supervision in the supermarket.) As the young adult gains greater independence across tasks and environments, reassess your acceptable level of risk* (Holtz, Ziegert, Baker, 2004).

Here is more advice from PSE professionals.

- *"Beware of unrealistic expectations for the child with special needs. Don't set a higher bar than for your typical kids. Their rooms don't have to be pristine and their sheets don't have to be perfectly white for the room to be good enough."*
- *"Start to see your son or daughter as a person in their own right, not an extension of yourself."*

Parents who have been strong advocates and have had the deepest involvement in the lives of their adult child with SD may find this advice disconcerting. In the past, you may have felt that nothing should be left to chance, every "t" crossed and every "i" dotted, but being overly involved on a day-to-day basis could undermine exactly what you have spent your life working for. You have been aware of appearances—you've had to be. Unless you were vigilant about it, the world would have reduced your child to a diagnosis (autism, Down syndrome, etc.)

Now, however, if you want your child to achieve the maximum level of independence, you may need to do things like:

- Bite your tongue and count to 10 when you see the disorder of your son's dorm room.
- Wait and see what happens when your daughter meets with her advisor and signs up for a class that you think will be lousy for her.
- Try to forget that you vowed never to allow your adult child to work in an industry that has become a stereotyped one for people with disabilities (think food, flowers, folding, and filth).

The messy room could be an indicator that he's comfortable at college, the class might be lousy but it won't kill her, and you may be surprised to listen to your child's enthusiastic reports of the training sessions for this hated industry.

Other advice from the professionals:

- *"If the school or program has rules, for example about a spending allowance or the number of phone calls that are recommended, realize that they are there for a reason."*
- *"View the staff as professionals teaching your child, not as 'hired help' taking care of your child."*

It is normal to want to smooth the way for your child in this new experience. How much could it hurt to call her a few times a day during the transition? How much could it hurt to send an extra $30.00 so she can go on a shopping trip with her new friends—haven't you been waiting years for her to have some friends? It is little enabling actions like this, however, that will eat away at the foundation of self-reliance you are hoping will be built. The world will not end if your son's third phone call of the day reporting a crisis goes to voice mail, your daughter won't be shunned forever if she can't go shopping this weekend, and next week she will learn (no doubt, with staff urging) to budget more carefully.

Programs spend a lot of time and give a lot of thought to rules and procedures, with the whole point being to help their students become as independent and personally competent as they can be. Family involvement, support, and input is always helpful; undermining is not.

PSE professionals also caution parents to be aware of the attitude that it is okay if your child's behavior is less mature behavior because she has a disability.

- *"Discourage childish interests (as much as possible) and encourage adult interests."*
- *"Don't allow certain behaviors just because your child has a disability. Beware of falling into the trap of 'Well, this is Billy, so that's okay.'"*

Unfortunately, the antiquated system of defining people with intellectual disabilities by their "mental age" continues. But let's remember that it was a ridiculous system when it was first presented and it's even worse now.

People with SD may be delayed in their emotional or psychological maturity. It may be very difficult for them to accept new interests or learn new skills. And certainly, they have the same right to spend their free time the way they want, just as anyone else does. But, there will come a time when the social price will be too high to pay. How comfortable would you be with an adult playing on a playground next to the small children in your life or hanging out in toy stores? How often would you choose to have lunch with a coworker who only wanted to talk about cartoons? You may need to help your adult child learn to engage in her less mature interests in the privacy of her own home or room, and guide her to use new, more socially acceptable ones in public. Don't think of it as having to give up an interest—think of it as expanding interests into new and interesting territory.

Handling odd behavior is a little more complicated. Obviously, some people with SD, like people without SD, haven't learned good social skills because they haven't been expected to use them. Some people with SD, like some people without SD, are simply rude!

But sometimes people with disabilities engage in unusual behaviors to minimize stress or anxiety. One way to handle such situations is to teach the young adult to explain why she needs to engage in a certain behavior. For example, a young woman with autism may explain that she rocks to relax or she may carry a card in her wallet that she can show others to explain that she wears sunglasses indoors because the light hurts her eyes. Due to an increase of information on television and depictions of people with disabilities in the movies, most people will be understanding and sensitive to unusual behavior when a disability is identified. Even if people don't fully understand, as Deborah Lipinski, a speaker with autism, once said, "No one ever died from second-hand self-stimming!" (Deborah herself wears an identification card while traveling, in case she becomes too overstimulated to explain her unusual behaviors.)

Good manners will also cover a multitude of sins. It is extremely critical that young adults with SD learn and use the basics consistently. Appropriate communication also makes people feel more comfortable and accepting. If the young adult uses an augmentative communication device or sign language, encourage her to communicate directly with people in the community (bank tellers, store clerks, people on the bus). Her matter-of-fact use of nonstandard communication will help it become standard for the people she sees every day.

One final piece of advice from PSE professionals to parents.

- *"Know the program your student is in or is entering. Expect 'realistic miracles.'"*

You remember the old adage "if it seems too good to be true, it probably is"? Don't expect that any postsecondary education experience is going to be perfect. As I spoke to students with significant disabilities all around the country, I heard the usual litany of complaints—too much work, not enough sleep or fun, parents and professors on their backs, boredom, arguments with peers, romantic dramas. Not every student I spoke to was delighted with his or her college experience. Not every staff person I spoke to was an inspired educator. Not every parent was 100 percent satisfied. In other words, PSE for students with disabilities is real life. Often, it won't be all it's cracked up to be.

In working with teenagers for many years, I have developed a mental trick for dealing with the complaints: most of the time, it is statistically impossible for everything about a situation to suck. Usually, something good is going on somewhere—it's just hard to see it when you are frustrated, tired, or having a bad week. Remind your adult child to hang in there. Resist the temptation to rescue her. An in-depth meeting with the staff, a transfer, or a withdrawal are always options, but they should not be your first option.

I've talked a lot about over-involvement of parents. A study on parental over-involvement was published in the *Journal of Developmental and Physical Disabilities* in June 2008. I have quoted, paraphrased, and given examples below to sum up how to support your adult child:

Don't:

1. Have tunnel vision in your outlook. ("I want this and only this.")
2. Overemphasize the functional age of your adult child rather than her chronological age. ("But she's really only like an eight-year-old.")
3. Believe you need to be involved in every decision. ("I'm taking her shopping for clothes.")
4. Make decisions based on your own needs, attitudes, or pride. ("No child of mine will work in a discount store.")
5. Distrust the staff working with your adult child. ("I know her best. These people don't care.")
6. Continue grieving your child's disability. ("If it weren't for her Down syndrome, she'd be in a real college.")
7. Exhibit anger and frustration and/or refuse to be satisfied. ("Never mind what's already been achieved. What's next?")
8. Communicate poorly. (Beat around the bush, and then be angry that things didn't happen the way you wanted.)
9. Be inconsistent and demanding. (No communication with program staff for months and then an enraged phone call over a small issue.)

Do:

1. Express appreciation. (Most professionals can live for weeks on a simple "Thanks for your hard work.")
2. Encourage your child to take risks. ("A spring break trip?! Well, let's talk about it.")
3. Place value on the chronological age of your child. ("She's twenty-three. We can expect this of a twenty-three-year-old woman.")
4. Hold a realistic view of your adult child's goals. ("She desperately wants to be a teacher, but can't earn a bachelor's degree. Maybe we can help her get a job as a classroom aide.")
5. Accept mistakes. (Know that the staff and your adult child have a lot to coordinate.)
6. Be emotionally independent. ("I am a person separate from my adult child.")

7. Be guided by facts rather than emotions. ("I know she's furious with the teacher, but what really happened?")
8. Be flexible. (Sometimes the desired class is full, and your child will need to register for another option.)
9. Believe in the importance of working together with staff and your child. ("We're all in this together.")

Believe in realistic miracles. There has not been a program invented that will "fix" your adult child's disability or smooth all of the rough spots. One single change will not make things better for the rest of her life. Your adult child with a disability, like an adult child without a disability, is a work in progress, and will be so throughout her life.

The Good, the Bad, and the Ugly

You're looking forward to the first holiday after your child with SD has started college. Maybe she is coming home or maybe this is the first time the family will see her after she has started taking courses at the community college. You are proud and excited. You have high hopes. The anticipated day or days arrive and your child is silent, surly, rude, or someone you just don't recognize. You find yourself thinking: "Who are you and what did you do with my kid?!"

Ah, rebellion against authority. I honestly believe Americans should not be so offended by it since that's how we became a country in the first place.

One of the best books I have ever read on the subject is *Letting Go: A Parent's Guide to the College Years* by Karen Levin Coburn and Madge Lawrence Kreeger. I read it shortly after my stepdaughter left for college and I gave it to my sister to read the next year when my nieces were preparing to launch. Although young adults with SD can be socially and psychologically delayed, they will go through the stages of breaking away eventually. The book also provides insight into what typical college students are experiencing. This insight can help you keep urging your adult child (and yourself) toward the most normal college experience possible.

So, what good can come of your adult child's foray into the world of higher education? Although the anecdotes I have heard will not qualify for inclusion in a research study, I have heard stories of the intellectual, social, and emotional growth of young people with SD, told by their proud and sometimes incredulous parents.

One father wrote to me about the changes that occurred in his son in his PSE experience.

His confidence skyrocketed. He finally has peers he can relate to—real friends. In April of this year, he casually mentioned that he was running to be the president of the [program's] student body. We were floored. Here was a kid who, nineteen months earlier, was extremely shy, had no real friends, couldn't look you in the eye when he talked with you, and usually stood at the outside edge of any group of kids, who was now asking his work supervisor to look over his campaign speech to help him improve it. The big day came and he made the wise move to wear a nice shirt and tie and real shoes. He won!

Afterward, I said to him that if he had told me when he entered [college] that he would have done this, I wouldn't have believed him. He stopped me, and, with a great amount of pride, said that he had been thinking the same thing. That self-awareness and sense of accomplishment was worth all of the effort and money we had spent on getting him to attend [college].

Epilogue
Removing the Stone

I used to know what mental retardation meant. For that matter, I used to know what college meant, too.

Both of these concepts had meanings etched in stone—college was for people who had demonstrated that they were smart enough to be there, and if a person was mentally retarded, well, college was not a reality.

I've learned that some of what I always knew to be true was not true.

I've learned that an intellectual disability is more than a number on an IQ test and that any disability is a part of a person's identity but not the whole of it. I learned that college is not a prize bestowed on young people who have proved that they are smart, but a place and a time of learning for people who want to become educated, contributing members of society. It is not just a time for people in their late teens or early twenties, but a time that many thinking people engage in throughout their lives.

Limiting attitudes toward people with significant disabilities remain, but those attitudes can change. When a concept becomes personal, attitudes change rapidly. All it takes is one person with significant disabilities in a class, on a campus, in a workplace, in a neighborhood, or in a family for individual attitudes to change. Despite my early feelings, attitudes are the most easily overcome obstacle facing young people with SD.

The real stones that continue to block the way to postsecondary education for people with significant disabilities are financing, inadequate preparation, and difficulties finding supports on campus.

Financing remains an enormous obstacle for many families, since the options are so limited. I hope that local school districts will begin to advocate for their students with SD to receive government grants and educational loans to finance their education. Perhaps local districts can become a "financial aid" agency of sorts, determining how much money it would cost to educate the students with SD in a district-run program and channeling that money either to a college-based program staffed by the district (as the Buffalo City School District has done), by direct pay to a program run by another organization, or by allowing the student with SD to purchase classes and services (speech, transportation, tutoring, note taking, etc.), which would allow him to create an inclusive, individually supported option at a college of his choice.

Most high schools would support these options for their special-needs students. But districts cannot support these developments without sufficient funding from state and federal governments. That means that there must be a change in attitude and expectations for students with SD from the level of federal government on down.

Very much like Head Start and other initiatives that help young children at risk for school failure, putting money into these ideas and programs will save the government money in the long run. Even if an adult with SD is not able to be completely independent, increasing the number of hours he can work, teaching him to travel alone, and eliminating his need for 24-hour-a-day supervision in a group home (paid for by public funds) will save money over the long haul.

Good preparation for postsecondary education must start in middle school, not just for students with SD but also for their families. As students with SD become a bigger part of higher education, I foresee a trickle-down effect in educational priorities that will benefit all students who are receiving extensive special education services. True, academic rigor has already started to become a part of programs for students with SD, but complete programs cannot stop there. Students with SD will need to become more knowledgeable about themselves, their rights, and their responsibilities.

Parents need to understand that their child's entitlement to appropriate education will end. Parents, students, and their secondary teachers need to have a full understanding of the role of adult services, the world of higher education, the demands of the twenty-first century workplace, and the community beyond the classroom, and they must aggressively prepare students with SD to meet the realities they will face.

Supports are still needed on campuses, but they are improving all the time. I check the www.ThinkCollege.net website at least once a week, and often discover that the list of schools offering opportunities for PSE to students with SD is growing. There are colleges and vocational training programs that are not listed on this site, but are providing exemplary supports and accommodations to individuals with SD. As more students with a variety of disabilities begin to attend college, colleges are becoming more accessible in their campuses and instruction.

There is such a difference in the options available to and the treatment of adults with SD who grew up before this age of acceptance and inclusion. I see them in the community; probably you do as well. Their elderly parents or paid care providers are able to bring them out to restaurants, public events, and stores now. Some blend in easily, going about their business. Others still act like or are treated like "children who never grew": eating kids' meals, getting balloons, taking trips to the toy store, or getting their faces painted at fairs. Often, they travel in small groups of others who have SD, usually with an attendant at least two decades younger than they are. If these situations and entertainments were truly their choice, I would shrug my shoulders and go about my business. But I suspect for many it is all they know, so it is not a true choice. How many of these adults with SD want something more out of life? Homes of their own, more privacy, a job, a spouse, the chance to plan their own schedule? Isn't that what we all want?

I also used to know for sure that if a person's body or mind was damaged due to illness, injury, or chromosome abnormalities, the damage was permanent. This assumption is also untrue. As every month goes by, I see more and more evidence that providing people with significant disabilities with opportunities to learn to make the world work extends their abilities further than we ever thought was possible. For example, people with Prader-Willi syndrome who live with the devastating consequences of an uncontrollable appetite as well as intellectual disability have been taught to live successfully in their own apartments, making responsible food choices and maintaining a healthy weight through an intensive teaching and behavior management program through the ARC of Alachua County, Florida, a development that no one thought possible because of the error in their genes. Perhaps the human mind can even learn to surpass these if given a chance.

Carol Dweck, in her book *Mindset,* writes of two mindsets—the fixed mindset and the growth mindset. Those who live their lives according to the fixed mindset believe that everyone is born with certain traits of intelligence, talent, and personality and that these traits are immutable—they simply are. That damaged chromosome? It just is and no amount of effort will change its effects. In fact, if you must expend effort, it must be a sign that you don't have what it takes in terms of intelligence or talent. Those who live their lives according to the growth mindset believe that all abilities and traits (including intelligence) can be changed and improved, but the change requires effort and openness to new challenges and ideas. Guess which mindset is supported by most of the professionals, parents, and students in this book?

I'll let Terrence have the last word. Terrence is a graduate of the College Based Transition Program at Buffalo State College. He spends a few days a month in Albany, New York working on two public policy committees on the rights of people with disabilities. Terrence learned to read only after leaving high school by contacting Literacy Volunteers. He continues to take classes at Buffalo State as an adult student. In his words: "There's always more to learn." In removing the stones to continuing education, we will allow other students to do the same. But first, forget everything you ever thought you knew for sure.

References &
Recommended Reading

Baker, Bruce L., Alan J. Brightman, Jan B. Blacher, Stephan P. Hinshaw, Louis J. Heifetz, and Diane M. Murphy. *Steps to Independence: Teaching Everyday Skills to Children with Special Needs.* 4th ed. Baltimore: Paul H. Brookes Publishing Company, 2005.

Basford, Katie and Candee Basford. Presentation at Cross Disability Post-Secondary Education Conference. Panel Discussion, May 19, 2007.

Biersdorff, Kathleen, Patricia Boman, and Tim Weinkauf. "Inclusive Post Secondary Education: Is It a Reality?" www.bridges4kids.org/articles/2004/4-04/STEPS4-04.html

Bruey, Carolyn and Mary Beth Urban. *The Autism Transition Guide: Planning the Journey from School to Adult Life.* Bethesda, MD: Woodbine House, 2009.

Buck, Pearl S. *The Child Who Never Grew.* Bethesda, MD: Woodbine House, 1992.

Citro, Teresa Allissa, editor. *Many Shades of Success: Other Views of Post-Secondary Options.* Lanham, MD: Rowman & Littlefield Education, 2004.

Coburn, Karen Levin and Madge Lawrence Kreeger. *Letting Go: A Parents' Guide to the College Years.* 4th ed. New York: HarperCollins Publishers, 2003.

Delmolino, Lara and Sandra L. Harris. *Incentives for Change: Motivating People with Autism Spectrum Disorders to Learn and Gain Independence.* Bethesda, MD: Woodbine House, 2004.

Doidge, Norman, M.D. *The Brain That Changes Itself: Stories of Personal Triumph from the Frontiers of Brain Science.* New York: Viking, 2007.

Dweck, Carol S. *Mindset: The New Psychology of Success.* New York: Random House, 2006.

Dybvik, Ann Christy. "Autism and the Inclusion Mandate: Daniel Experiences the Regular Classroom." *Education Next.* Number 1, 2004.

Field, Sharon. "Self Determination: Assuming Control of Your Plans for Post Secondary Education." GW Heath Resource Center. www.heath.gwu.edu

Flannery, K. Brigid, Paul Yovanoff, Michael R. Benz, and Mary McGrath Kato. "Improving Employment Outcomes of Individuals with Disabilities Through Short-Term Postsecondary Training." *Career Development for Exceptional Individuals.* Volume 31, Number 1, pp. 26-36. May 2008.

Ford, Ann and John-Richard Thompson. *On Their Own: Creating an Independent Future for your Adult Child with Learning Disabilities and ADHD, A Family Guide.* New York: Newmarket Press, 2007.

Gardner, Daniel, ed. "The Student with a Brain Injury: Achieving Goals for Higher Education." Washington, DC: HEATH Resource Center, 2001. www.heath.gwu.edu

Getzel, Elizabeth Evans and Paul Wehman. *Going to College: Expanding Opportunities for People with Disabilities.* Baltimore: Paul H. Brookes Publishing Company, 2005.

Gray, Kenneth C. and Edwin L. Herr. *Other Ways to Win: Creating Alternatives for High School Graduates.* 3rd ed. Thousand Oaks, CA: Corwin Press, 2006.

Holtz, Kristen D., Amanda K. Ziegert, and Cynthia D. Baker. *Life Journey Through Autism: A Guide for Transition to Adulthood.* Organization for Autism Research and Danya International, 2004. www.runforautism.org/resources/reading/documents/TransitionGuide.pdf

Jorgansen, Cheryl. "The Least Dangerous Assumption: A Challenge to Create a New Paradigm." *Disability Solutions*. Volume 6, Issue 3, Fall 2005.

Kauffman, James M. and Daniel P. Hallahan, editors. *The Illusion of Full Inclusion: A Comprehensive Critique of a Current Special Education Bandwagon.* 2nd ed. Austin, TX: Pro-Ed, 2005.

Kaufman, Leslie. "A Dream Not Denied - Just a Normal Girl." *New York Times*. November 5, 2006.

Kleinfeld, Judith, Barbara Morse, and Siobhan Wescott, editors. *Fantastic Antone Grows Up: Adolescents and Adults with Fetal Alcohol Syndrome*. Fairbanks: University of Alaska Press, 2000.

Kronman, Anthony T. *Education's End: Why Our Colleges and Universities Have Given Up on the Meaning of Life*. New Haven: Yale University Press, 2007.

Lavoie, Richard. *It's So Much Work to Be Your Friend: Helping the Child with Learning Disabilities Find Social Success*. New York: Simon and Schuster, 2005.

McGrew, Kevin S. and Jeffrey Evans. "Expectations for Students with Cognitive Disabilities: Is the Cup Half Empty or Half Full? Can the Cup Flow Over?" (Synthesis Report 55). Minneapolis, MN: University of Minnesota National Center on Educational Outcomes, 2004. cehd.umn.edu/nceo/OnlinePubs/Synthesis55.html

McGuire, Dennis and Brian Chicoine. *Mental Wellness in Adults with Down Syndrome: A Guide to Emotional and Behavioral Strengths and Challenges*. Bethesda, MD: Woodbine House, 2006.

Moore, Abigail Sullivan. "A Dream Not Denied: Students on the Spectrum." *New York Times*. November 5, 2006.

National Collaborative on Workforce and Disability. *The 411 on Disability Disclosure: A Workbook for Youth with Disabilities. Washington, DC: Institute for Educational Leadership, 2005.* www.ncwd-youth.info/resources_&_Publications/411.html

Organization for Autism Research, Danya International, Inc., and Southwest Autism Research and Resource Center. *Life Journey Through Autism*. Arlington, VA: Organization for Autism Research, 2006.

Palmer, Greg. *Adventures in the Mainstream: Coming of Age with Down Syndrome*. Bethesda, MD: Woodbine House, 2005.

Peak Parent Center. *Accommodations and Modifications Fact Sheet.* www.peatc.org/peatc.cgim?template=peakaccom

Planty, Michael et al. *The Condition of Education 2008.* Washington, DC: National Center for Education Statistics, 2008.

Planty, Michael et al. *The Condition of Education 2009.* Washington, DC: National Center for Education Statistics, 2009.

Roffman, Arlyn. *Guiding Teens with Learning Disabilities: Navigating the Transition from High School to Adulthood.* New York: Random House, 2007.

Scheiber, Barbara. *Fulfilling Dreams: A Handbook for Parents of People with Williams Syndrome.* Royal Oaks, Michigan: Williams Syndrome Association, 2002.

Schwier, Karin Melberg. *Couples with Intellectual Disabilities Talk about Living and Loving.* Bethesda, MD: Woodbine House, 1994.

Sforza, Teri, Howard Lenhoff, and Sylvia Lenhoff. *The Strangest Song: One Father's Quest to Help His Daughter Find Her Voice.* Amherst, NY: Prometheus Books, 2006.

Sicile-Kira, Chantal. *Adolescents on the Autism Spectrum: A Parent's Guide to the Cognitive, Social, Physical, and Transition Needs of Teenagers with Autism Spectrum Disorders.* New York: The Berkley Publishing Group, 2006.

Simons, Jo Ann. "Thinking about Tomorrow: The Transition to Adult Life." *Disability Solutions.* Volume 6, Issue 1. September/October 2004.

Siperstein, Gary N., Robin C. Parker, Jennifer Norins Bardon, and Keith F. Widaman. "A National Study of Youth Attitudes Toward the Inclusion of Students with Intellectual Disabilities." *Exceptional Children.* Volume 73, No. 4, pp. 435-455. 2007.

Uditsky, Bruce, and E. Anne Hughson. "Inclusive Post-Secondary Education for Students with Significant Developmental Disabilities: Challenging Legal, Moral and Pragmatic Assumptions." www.nl.edu/dse/docs/Uditsky%20and%20Hughson.Inclusive%20post-secondary%20education.pdf

Van Ingen, Daniel J., Linda L. Moore, and Joseph Am Fuemmeler. "Parental Overinvolvement: A Qualitative Study." *Journal of Developmental Disabilities.* Volume 20, Number 5. October 2008.

Walker, Pamela M. and Patricia Rogan. *Make the Day Matter: Promoting Typical Lifestyles for Adults with Significant Disabilities.* Baltimore: Paul H. Brookes Publishing Company, 2007.

Weinkauf, Tim. "College and University? You've Got to Be Kidding: Inclusive Post-Secondary Education for Adults with Intellectual Disabilities." *Crossing Boundaries: An Interdisciplinary Journal,* Volume 1, Number 2. Spring 2002.

Yuan, Frances T., Linda Brennan, Patricia Morrissey, Carole Noveck, Fran Osten, Threshold Program Faculty. *Beyond Threshold: A Follow-Up Survey of Graduates.* Cambridge, Massachusetts: Threshold Program at Lesley University, October 2006.

Resources

· ·

Postsecondary Education for Students with SD

College Resources for Students with Autism
autismandcollege.googlepages.com

Going to College
www.going-to-college.org
   (Website for college-bound students with disabilities with online videos that teach about exploring interests, requesting accommodations, choosing a college, what to expect in college, etc.)

Individual Supports for College Success
On-Campus Outreach
www.education.umd.edu/oco

Online Clearinghouse on Post-Secondary Education for Individuals with Disabilities
HEATH Resource Center
George Washington University
2134 G St., NW
Washington, DC 20052
202-973-0904; 202-994-3365 (fax)
askHEATH@gwu.edu
www.heath.gwu.edu
   (Resource papers, fact sheets, directories, and other publications on transition resources, postsecondary education, career-technical education, financial aid.)

ThinkCollege
College Options for People with Intellectual Disabilities
Editor Nancy Hurley
www.thinkcollege.net

Transition Coalition
University of Kansas
Dept. of Special Education
1122 W. Campus Rd., Rm. 521
Lawrence, KS 66045
785-0864-0686
www.transitioncoalition.org
 (The website has a searchable database of 18-21 programs—community-based transition programs in age-appropriate settings for students with disabilities aged 18-21. Assorted publications on transition issues are also available.)

• •

Testing

The ACT Test
Services for Students with Disabilities
www.act.org/aap/disab/index.html
319-337-1332

College Board (SAT) Accommodations
Services for Students with Disabilities
P.O. Box 6226
Princeton, NJ 08541-6226
609-771-7137
ssd@info.collegeboard.org
professionals.collegeboard.com/testing/ssd

Fairtest
The National Center for Fair and Open Testing
15 Court Square, Ste. 820
Boston, MA 02108
857-350-8207
www.fairtest.org
 (Maintains a list of colleges and universities that don't require ACT/SAT for admission.)

Transition Issues

Person-Centered Planning Education Site
Employment and Disability Institute
Cornell University
School of Industrial and Labor Relations
Ithaca, NY 14853
607-255-7727
www.ilr.cornell.edu/edi/pcp

The Research and Training Center on Community Living
rtc.umn.edu/main

Student-led IEP meetings
InterAct
College of Teacher Education & Leadership
Arizona State University West
6515 North 12th Place
Phoenix, AZ 85014
www.studentledipes.org

Youthhood.org
www.youthhood.org
(Website for young adults with disabilities to use in exploring transition issues.)

Finances

Autism-related Scholarships
www.collegescholarships.org/health/autistic-students.htm

Cerebral Palsy-related Scholarships
www.collegescholarships.org/health/cerebral-palsy.htm

Epilepsy-related Scholarships
www.collegescholarships.org/health/epileptic-students.htm

Financial Aid for Students with LD and other disabilities
www.ncld.org/content/view/1441/456289

Free Application for Federal Student Aid
800-4-FED-AID (433-3243); 800-730-8913 (TTY)
www.fafsa.ed.gov/what010.htm

Internal Revenue Service
800-829-3676
www.irs.gov/publications/p502/ar02.html
(Publication #502, "Medical and Dental Expenses," which covers deduction of qualified special education tuition, can be downloaded from the website above, or ordered by calling the 800 number.)

Introduction to 529 Plans
U.S. Securities and Exchange Commission
www.sec.gov/investor/pubs/intro529.htm

Vocational Training and Jobs

DisabilityInfo.Gov
www.disabilityinfo.gov
(The home page includes a link to a great deal of information on vocational rehabilitation services, including links to each state's agencies.)

Social Security Administration
Office of Public Inquiries
Windsor Park Bldg.
6401 Security Blvd.
Baltimore, MD 21235
800-772-1213; 800-325-0778 (TTY)
www.ssa.gov/disabilityresearch/wi/pass.htm
(Visit the website above for information on the Plan to Achieve Self Support, PASS, for SSI recipients who want to save money to achieve a work goal without jeopardizing their benefits.)

Job Corps
200 Constitution Ave., NW, Ste. N4463
Washington, DC 20210
202-693-3000
national_office@jobcorps.gov
www.jobcorps.gov

One Stop Career Centers
877-US2-JOBS (872-5627); 877-889-5627 (TTY)
www.careeronestop.org

Appendix A

Advice for Students with Disabilities about College Accommodations[1]

Top 5 Tips for Working with the Office of Disability Support Services in College

1. Familiarize yourself with your rights under Section 504 of the Rehabilitation Act and the Americans with Disabilities Act. Your rights are very different than they were under the Individuals with Disabilities Education Act (IDEA), which protected your rights in high school. (See www.thinkcollege.net for a table on the differences between high school and college.)

2. Contact the Office of Disability Support Services (ODSS) at your college as soon as you are accepted to college. Academic accommodations may take time to arrange. Don't wait until you arrive on campus or you may have to wait weeks to get accommodations.

---

[1] with thanks to Stephen Simon, Director of Syracuse University's Office of Disability Services

3. Get used to using educational technology, such as a Kurzweil reading program, voice recognition software, etc. ODSS uses this technology frequently to provide accommodations.

4. Know your disability (by diagnosis), how your disability affects your ability to learn, and what accommodations you need.

5. Make sure your parents understand how their role in your education will change. They will no longer be your primary advocates, although they may help you with advice and problem solving. You must be prepared to advocate for yourself.

Other Important Information:

- When you go to the ODSS to request academic accommodations, bring a copy of your most recent psychological testing report. Check your college's website for any additional information you may need to document your disability or accommodations (for example, a doctor's note or letter from a psychologist). You may bring a copy of your IEP, but most of the time your IEP will not be enough documentation to get accommodations. It may be helpful to bring it with you to provide information about your learning style and accommodations that have worked in the past. However, the college does not have to follow your IEP—there are no IEPs in college!

- The ODSS will look at your documentation for a diagnosis and your learning profile. Even with accommodations, you must be able to "meet the fundamental requirements of the degree program." ***The college maintains the right to determine accommodations.*** It does not have to waive or substitute requirements for you (for example, math or foreign language courses) even if they were waived in the past. If a math course or language other than English is a fundamental requirement of your degree, you must take the course and earn a passing grade. Make sure you understand the difference between accommodations and modifications.

- ODS can help with any accommodations needed on campus. For example, if you need a single room in the dorm because of medical equipment or to deal with sensory issues related to autism spectrum disorder, the ODSS can help you get this accommodation. For needed accommodations to the physical environment (such as an accessible classroom or special dietary needs in the cafeteria) notify the ODSS as soon as possible!

- ODSS can also help with accommodations that are somewhat unusual. For example, if a student uses an augmentative communication device or has tics due to Tourette Syndrome, the ODS can help to facilitate understanding in the classroom by providing information to the professor and other students in the class. If you need preferential seating so that you are near an exit to accommodate an anxiety disorder or priority registration because you are a part-time student after a traumatic brain injury, the ODSS can help you arrange these accommodations.

- There are no one-to-one aides in college, unless you have hired them yourself. A support person may be allowed to attend class with you if there is a legitimate reason. For example, the college might allow a nurse's aide to accompany you if you have a tracheotomy and need someone to suction you or if you have a severe seizure condition. But you need to work with the ODS to make an accommodation of this kind happen.

- Regardless of the nature of your disability, you must follow the student code of conduct. Being diagnosed with intermittent rage disorder, for example, may be a reason for fighting, but not an excuse. You can be asked to leave the college if you violate the code of conduct, even if you have a disability.

Appendix B
Advice to Students with Acquired Brain Injury (ABI)

Every 15 seconds, someone in the United States sustains a brain injury. Nearly 5.3 million Americans currently live with disabilities resulting from such injuries, the highest incidence occurring among youth and young adults between the ages of 15 and 24. Because individuals within this age group typically are preparing for postsecondary education or are of traditional college age, students with brain injuries are a growing presence on college and university campuses and within other post secondary programs (Gardner, 2001).

Early in my career, I had the opportunity to work with teenagers and young adults who had acquired brain injury (ABI).[1] I particularly remember that these young people felt as though they were neither fish nor fowl. They were people with disabilities, but did not feel at home in the disabled community, and they no longer fit into the "normal" world. There are a few programs that are specifically designed

---

[1] Acquired Brain Injury is a term that is inclusive of traumatic brain injury or TBI, which is caused by violent trauma to the head and injuries caused by illness or lack of oxygen to the brain.

for students with ABI where they may find the support of peers struggling with similar issues. Students with ABI can also attend college in an individually supported inclusive model.

College students who have an acquired brain injury due to an accident, an illness, or a war-related injury are in an unusual situation when it comes to postsecondary education. These students may have been admitted to college as regularly enrolled undergraduates prior to their injury, or they may have sustained their brain damage many years before seeking admission. Many young veterans injured between the ages of 18 and 25 may have deferred college to serve in Iraq or Afghanistan. These students are unusual in my discussion of this topic because they spent a significant portion of their lives as nondisabled students and now must learn the complexities of managing higher education as a person with a disability.

I had the opportunity to discuss this topic with Dr. Richard Dressler, the director of the Acquired Brain Injury Resource Program (ABIRP) at Western Kentucky University.

"Students with head injuries tend to fall through the cracks," Dr. Dressler said. "These students need to know what their choices are and what they can realistically obtain." He urged students with ABI to follow the same steps as other students with disabilities. That is, they should contact the college for information about accommodations, find out about resources available on campus for assistance, and communicate their needs to professors. But they should also contact their local brain injury association for additional help and information. People with ABI often experience severe difficulties with memory, distractibility, executive functioning, planning ahead, frustration tolerance, and sorting out main ideas from details. All of these issues may interfere with success in college.

Dr. Dressler recommends that students with ABI consider online courses to begin or to continue their college studies. Particularly for students who struggle with distractions in the classroom or who have physical disabilities related to their ABI, online courses can offer the best of the college world.

Dr. Dressler also emphasizes the need for the student and her parents to accept the new limitations of living with ABI. "For some students, earning a two-year certificate might be more realistic than earning a four-year degree." Students with cognitive damage from an ABI can also enroll in any of the nondegree programs I describe in Part

2 of this book if they meet the admissions criteria and the program can address their goals. Students with ABI who are still undergoing intensive rehabilitation (speech therapy, physical therapy, occupational therapy) may not be able to find these services through a college program.

Colleges and universities with programs that specifically support students with ABI with academic support and cognitive retraining include:

- Coastline Community College, Fountain Valley, California;
- San Diego Community College, San Diego, California;
- Santa Monica College, Santa Monica, California;
- University of Central Florida, Orlando, Florida;
- Western Kentucky University, Bowling Green, Kentucky (Acquired Brain Injury Resource Program or ABIRP).

Glossary

Accommodation: A change in how academic information is accessed or completed without substantial change to the level, content, or performance criteria expected of all students. The use of a note taker, the services of a sign language interpreter, using Braille or large print materials, having extended time to complete assignments and tests, or environmental alterations (e.g., an elevator, change in lighting, a ramp, an accessible restroom, a quiet room for testing) are examples of accommodations.

Americans with Disabilities Act (ADA) of 1990: A law that prohibits discrimination on the basis of disability in employment, state and local government, public accommodations, commercial facilities, transportation, telecommunications and the United States Congress. A person with a disability is defined as: (1) having a physical or mental impairment that substantially limits one or more major life activities, or (2) having a record of such an impairment, or (3) is regarded as having such an impairment.

Audit/auditing (a course): To attend a class for participation, but not for credit. Most postsecondary institutions charge a fee for auditing a course.

Best Buddies: A not-for-profit organization founded in 1989 by Anthony Kennedy Shriver to promote one-to-one friendships between students with and without intellectual disabilities. The organization has 1,400 chapters in middle schools, high schools, and colleges in the United States and across the world.

BOCES (Board of Cooperative Educational Services)/educational collaborative: A group of school districts that combine resources to provide educational services to students, including special education services.

Circle of Friends or Circle of Support: A group of people who meet on a regular basis to provide ongoing support to a person with a disability in order to help him achieve his dreams and goals. Members may include, but are not limited to, family, friends, service providers, teachers, church members, and coworkers of the person with a disability. The members meet voluntarily (rather than as paid professionals) to support the person with a disability who is called a **focus person.**

Free and Appropriate Public Education (FAPE): A requirement under the Individuals with Disabilities Education Act (IDEA) which states that a student with a disability must receive education services appropriate to his or her needs at public expense from kindergarten through age 21 or until he receives a high school diploma (whichever comes first). The student may receive services at a public or private school.

Hidden Curriculum: A term that refers to social behavior that is expected in situations, but is not specifically taught or articulated. For example, most students do not need to be taught explicitly that Mrs. X is more likely to impose a consequence when a classroom rule is violated than Mr. Z and that they need to control their behavior in her classroom. Students with autism spectrum disorders often struggle to "read" these situations accurately and to respond appropriately.

Matriculate: To be admitted (usually as a degree-seeking student) to a postsecondary institution.

Modification: A change in what a student with disabilities is expected to learn compared to students without disabilities. Examples include: reading a simpler textbook, making a poster instead of writing a paper, and completing fewer assignments and meeting fewer class objectives than students without disabilities.

Office of Disability Support Services (ODSS): The office at a postsecondary program that coordinates reasonable accommodations for college students, such as note taking, test accommodations, readers or reading software for tests or textbooks, etc. Students with disabilities need to contact the ODSS on campus and keep in contact with the office in order to secure on-going accommodations.

Person-Centered Planning: A process by which a person with a disability determines what goals, plans, and dreams he or she has for life and what services and supports are needed to achieve them. There are a variety of person-centered planning tools, including Circles of Support/Circles of Friends, Planning Alternative Tomorrows with Hope (PATH), MAP, Personal Futures Planning, etc., all with the common goal of having the person with a disability decide what he or she wants and choose the services that are needed, rather than fitting into a specific program or limited choice of options.

Public Accommodation: A place such as a school, store, theater, or restaurant that is generally open to the public. The ADA prohibits discrimination against people with disabilities by public accommodations.

Section 504 of the Rehabilitation Act: A law that prevents the exclusion of, the discrimination against, or the denial of benefits to any qualified individual with a disability from any program or activity that either receives federal financial assistance or is conducted by any executive agency or the U.S. Postal Service. Section 504 and the ADA are the two federal laws that require postsecondary education programs to provide reasonable accommodations to students with disabilities who are otherwise qualified to attend the program.

"Soft Skills": A term that refers to the emotional, social, and personal skills that an individual needs in order to work successfully with others and to maintain personal motivation. The skills are called "soft skills" as opposed to "hard skills" that can be taught, such as running a cash register, sewing, using a computer, welding, etc.

Index

ABOUT THE AUTHOR

• •

Diana M. Katovitch has been working with children and teenagers with disabilities in various capacities since 1982, and has been teaching special education in New York state public schools since 1990. She is a graduate of Syracuse University and The State University of New York (SUNY) Cortland. Frustrated that many of her students were not meeting their adult potential, she became intrigued by the idea that higher education was possible for students with significant learning and intellectual disabilities. She lives with her husband, Dale, and children, Celie and Sam, in Union Springs, New York.